BOURBON
·EMPIRE·

BOURBON

·EMPIRE·

THE PAST and FUTURE of
AMERICA'S WHISKEY

REID MITENBULER

VIKING

VIKING
Published by the Penguin Publishing Group
Penguin Random House LLC
375 Hudson Street
New York, New York 10014

USA | Canada | UK | Ireland | Australia | New Zealand | India | South Africa | China
penguin.com
A Penguin Random House Company

First published by Viking Penguin, an imprint of Penguin Publishing Group, a division of
Penguin Random House LLC, 2015

ISBN 978-0-670-01683-9

Printed in the United States of America
1   3   5   7   9   10   8   6   4   2

Set in Adobe Caslon
Designed by Spring Hoteling

To Lauren

· CONTENTS ·

What's truer than truth? The story.

—old Jewish proverb

There's the story, then there's the real story, then there's the story of how the story came to be told. Then there's what you leave out of the story. Which is part of the story too.

—Margaret Atwood

· INTRODUCTION ·

BENEATH THE CHAR

In 1964, a handful of U.S. congressmen found themselves in an awkward situation. A pending resolution to declare bourbon a distinctive product of the United States sat on their desks, and while most would pass it immediately, a few had reservations. The measure would convert this humble whiskey into an American classic on par with baseball or apple pie, and some legislators needed a little more justification from House staffers before granting this kind of lofty recognition. Of course, bourbon's modest pedigree wasn't their biggest concern: behind the measure lurked lobbyists for an industry with a shoddy reputation. During the previous decade, the Justice Department had investigated the predatory and monopolistic business tactics of the handful of companies, known as the "Big Four," that controlled almost three-quarters of the liquor trade. There had also been a Senate investigation—known as the Kefauver Committee—that had revealed links between Big Four executives and organized crime chiefs dating back to Prohibition-era bootlegging. Surely, a resolution glorifying bourbon as an American original wasn't great use of political capital. Nevertheless, any misgivings between the lawmakers and lobbyists were eventually smoothed out—no doubt in a way that involved drinking a lot of bourbon—and the resolution was passed.

The next day, news of bourbon's coronation as an American icon made a scant media blip on the back pages of a few newspapers, and the resolution was soon forgotten.

A half century later, that legislation has risen above its inauspicious beginnings to become famous. Marketers and food writers love to burnish bourbon's credentials by reminding drinkers that even Congress, in all its awesome authority, has officially declared the spirit a unique part of America's heritage. For them, the resolution is a stamp of approval, verifying that the values implied by the frontier iconography found on countless bourbon bottles are inherently American: individualism, self-sufficiency, practicality, and guts. It means that these truths, which we Americans hold to be self-evident, are unquestionable and true. In 2014, after the National Archives loaned the original resolution to the Kentucky Distillers Association for display, the trade group's president even went so far as to tell a crowd of onlookers that the document was "the Declaration of Independence for bourbon. . . . It's one of the most cherished pieces of our history."

But like all good American legends—Paul Bunyan, Johnny Appleseed, the Headless Horseman—the resolution's story has become embellished over time. In the years following its passage, people started dressing up its language, swapping the dry legalese of "a distinctive product of the United States," which did little more than clarify bourbon's place of production, with the punchier "America's Native Spirit." This zippier but inaccurate wording would help create a folksy sense of pageantry around bourbon, a little hokey but definitely better for marketing. Today, the catchier but misquoted language has become the norm. In 2007, when Kentucky senator Jim Bunning sponsored a bill to declare September "National Bourbon Heritage Month," the legislation he introduced to Congress not only misquoted the original resolution, it added sentimental language connecting the spirit to a loftier set of ideals than the original resolution ever intended: "family heritage, tradition, and deep-rooted legacy."

But regardless of how much bourbon truly deserves these accolades, it wasn't sentiment or patriotism that inspired the 1964 legislation. It was business, and a cutthroat one at that. The true driving force behind the resolution was actually a man named Lewis Rosenstiel, head of Schenley Distillers Corporation, part of the Big Four and one of the largest liquor companies in the world. The impetus for his move had happened more than a decade earlier, when Rosenstiel mistakenly evaluated that the Korean War would create whiskey shortages like those suffered during World War II. In preparation, he ordered his distilleries to produce at full blast, helping push total stocks of American whiskey held in storage past 637 million gallons, enough to supply national demand for nearly eight years. When the war quickly ended without the shortages Rosenstiel had anticipated, his surplus gave him control of roughly two-thirds of the nation's aged whiskey stocks, according to his competitors. This was a disaster from a business perspective—Americans were drinking plenty of whiskey, but demand was dwarfed by supply. Since bourbon evaporates at a rate somewhere between 3 and 7 percent a year while it ages in wooden barrels, much of Rosenstiel's investment threatened to vanish into thin air before he could sell it.

Rosenstiel had spent tens of millions of dollars on creative ad campaigns and lobbied Congress for changes to industry regulations that would make it easier for him to sell his whiskey. Even though most of his lobbying initiatives were good for the industry as a whole, such as tax breaks, some had met fierce resistance from Rosenstiel's Big Four counterparts. Whenever these other executives assessed that a looming rule change might give Schenley an unfair advantage—even though it might be good for the whiskey trade in general—they'd undermine it within the Distilled Spirits Institute, the industry's main lobbying group.

During one such impasse in 1958, over a change in tax codes, Rosenstiel responded by forming his own renegade lobbying organization, which he called the Bourbon Institute. Running the organization for him was retired navy vice admiral William Marshall, a man who had commanded a destroyer at Omaha Beach during the Normandy invasion. Marshall folded the resolution into the lobbying group's broader strategy of giving bourbon international trade protection so Rosenstiel could expand into overseas markets. In being declared "a distinctive product of the United States," bourbon would be afforded the same regional trade designations as scotch whisky, French cognac, and champagne, giving U.S. producers like Rosenstiel a competitive advantage abroad. It would also prevent U.S. merchants from importing products called bourbon from overseas, protecting the domestic market from unwanted outsiders (one of the resolution's few congressional opponents was indeed a New York politician representing two Manhattan heiresses earning royalties from imports of a cheap "bourbon" made at a distillery in Juárez, Mexico).

Before the 1964 resolution passed, Rosenstiel put in place the rest of his overseas sales strategy. He sent a case of bourbon to every U.S. embassy in the world and spent $35 million on a global marketing campaign. It was all a gamble—bourbon had little name recognition in foreign markets—but Rosenstiel was a solid bet to reverse that trend. By this point, he had been involved in the liquor trade for nearly a half century and hadn't encountered much failure. He was a tough operator who had made his bones in the industry during the lawless years of Prohibition, the same decade when U.S. president Calvin Coolidge declared, "The chief business of the American people is business." That quote would eventually become famous and no doubt was still ringing in Rosenstiel's ears when Congress passed the 1964 resolution. Of course, by that point this corporate titan was already one of the richest men in America.

· · ·

Like no other American product, bourbon embodies capitalism—a word that's dirty to some, beautiful to others, but has nonetheless shaped our political and cultural life as much as it determines how we do business. Early styles of American whiskey, bourbon among them, allowed farmers to preserve the value of surplus grain crops by converting them into spirits. This liquid soon became the frontier's de facto currency, knitting together America's early economy. Then, when the question of taxing these spirits erupted during the Whiskey Rebellion of 1794, the ideologies of Alexander Hamilton and Thomas Jefferson clashed in a battle to define the soul of American business. While the debate roared, the trappings of a cottage industry gave way to factories and, according to business lore, the term "brand name" entered the American lexicon as distillers began differentiating themselves from one another by branding their names onto the ends of whiskey barrels. The evolution wouldn't be complete, however, until bourbon, that spirit born on the frontier, would come of age on Madison Avenue. The style of modern marketing it helped create would define the system of commerce that America would eventually spread across the globe.

But just as bourbon helped shape U.S. history, it was also shaped by it. The spirit's recipe was determined by the migration of Americans drifting west to places where corn, its main ingredient, was more prevalent than the grains primarily used in other whiskey styles such as rye. Most of bourbon's flavor also comes from aging in wooden barrels, which was an outgrowth of America's shifting trade patterns: as the empire expanded, people noticed that whiskey shipped in barrels on relatively longer voyages tasted better after absorbing flavors from the wood. America's Industrial Revolution brought scientific advances that would change bourbon, just as other technological innovations today keep doing. Finally, there's government lobbying. This strange art—which helps guide the "invisible hand" that economist Adam Smith credited with building the wealth of nations—always has, and always will, affect whiskey by influencing production standards, regulations, and profits.

None of this history, however, is brought up in the dry language of the 1964 resolution. The declaration doesn't explain how bourbon is the tale of a nation told on a condensed scale: the humble origins, ambition and promise, innovation driven by necessity, the dizzying wealth, corruption, downfall, and redemption. Nor did the legislation mention that textbook history and the carefully cultivated myths of the whiskey industry are often overshadowed by stories as shocking as they are impressive: the nation as it really works, built by men like Lewis Rosenstiel as well as the frontier icons you find on many bourbon bottles. We hold up bourbon as a mirror of the America psyche, but the images it reflects—seen on whiskey labels that portray our evolving attitudes toward race, class, sex, and religion—always confound expectations.

Other drinks have concrete images—beer is for the everyman even when it's expensive and hyper-crafty, while wine is typically considered sophisticated and swanky even when you buy it at a gas station. Bourbon, though, is a shapeshifter. It can be a refined drink or it can be rough, depending on how it's served and who's drinking it. Sometimes it conjures up images of old men sitting around in deep leather chairs, power brokers who spend their time in rooms decorated with oil paintings of other old men with good posture and impressive facial hair. At other times it makes you think of cowboys getting arrested—one fun but probably untrue bit of drinking lore even claims that the expression "a shot of whiskey" originated from how much whiskey cowboys got for trading a round of ammunition at the saloon.

Of course, these old stereotypes are fast changing. Today, women have cracked into the old boys' club and are just as likely to drink whiskey as men, while the rowdy cowboys are replaced by whiskey geeks who sniff cautiously at the edges of their glasses before dutifully noting aromas of "hibiscus," "buttery oak," or "stewed fruits" in their tasting notebooks.

Speaking of tasting notes, voluminous pages of these can be found in many other fine books that scrutinize and rank individual brands. These sources are a helpful first step for understanding whiskey, but I ultimately believe that examining the spirit's history is the best guide. Rankings are subjective, arbitrary, and vulnerable to the industry's marketing efforts. Certain qualities—the length of time a whiskey is aged in a barrel, proof, the grains used in different recipes—have come to be more appreciated than others. And why is that exactly? The answer is for reasons aside from what actually gives us the most pleasure. We taste with our minds as much as our senses, and perceptions of status and image—the products of economics, politics, and culture—dictate many of our "rules" about connoisseurship.

For instance, when Lewis Rosenstiel was lobbying for the 1964 resolution, he was also investing $21 million ($167 million today) on ad campaigns to reeducate the palates of drinkers toward particular whiskey styles of which he held vast surpluses. Some of it was good, but some of it wasn't—it didn't matter, he simply needed to get rid of the stuff. Nevertheless, you can still see the fallout from those ad campaigns today when celebrity chefs or the other various apparatchiks of the foodie-industrial complex offer questionable advice about what to buy or what is the "best." Much of this talk is just white noise, doing little to demystify the array of bottles on store shelves today. Knowing the history, though, and how some of these "rules" came to be, clears the marketing fog and helps us make our choices more objectively. Fortunately, the lessons are usually refreshing, revealing the best bottles to be hidden gems, and not always the ones that are the most expensive or discussed.

. . .

Even though the true origins of the 1964 resolution aren't particularly romantic, the document's sentimentalized meaning has become today's reality. This has helped drive bourbon's resurgent popularity this century, a comeback that is often credited to the drink's "authenticity," a term used to describe unbroken heritage and trueness. We often imagine that bourbon connects us to a past that was somehow less complicated, and we've turned to it for relief from modern confusion. Bourbon's sales this century have spiked to their highest level since Rosenstiel's 1964 resolution, and I don't think it's coincidence that the uptick has come during times of confusing change. The economy is booming, but the new industries are tearing asunder the old ones and leaving inequality in their wake. Our political leaders are smart products of the meritocracy, but Washington seems more angry and gridlocked than ever. And while technology today better connects us, it has also managed to disconnect us, replacing actual conversation with the numb glow of tiny screens. Some pundits speculate that these changes spell the decline of the American Empire, but I have no idea if this is true or not. What I do know is that we could all probably use a drink of bourbon right now.

In this way, bourbon is comfort food. As the world becomes more complex, bourbon remains simple—its foundation is little more than a balanced combination of grains, mostly composed of corn, that is fermented and distilled into alcohol. It also remains gloriously inefficient as the ruthless efficiency of new industries unsettles the modern economy—the better part of a decade is required to make it well, as it sits quietly in charred oak barrels absorbing flavor from the wood and waiting patiently to be ready. And as the workplace scrambles around on increasingly shorter deadlines, bourbon refuses to be rushed—drinking it is an exercise in slow sipping, just letting the concentrated bursts of honey, spice, and vanilla flavors unwind on your tongue. The heat of its alcoholic power rewards those who patiently savor it, and punishes those who drink it too fast.

But even though bourbon connects us to the bedrock values of our past, the stories used to establish our ideas of heritage and authenticity are not always what they seem, as the story behind the 1964 resolution demonstrates. Take, too, Bulleit, a brand that is owned by Diageo, today the world's largest spirits company and the outfit that would eventually acquire a good portion of Schenley's portfolio following Rosenstiel's retirement and a few other rounds of corporate takeovers. In advertisements, Bulleit bills itself as "frontier whiskey" and "The Last of the Great Bourbons." It has one of the most eye-catching bottles on the liquor-store shelf: shaped like a tombstone, with a font reminiscent of "Wanted: Dead or Alive" posters, it was even used as a prop in HBO's Old West period drama *Deadwood*. But the truth behind the brand is a little different: Bulleit didn't first hit store shelves until the 1990s, its backstory as a frontier original the result of clever marketing. The giant British corporation that owns Bulleit (Diageo) as of 2014 contracted production of the bourbon out to a competing company (Four Roses in Kentucky), which itself is owned by a foreign conglomerate based out of Japan (Kirin Brewing Company).

Nothing here really screams "frontier" or conjures up notions of what most people would probably define as "authentic." But this isn't meant to pick on Bulleit—not only do most brands stretch the truth to create a sense of heritage, but many go much further. Michter's suggests that its lineage traces back to 1753 and that George Washington served whiskey made by the company to his troops during the Revolution. It's a powerful story, but the modern version of the brand actually only dates to the 1990s. The company behind it originally didn't even make its own whiskey—it simply purchased spirits from outside suppliers (which were typically very good) and sold them under its own label. The name Michter's came from the resurrection of a lapsed trademark created in the mid-twentieth century by an advertising executive named Lou Forman who had combined the names of his two sons, Michael and Peter. For Michter's, the decidedly unromantic story of its true beginnings needed a little glamour, which the George Washington tale provided.*

To some, these details about popular labels like Bulleit and Michter's rob the brands of their integrity. Perhaps, but integrity aside, the facts behind these brands don't necessarily deprive them of their authenticity; they simply indicate what bourbon and the industry surrounding it have been for a long time. Even in the nineteenth century, at the dawn of modern liquor marketing, brands began creating fake backstories they used to appeal to customers' desire for heritage and history. These fanciful tales are very much a part of bourbon's authentic legacy, and have proved essential to many brands' success. Almost none of the stories or dates on bourbon bottles are true, but asking, "Is the story true?" sort of misses the point. Instead, ask, "Is it good?" Even if it's not, the bourbon inside the bottle usually is.

Besides, the honest truth is that you probably wouldn't want to let most authentic frontier whiskey touch your lips. It was often an inconsistent nightmare of quality that could have raised a corpse from a concrete grave, made by amateurs selling it as a bulk commodity and hiding its taste with other ingredients in cocktails. Whiskey sold on the American frontier passed no government regulations and was doctored up to appear older than it was with chemicals that today are used to embalm cadavers. Nostalgia is a powerful force, but the whiskey you

*In 2012, Michter's began planning construction of a distillery in the Shively section of Louisville to start producing its own spirits. By early 2015, it was nearing completion.

most want to drink is the modern stuff made after bureaucrats, not frontiersmen, tediously passed the Pure Food and Drug Act in 1906.

But even though reality is often less romantic, it's usually more interesting. Beneath the slick surfaces of America's greatest tales dwell contradictions and surprising truths that make the stories real. The Declaration of Independence states that "all men are created equal," but is signed by men who owned slaves. Daniel Boone made the coonskin cap a symbol of rough-hewn frontier independence, but he refused to wear one himself because he thought them "uncouth" and that top hats made of beaver fur were more dignified. Thomas Jefferson is beloved by bourbon drinkers because he established policies that helped whiskey production thrive in the decades after his presidency, but he called the drink a social "poison" and tried to persuade Americans to switch to wine instead.

Bourbon is likewise brought to life by its contradictions. It has one foot in the agricultural realm, made from grains harvested from fields, but another foot in the industrial realm, distilled in places that have always resembled the factories of their eras. Take as another example today's craft distilling movement: it is full of people reclaiming whiskey's individuality from corporate conglomerates, but many of those giant corporations started as craft outfits themselves, growing big because they made a good product, which isn't something that can always be said of whiskey's counterparts in the beer or meatpacking industries. In fact, big companies often make the most coveted bourbon brands, and our conversations about whiskey within the confines of the craft movement demand a different type of discussion than we have about other foods.

The most beguiling aspect of bourbon, however, is found in the stories of the people who really built the industry, rather than the ones with their names on the bottles. Lewis Rosenstiel sold millions of gallons of whiskey in his lifetime but never got a brand named after him or his picture on a bottle. Admittedly, the label might have looked funny: Rosenstiel wore the kind of amber-tinted glasses most people associate with the fashion sense of bookies working in Atlantic City during the

1970s. Plus, his stare was crooked, the result of his getting kicked in the face as a teenager. It was this injury that actually got Rosenstiel into the liquor business in the first place—he figured it ruined his chances of becoming a professional football player, so he dropped out of high school and went to work at his uncle's distillery in Kentucky.

Even if Rosenstiel had attempted to name a brand after himself, one of the four Madison Avenue advertising agencies on his payroll probably would have advised against it. Nobody wants to drink something honoring the guy at the top of the food chain. The ad men no doubt would have reminded Rosenstiel that bourbon is one of those rare objects into which America invests its own image. This, they would have said, should always be a picture of ideals and aspirations—how we want to be seen—rather than a picture of shrewd operators such as himself. Not only that, but the prejudice of Rosenstiel's times might have sniffed at his Jewish name. This sort of obstacle had already been dodged by a long history of other notable Jews who had responded to bigotry by building their fantastic success on the names of long-dead WASPs such as Elijah Craig and Evan Williams, men who had nothing to do with the liquor in the bottle but at least conformed to stereotypes. Of course, Rosenstiel had other image considerations as well: he was indicted, although never convicted, on bootlegging charges during Prohibition. And there were stories of his legendary sexual adventures—with men and women alike; he did nothing on a limited scale—at epic parties he threw at his home that were attended both by politicians and underground crime figures.

In terms of how Rosenstiel changed whiskey as a product, his legacy on that front is also a little controversial. He presided over vicious consolidation rounds that put many distillers out of business and caused many unique bourbon styles to go extinct. But with this said, Rosenstiel is also part of the reason why many bourbons today taste as good as they do. On the lobbying front, he was a driving force to change industry regulations over taxation—dictating how long distillers could age bourbon and still make a profit—that are directly responsible for the existence of some of today's most noteworthy brands.

But here's the greatest irony: even though Rosenstiel didn't make it onto a bottle, he would have fit in well with the frontiersmen who did. Like them, he was an ambitious bootstrapper and a gambler who won more than he lost. He was a *shtarker*, the Yiddish term that's used, half in admiration and half in fear, to describe somebody who will always get the job done and never apologize about how it was accomplished. Rosenstiel might have been accused of lining the pockets of a few politicians, including Lyndon Johnson, but he also gave $100 million to philanthropic causes; and while fierce to his enemies, he was loyal to his friends. Rosenstiel was full of contradictions, but that's just another way of saying that he was an American, and just one in the kaleidoscopic cast of Americans who have made bourbon what it is. Of course, just to be fair, it *was* Rosenstiel who was most responsible for convincing Congress to designate bourbon "a distinctive product of the United States."

Our native spirit, indeed.

· CHAPTER ONE ·

BIG BANG

The earliest days of bourbon whiskey likely date to a Virginia swamp where roughly a quarter of America's colonial population was massacred in 1622 during the Powhatan Uprising. Almost four hundred years later, a visit to the swamp is much more pleasant. The Berkeley Plantation, about twenty miles upriver from Jamestown, sits in the middle of it, and was briefly the home of Captain George Thorpe, one of the first Americans believed to have distilled liquor from corn. The finer details of his efforts are vague, which can sometimes give Thorpe's story the feel of a legend, but what is certain is that he was eagerly exploring the New World's potential riches when the native grain caught his eye. In America, corn grew better than the barley that Europeans used to create beer and spirits, and Thorpe wondered if it could be used instead. Berkeley today is a working museum, and historians speculate that the carpet of grass where I'm standing on the day I visit is where Thorpe had his original still, and also where attackers during the uprising bludgeoned him to death and dismembered his corpse.

Before his unfortunate demise, Thorpe was a living paradox. Here was a New World fortune seeker who condemned his fellow colonists' bigoted attitude toward American Indians. A humanitarian as well as an inquisitive explorer, Thorpe was enthusiastic about his new home and its native people. Where his countrymen were skeptical of

America's native corn, Thorpe wrote back to London championing the grain, hoping it could be used for a drink that would raise morale and reduce the death rate caused in part by unsafe drinking water. He owned a still but he wasn't a professional distiller looking to create an industry—America for the next century would consist mainly of cottage industries supporting the larger economies of Old World empires busily carving up the continent. Rather, Thorpe was a curious amateur feeling out his new home, trying to re-create the comforts of his past life in England by experimenting with an unfamiliar grain. His early efforts likely tasted more like paint thinner than what we'd today recognize as bourbon. Regardless, the act of distilling a distinctive New World grain was a break from Old World tradition and the first step toward a uniquely American whiskey. A forerunner of the more refined corn-based whiskey that would evolve centuries later, here was bourbon's "Big Bang."

. . .

The Berkeley Plantation where Thorpe lived began in 1619 as a kind of suburb to the original Jamestown settlement, which was established a decade earlier when the very coast itself was considered the frontier. Thorpe and other settlers moving to Virginia in those first decades were taking a risky and dangerous gamble into a "howling wilderness" ravaged by famine, disease, and even rare cases of cannibalism. Travel agents, had they existed at the time, likely would have steered clients elsewhere.

Thorpe's name isn't attached to any modern whiskey brand—his grisly death doesn't make for sparkling ad copy—and nobody has bothered to spend the budget to put his name in lights. This is partly because his achievements came too early—whiskey wouldn't become popular in America until almost two centuries after his death. Until then, it was a bit player in an ensemble dominated by ale, cider, and other spirits such as rum. When whiskey finally emerged from the shadows in the late eighteenth and early nineteenth centuries, other distilling icons—people from the Ohio River Valley states where the frontier had migrated—found the spotlight instead. By the middle of the twentieth century the whiskey industry would consolidate largely within Kentucky and Tennessee, and distillers in these places naturally chose to tell the stories of hometown favorites instead of people like Thorpe. This has diminished his legacy; most of today's books about whiskey only put Thorpe's name in the footnotes, if they mention it at all.

But Thorpe's Berkeley home is likely where the idea of producing spirits from a grain unique to America first appeared. In the centuries after his experiment, the rules and standards for making bourbon, the most iconic of American whiskies, were slowly developed and codified. For a spirit to be called bourbon today, federal regulations dictate that it has to be made within the borders of the United States (not just Kentucky); it must be at least 51 percent corn, and it has to be aged in charred new oak barrels. The remainder of the grain mixture used is up to the distiller, but typically includes a small amount of malted barley and a bit of rye, which provides a spicy kick to balance the corn's sweetness (wheat is sometimes used in place of rye for a softer effect). The proofs at which it is distilled, barreled, and bottled are also carefully regulated.

It's a lot of rules, but this is what makes Berkeley so special. It's where George Thorpe started everything before any of the rules were even written.

. . .

A native of Gloucestershire, England, George Thorpe was a well-connected lawyer who had served in Parliament before partnering with three other men to form a private colony in Virginia then known as the Berkeley Hundred. He sailed from Bristol for America in 1619, leaving in England his wife, an eight-year-old daughter, and three young sons, all of whom he planned to send for once he was established across the Atlantic. After nearly three months at sea, he arrived in Virginia aboard the *Margaret*.

There was plenty of booze aboard the *Margaret*: "5½ tuns of beer,

6 tuns of cider, 11 gallons of sack, 15 gallons of aqua vitae, etc," according to ship records. "Aqua vitae" referred to distilled spirits, a term that is often dated to the fourteenth century and credited to a physician and alchemist at the University of Paris named Arnaud de Ville-Neuve. Ville-Neuve was obsessed with unlocking the secrets—including health benefits and the possibility of achieving immortality—presented by the distillation of alcohol. He suspected that alcoholic spirits were the concentrated essence of sunlight, funneled into fruits and grains that were later fermented and distilled. He wrote that aqua vitae was "a water of immortality. . . . It prolongs life, clears away ill humors, revives the heart, and maintains youth." The term meant "living water" and translated to *akvavit* in Swedish, *eau de vie* in French, and *usquebaugh* in Gaelic. The Gaelic version became *uisge-betha*, was eventually shortened to *uisge*, and finally became *whiskey*, referring to the spirit that people in the British Isles distilled from a coarse beer made out of fermented grains, predominantly malted barley.*

It's unclear if the aqua vitae aboard the *Margaret* was actually whiskey (distilled from grain) or if it was gin (also typically distilled from grain but flavored with juniper and other aromatics), brandy (distilled from fruit), or rum (distilled from sugarcane by-products like molasses). Old historical documents have a confusing tendency to use spirit names interchangeably.† In any case, more important than the specific nature of the spirits on board the *Margaret* is the fact that they were a part of the first Thanksgiving, which the Berkeley Plantation staff today emphasizes happened here more than a year before the Pilgrims' better-known celebration at Plymouth, Massachusetts. On December 4, 1619, the group's

---

*Ireland and the United States typically use the spelling "whiskey," while Scotland and Canada typically use "whisky." One legend suggests the reason for this is because stingy Scottish printers didn't want to waste the extra letter, although the real reason is unknown. America's Maker's Mark bourbon uses the *whisky* variant to honor the Scottish roots of the brand's creator.

† For instance, distilling manuals from the eighteenth century often provide recipes for "usquebaugh" that modern drinkers would likely recognize as kinds of gin. Likewise, Americans in the nineteenth century sometimes used the word "rum" to describe what was in fact whiskey (or any other spirit, for that matter).

leader, Captain John Woodlief, led everyone to a grassy clearing to give thanks and enjoy the stale remainders of the ship's provisions, including the aqua vitae.

This significant historic event is commemorated today with a humble brick gazebo festooned with plaques, reminding visitors that Virginia's Thanksgiving came first, specifically "One year and seventeen days before the Pilgrims," which can also be read to mean, "Take that, Massachusetts."

The tale paints a far different picture of the first Thanksgiving that most Americans learn in elementary school. In the Berkeley version, the settlers make do with scraps. Every year since 1958, Berkeley has reenacted this more truthful version of Thanksgiving, although guests today have the option of swapping out the scraps for catered fare. In 1963, President John F. Kennedy even issued an official proclamation acknowledging that Virginia, and not just Massachusetts, laid claim to the nation's earliest Thanksgiving heritage, but nobody really noticed— the story was already written.

About eighty yards beyond the first Thanksgiving site sits a large cornfield. When Thorpe first arrived in Virginia, the importance of corn quickly became evident. It grows well here, and American Indians in the area cultivated three principal varieties of the grain as an important foundation of their diet. The term *maize* translates to "that which sustains us," and the crop had helped save many of America's earliest white settlers from starving to death. Even so, many English back in London remained prejudiced against the grain. One European even wrote that maize was "fit only for beasts."

But Thorpe embraced the corn. Part of his mission to America was to experiment with new crops, such as tobacco and silk, and corn represented a potential cash source. He learned to grow it from the natives, a group who had captured his sympathy when he still lived in London and had hired a manservant who as a youth had traveled across the Atlantic as part of the Indian princess Pocahontas's entourage. Thorpe was impressed by the boy, and upon his arrival in America began organizing a university for natives, to convert them to Christianity and teach them about English life. Students at the school supported themselves by farming corn.

Thorpe took his role with the school seriously and, missionary zeal notwithstanding, was relatively liberal for his time. He condemned the rampant prejudice of his colonial counterparts, arguing that kindness was needed to gain the natives' trust. Backed by the colonial government, Thorpe curried favor with the Indians in ways that bothered some of his fellow colonists. He sternly punished subordinates who offended the natives and modified the rules so Indians could roam the colony freely. When Indians complained about two rowdy English mastiffs, Thorpe had the dogs hanged in public. To attract needed support from the powerful Powhatan Confederacy tribal leader Opechancanough, a large and commanding man whose name in Algonquin means "He whose soul is white," Thorpe replaced his traditional hut with an English-style house. The home included keyed locks that the Indian leader reportedly amused himself with for hours, locking and unlocking the unfamiliar devices hundreds of times over. Studying these gadgets designed to prevent theft and invasion, Opechancanough only could have taken them as an omen.

By this point, Thorpe had fully adopted corn as part of his new life, despite the occasional scorn of his countrymen back home. Running short of traditional ingredients to make his precious English beer, he realized that nature had gotten the last word, and decided to swap America's abundant corn for scarce malt. As the cargo manifest of the *Margaret* indicates, beer was more popular with the first colonists than spirits, even though it was more difficult to ship, took up greater space, and spoiled much faster. A reminder of home, beer was worth the bother, even if recipes had to be padded with things like corn, pumpkins, parsnips, and pinecones. Thorpe wrote in a letter to friends back in London that he actually preferred his "drink of Indian corn" to proper English beer, which they no doubt considered a hick thing to say. He was becoming an American.

But the colony was a restless place, better suited for a more efficient drink that lasted longer and weighed less. Records from a year after Berkeley's founding show beer imports falling and aqua vitae imports more than quadrupling. Medical thinking of the day held that distilled spirits were a good way to battle North American climates that were vulnerable to drastic swings in temperature. People believed that when a person sweated in warm weather, heat was drawn from internal organs and needed replacement, which hot liquor provided. In cold weather, the liquor provided warmth. Writing to his friend John Smyth back in London, Thorpe lamented the high mortality rate, the questionable water, and other colonists' complaints about the lack of a "good drink." This he hoped to change.

Between the first Thanksgiving site and the cornfield lies a grassy plot near a spring where Berkeley's staff speculates Thorpe kept his still. Marking it today is a whiskey barrel converted into a drinking fountain, alongside a sign that reads, "First Whiskey Distillery 1621." Other than this, the distillery is a ghost—records indicate that Thorpe had a copper still and make vague references to distilling, but are spare with finer details.

Similar distilling operations from the era, however, give us a pretty good idea of how Thorpe might have made whiskey, which follows a similar process today. He would have begun by drying his corn and then grinding it into a flour resembling cornmeal. Then it was time for cooking, the flour mixed with hot water to become a thin porridge that distillers call a "mash." The mash sat until wild bits of yeast landing in it turned the liquid into a bubbling broth called a "sweet mash." This process of fermentation can last for a few days, and when it peaks, the surface of the mixture is alive and warm as yeast spores furiously devour sugars and convert them into alcohol. During this stage, thousands of small bubbles explode on the surface. They release fumes that, from a distance, smell like fresh bread. Move in closer, and the smell gets more tangy, like sourdough starter. Stand directly over the frothy mix, and the little exploding bubbles release fumes so barely alcoholic they'll gently sting your eyes.

Of course, this is what happens when the process goes well. Sometimes it doesn't. In Thorpe's time, the primitive nature of equipment and methods sometimes prevented the magic from happening. Temperature was often an issue, and to keep the fermentation warm in cold weather, steaming manure might have been packed around the vats. If a batch resisted fermentation, it wasn't out of the question to add the carcass of a dead animal to kick-start the process.

But for now let's just assume that everything went well for Thorpe. Once the bubbling was finished, the fermented mash—resembling a thin-tasting beer absent of the lightly bitter flavor of hops—was ready for distillation. It went into a pot still sealed at the top with a thin piece of copper tubing called a *worm* that extended out and passed through a barrel of cool water. A low, even fire was built underneath the contraption, vaporizing the alcohol and pushing it through the worm, where it cooled and condensed back into a liquid. This clear liquid was likely distilled again through the same still to increase the alcoholic concentration, although more sophisticated stills today usually have a second distilling piece called a "doubler" to do this.

The clear liquor emerging from the second distillation is commonly referred to as "white dog."* It's an artful term that gives a pretty good impression of how it tastes. The nose carries the husky aroma of concentrated corn, and the taste has a hot bite that can force a sputtering cough from drinkers. The distiller's goal when producing white dog is to capture the cleanest middle portion of the distilling run, separating it from the ends, which contain chemical compounds such as congeners and aldehydes that enhance flavor when present in small quantities, but can also ruin it if there are too many. (The middle portion of the run is sometimes called "the hearts," while the ends are referred to as "heads," "tails," or "feints.") When white dog is done right, grain notes shine through and the spirit is drinkable, but that takes skilled knowledge and a lot of practice. Like most things, it's hard to get right the very first time, and most modern drinkers would probably find Thorpe's whiskey about as pleasant as getting stabbed in the mouth by a screwdriver used to pry the lid off a gas

---

* Americans tend to call it white dog; Scottish distillers prefer the term *new make.*

can. He wasn't making it for connoisseurship, he was making it to survive. The thinking of the day considered spirits a form of medicine, their alcoholic content a guard against unsafe drinking water. Surpluses of it could also be traded—for anything, really, but particularly for the Indians' land, as many of Thorpe's fellow settlers would soon learn.

A few years of aging in wood barrels greatly improves white dog, and it's at this stage that whiskey acquires its brown color and much of its flavor. The original set of colonists at Berkeley included a cooper, who might have made barrels for storing and transporting whiskey, although we can't know if they were ever used for that purpose. (Thorpe's spirit was likely stored in ceramic jugs, which lose less to evaporation than porous wooden barrels.) Even if barrels had been used, they probably weren't charred on the inside, which greatly improves flavor by caramelizing sugars in the wood that are later absorbed by the liquid (the technique wasn't widely common for aging whiskey until the nineteenth century). Thorpe's rough whiskey was probably made palatable by adding fruit or spices.

Thorpe didn't live at Berkeley long enough to refine his whiskey-making techniques or write much more about his experiments. It wasn't his main priority, and he didn't indicate if he sold it to other settlers or traded it. He was busy with his other pursuits, and had made promising steps to improve relations with the natives. Some natives were even regularly hosted in colonial homes for dinner, although for most it was probably less an act of friendship than of cultivating a labor supply for the growing expanse of plantations.

Thorpe had also grown closer to Opechancanough, who dropped hints that he was interested in converting to Christianity. Pleased with the development, Thorpe reported optimistically back to London.

Opechancanough's gestures, however, were a ruse—he was following the age-old practice of keeping friends close, but enemies closer, and the Indian leader was in fact inwardly seething from a decade's worth of slights from his new neighbors. The list was long, and alcohol was involved.

Tribes in eastern North America were some of the few peoples on earth with no traditions based around alcoholic beverages (southwestern tribes, on the other hand, had been acquainted with fermented corn drinks long before Spanish explorers introduced brandy). For these eastern Indians, such as Opechancanough, their first sips of the intoxicating liquid must have been as startling as watching the first masts of European ships puncture the horizon. Many tribes invented new words to describe alcohol's effect, but unfortunately those initial experiences were rarely positive. One of the first came in 1607, when Jamestown settler Christopher Newport—a university would be named for him many years later—sailed upriver toward the eventual Berkeley site and shared some of his liquor with a local chieftain. The chieftain fell into a stupor and thought he had been poisoned. Seizing the opportunity, Newport pretended to mumble some magic words over the Indian leader and told him he'd be better by morning. After the chief sobered up, Newport was billed as a miracle worker. Similar forms of trickery eventually evolved into a ritual of drunken trade negotiations that often ended with Native Americans giving away huge tracts of land for little in return. Years later, one settler put it bluntly: "When the object is to murder Indians, strong liquor is the main article required, for when you have them dead drunk, you may do to them as you please, without running the risk of losing your life."

During the next decade, Opechancanough watched as whites pushed 140 miles up the James River, the edges of their plantations creeping like high tide. He bided his time through 1621 and into the early months of 1622, but the writing was on the wall. Letting the new neighbors stay would be cultural suicide. Despite his best intentions, Thorpe was Opechancanough's enemy. The school he was planning was a declaration that native tradition and religion were in the crosshairs. "Integration" really meant subjugation and extinction.

On March 22, 1622, the day started as normal. Native men brought game and fur onto the plantations to trade. Some joined the colonists for breakfast. Others mingled in the fields and workshops. It was business as usual, although some of the colonists had received word from rival tribes that Opechancanough was planning an attack. Thorpe, for his part, was at home when a servant, suspicious of the natives' behavior, urged him to get away. Thorpe casually dismissed the advice, as he often did at what he considered other colonists' poor understanding of native customs.

It was advice he should have taken. Shortly thereafter, the natives struck, grabbing whatever tools or weapons lay at hand, and began slaughtering colonists in a coordinated attack throughout the countryside, killing at least 347 out of the colony's total population of roughly 1,240. Thorpe was afforded special treatment, his body mutilated after he was bludgeoned to death. The note back to his family in London was carefully circumspect about the finer details, although some historians speculate he was dismembered. Some old history texts claim the natives were drunk on Thorpe's whiskey when they attacked, a baseless claim completely rejected by Berkeley's staff.

The colony took revenge, and their policies toward the natives hardened, spinning into a cycle of violence. Opechancanough was captured more than two decades later when he was nearing one hundred years of age and had just orchestrated another uprising. While he was imprisoned in Jamestown, his guard shot him in the back. Today the primary reminders that his culture ever even existed are found mainly in the names of the rivers, national parks, and military bases—Rappahannock, Shenandoah, Quantico—that you pass as you drive down the I-95 expressway that hugs the eastern coastline.

· · ·

The beginning of whiskey in America wasn't spectacular, and as Thorpe's fate and the probable quality of spirits made from his corn drink can attest, there was still a long way to go. Thorpe would probably be gobsmacked at modern bourbon, the sweetly oaked stuff of today a vast departure from the harsh first drippings that dribbled from his still. Improvisational attempts at distilling other fermented grains into spirits had occurred long before Thorpe's time, and remained improvisational well over a century after his death. These ancient spirits carried an assortment of names, many of them variations of the Gaelic *usquebaugh* that would later morph into "whiskey": *uisce betha* (1405), *uskebaeghe* (1581), *uscough baugh* (1600), *usquebagh* (1682), *usquebae* (1715). One manual from 1731 gives a recipe for *usquebaugh* that resembles a kind of primordial gin, consisting of malted barley steeped with sugar, cloves, coriander, and cinnamon.

These spirits were made on both sides of the Atlantic but were minimally if at all aged, aside from any flavor they picked up from barrels used for transport. Other distilling manuals from the eighteenth and early nineteenth centuries show that Americans regularly channeled the innovative practicality that Thorpe had exhibited with corn. They experimented by fermenting and distilling whatever surplus crops lay at hand: carrots, turnips, whortleberries, maple syrup. In most cases, the rough edges of the unaged results were masked with herbs and flavorings.

In the decades before the American Revolution, however, all of these other spirits were vastly overshadowed by rum, made from sugarcane and molasses shipped from British-controlled parts of the Caribbean to distilleries in the rapidly industrializing coastal cities of the colonies. The sugarcane by-products would have gone to waste otherwise, thus making rum an essential and practical tool used by the Crown to knit together the various economies of its scattered empire. But as war between the colonies and England threatened the rum trade, whiskeys more closely resembling those we are familiar with today—made from the native grains of a nation verging on independence—shifted into position.

· CHAPTER TWO ·

RYE AND REVOLUTION

In 2007, Washington, D.C., buzzed with talk about the resurrection of George Washington's lost whiskey recipe. His distillery at Mount Vernon, only a few miles from the capital, had just been rebuilt and was holding its grand opening. The first bottle of whiskey coming off the stills was going to be auctioned to the highest bidder, and many came to watch the competition.

Washington notables roamed the event grounds alongside about fifty reporters and photographers. Prince Andrew, the Duke of York, was present to cut the ribbon and promote Scottish-U.S. ties with a tribute to James Anderson, the Scottish farm manager who originally convinced George Washington to build the distillery after he returned home from the Revolutionary War. The first president was persuaded, and for a brief period his operation was America's biggest whiskey distillery. The winning bidder for the first bottle from the rebuilt still would own a piece of history, one connecting whiskey to the most famous founding father and the nation's earliest heritage.

Marvin Shanken, impresario publisher of *Wine Spectator* and *Cigar Aficionado*, was there for the auction. Shanken had electrified international headlines two decades earlier when he entered a bidding war with the billionaire Malcolm Forbes for a bottle of French wine that had supposedly belonged to Thomas Jefferson. Shanken was a bushy but charming pleasure seeker, a man given to dropping serious coin in pursuit of the good life. Once, after his wife forbade him from smoking cigars in their Manhattan apartment, he bought the adjacent unit and turned it into a smoking lounge. At the auction, there was no doubt he'd go to similar great lengths to get the first bottle of Washington's whiskey. After the bidding started, Shanken didn't disappoint, securing the bottle for a cool $100,000. It was by far the highest price anyone had ever paid for an American whiskey.

At the time of Shanken's winning bid, most Americans were blithely unaware that the first president had been involved in the whiskey industry at all, let alone that he was the nation's biggest distiller. Washington's distillery burned down a decade after his death in 1799, and a blanket of weeds soon covered the rubble. After that, it was effectively wiped from the nation's collective memory. A few anti-Prohibition advocates tried to resurrect the memory of Washington's distillery a century later, but were shouted down by a powerful temperance movement claiming the first president's ties to whiskey would tarnish his reputation, although it was probably more worried that the connection would undermine its own cause.

Thus the distillery sat dormant until archaeologists stumbled upon the old site in 1995. By then, Prohibition was a faded memory and whiskey was starting to enjoy renewed popularity. Its cultural cachet restored, Americans no longer had qualms about linking whiskey to the most famous founding father, who personally helped engineer the nation's transformation from a country of rum drinkers into whiskey drinkers. The whiskey industry's chief lobbying group, no doubt sensing the powerful appeal of reestablishing a deep connection to George Washington, quickly made plans to rebuild the distillery as a working museum and tourist attraction.

The rebuilt distillery at Mount Vernon sits a couple of miles away from Washington's main home so its gristmill can utilize the passing currents of a nearby stream. The entire operation was originally part of an eight-thousand-acre working plantation that made the first president one of the wealthiest men in Virginia. Construction of the main house began in 1757, shortly after Washington suffered his second major defeat for election to the Virginia House of Burgesses. Sizing up his losses and pondering his next steps, he blamed the defeat on his failure to effectively accomplish what many called "swilling the planters with bumbo."

What this meant was that he had failed to ply voters with alcohol, a common if illegal practice that politicians from the era referred to as "treating." The colonies inherited the habit from England, and it became an essential part of the American political process well into the nineteenth century. James Madison, who lost an election in 1777 to a candidate who gave out more free alcohol to voters, would later write that voters traveling long distances to polling stations expected their trips to be rewarded with more than just democracy. Washington was savvier when he ran again in 1758. He swilled the planters with enough booze to win Frederick County with 310 votes to his opponent's 45.

"Bumbo" wasn't a nickname for whiskey or even a generalized term for alcohol. It was a rum-based drink made with sugar and spices such as nutmeg or cinnamon. Rum dominated the colonial drinkscape before it was usurped by whiskey following the Revolution, and tavern records from the time regularly show it outselling all other drinks combined. It was both the colonists' favorite drink and a perfect symbol of colonial economics and politics. Made from sugarcane and molasses shipped from British-controlled parts of the Caribbean to commercial distilleries popping up in rapidly industrializing parts of New England, rum provided a mechanism for the Crown to integrate its empire by pairing the distinct talents of its far-flung points—New England had the customer base and distilleries, the Caribbean had an abundance of cheap molasses. By 1763, Boston brimmed with more than thirty rum distilleries, and nearly a thousand ships each year brought the drink in and out of its harbor. Rum and molasses composed 20 percent of the city's imports, making it the region's leading industry.

The brisk trade, however, was plagued by imbalances, and colonists relied on British imports more than the reverse. The colonists paid for their imports with gold and silver, then suffered currency shortages when England didn't buy anything in return. Credit was one answer, but English financiers hesitated to invest in remote projects, forcing many colonial merchants to barter using rum when cash was short. The spirit was easy to make, relatively simple to ship, and maintained a value that fluctuated less than paper money.

As colonists increasingly used rum as a barter tool for international trade, the British soon introduced tariffs to ensure they got a fair share of the growing profits. The Molasses Act was passed in 1733, prompted by British sugar planters who pulled strings in Parliament to establish duties making colonial imports of French and Spanish molasses more expensive than British molasses from the West Indies. Unfazed, colonists shrugged off the duties and spent the next three decades simply smuggling the cheaper molasses. Corrupt British customs officials usually doctored the paperwork.

In 1764, England became more serious when it passed the Sugar Act. The measure increased the price that New England rum distilleries paid for molasses by further curtailing foreign imports, and was once again a maneuver by Parliament to help its cronies in the Caribbean. But whereas the colonists had considered the Molasses Act a mere nuisance, the Sugar Act touched a nerve. It landed amid an economic depression, closing many distilleries and forcing the rest to muddle along, enduring higher costs. Colonists began carving time out of their busy smuggling schedules to protest and begin writing pamphlets. One title breathlessly said it all: *Reasons Against the Renewal of the Sugar Act as It Will Be Prejudicial to the Trade Not Only of the Northern Colonies But to Those of Great Britain Also.*

The colonists' outcry convinced England to roll back parts of the act, but that did little to settle the matter. They were now talking, organizing, and warming up the presses. England, working to prevent the colonists from becoming emboldened by their victory, quickly imposed other taxes. The Sugar Act was replaced by the Stamp Act, which was an even more burdensome tax on all varieties of printed papers, including newspapers, playing cards, contracts, and pamphlets with ridiculously long titles.

Colonists responded with a shorter message: "No taxation without representation."

On the brink of war, just two months before the battles at Lexington and Concord, a group of British soldiers marched toward Salem, Massachusetts, and were confronted by an angry mob blocking the only bridge into town. A colonist named Joseph Whicher stepped forward from the crowd and dared the soldiers to fight, pulling back the sides of his shirt to reveal his bare chest. A British soldier glanced him with his bayonet—it was just a little warning telling the colonist to back off, but enough to spill a thin line of blood down the front of Whicher's shirt. The Revolutionary War's first blood was drawn, and from a man who happened to be the foreman of a local rum distillery, a spirit that was about to be ousted in favor of whiskey.

. . .

George Washington was a moderate drinker, usually preferring the expensive Madeira or brandy favored by many in his high social class. But most Americans enjoyed the ubiquitous rum, including the regular troops serving under Washington in the war, who were given a daily four-ounce ration of the spirit for morale and health. Shortly after the war started, however, British blockades of molasses shipments from the Caribbean created shortages of the drink. When American major general Horatio Gates prepared to fight the British in South Carolina during the summer of 1780, as British troops swept up the coast from the south in a series of successful offensives, he found his rum supplies bare. He did, however, have plenty of molasses. Figuring the raw material of rum was better than nothing, Gates distributed the sweet goo among his men without realizing it was a laxative. He ultimately lost to the British.

Rum soon became a political target. In the middle of the war Congess moved to levy import duties on molasses, but the measure, which required unanimous consent, was blocked by a Rhode Island delegation protecting rum distilleries in the state. That was rum's last political victory, however. Once the federal government was established at the war's end, Congress, which didn't need unanimous consent anymore, put the rum and molasses duties in place.

Rum was falling fast, and per capita consumption during the war dropped by more than half. Pushed by necessity to find alternatives, the United States began acquiring a taste for whiskey, a more patriotic alternative made from domestic grain. After patriot troops lost a well-fought battle to the British at Germantown in October 1777, Congress sent the fighters thirty casks of whiskey as a reward. The French, equally impressed by the patriots' fighting at the battle, as well as at Saratoga, decided to assist the struggling rebellion. Americans repaid the gesture by naming an assortment of frontier areas for French towns and people. These included Bourbon County in present-day Kentucky, which in the following decades would emerge as an important whiskey-producing area.

As the fighting raged, Washington lobbied Congress for the construction of public distilleries in different states, writing in one letter that "It is necessary, there should always be a Sufficient Quantity of Spirits with the Army." During the winter at Valley Forge, where vicious bouts of dysentery and typhoid killed around 20 percent of the twelve thousand troops, rum shortages were particularly bad, forcing Washington to constantly reallocate supplies. Eventually, he ordered the switch to whiskey. While ration orders had previously stipulated rum specifically, Washington broadened them to read, "One gill of whiskey or spirits, as or when they are available."

America's transition to whiskey was also sped along by backwoods settlers who became some of Washington's favorite fighters in the war. Even as combat raged, Americans continued to migrate west, where they often protected the Continental Army's flank by fighting Indians recruited by the British. The frontier, however, was isolated from shipments of rum or the raw materials needed to make it. In contrast, it was an ideal place for whiskey: water flowed, grain grew, and plenty of wood was available to burn under the stills. Many of the settlers were also skilled at the practice, hailing from a variety of European backgrounds—German, Scottish, Irish, Scotch-Irish—that all had strong legacies of distilling either brandy or grain spirits.

Of the entire contingent, the Scotch-Irish best embodied the characteristics that proved most useful to Washington in turning the tide of the war. Most had left Europe on bad terms and were intensely patriotic and loyal to the cause of American independence. They hated the British, questioned all authority, and had honed their fighting abilities back in Europe by resisting whiskey taxes levied by an oppressive government. Neither technically Scotch nor Irish, the Scotch-Irish were poor Protestants also known as Ulstermen, a name given them by King James I starting in 1610 when he sent them to Ulster, a rowdy Catholic region of Ireland, to "tame" the "wild Irish" living there and help spread Protestantism. The move came shortly after the Crown had dragged the remote enclave into submission after a protracted struggle, and the Scotch-Irish became outcasts living among other outcasts as both groups struggled to survive.

The Scotch-Irish turned to whiskey for income, building their reputation as distillers. The Scotch and Irish whiskey styles for which the British Isles would later become famous, however, were still a long way from their modern forms. Today, both are made primarily, though not always entirely, from barley. Other differences depend on many factors: How is the grain malted, and with what kind of fuel? (With scotch, burning peat is often, though not always, used to dry the grains, infusing the whisky with the essence of the loamy bogs from which the peat is harvested.) What kind of still is used, and how? (Irish whiskey is typically, though not always, triple distilled.) How is the spirit aged? (Different kinds of barrels are used, many of them repurposed after aging sherry or bourbon.) These decisions are made by the producers and, like bourbon, it wouldn't be until much later that Europe's most famous whiskey styles would become fully defined or regulated by their own sets of rules and standards.

As the Scotch-Irish refined their whiskey craft in their new home, the Crown buried them under indignities. They had converted peaty countryside bogs into farmland, introduced the potato, built deepwater ports that turned Belfast into northern Ireland's shipping hub, and established thriving woolen and linen industries. Their English counterparts couldn't keep up, and Parliament soon passed laws to limit trade and increase rents. When the Crown passed a tax on whiskey to help fund a civil war elsewhere in the country, the Scotch-Irish began celebrated careers as whiskey smugglers and moonshiners, the latter term derived from their nighttime smuggling of spirits from Holland and France onto the British coast. They didn't hesitate to kill revenue collectors and organized into gangs to battle any larger forces sent to enforce the whiskey tax.

America beckoned. Starting around 1717, large waves of Scotch-Irish streamed into the Carolinas and Pennsylvania. From there, many drifted into remote western territories where, unbothered by authority, they lived as they pleased and put their indelible stamp on the land. John Steinbeck many years later would write in *East of Eden*, "The names of places carry a charge of the people who named them, reverent or ir-reverent, descriptive, either poetic or disparaging." The Scotch-Irish gave the American places where they made whiskey names like Gal-lows Branch, Cutthroat Gap, or, in one instance, Shitbritches Creek. In Lunenburg County, Virginia, they even named two streams Tickle Cunt Branch and Fucking Creek. They often called themselves "red-necks," an old Scots border term for Presbyterians. Another title they used for themselves was "crackers," a term that came from the Scots word *craik*, which literally means "talk," but was typically used to de-scribe the kind of loud bragging that usually leads to a fight.

The Scotch-Irish in America intimidated easterners who failed to understand why these backwoodsmen would actually choose to live in the howling wilderness. During their odd visits back east, these people from the frontier wore buckskin and spoke of living among In-dians while at the same time killing them. Many seemed to prefer this dangerous life. They emerged only periodically from the woods, sport-ing long greasy hair and rifles that proved deadly accurate against tiny squirrels or other humans. They were accomplished killers whose skills at fighting were matched only by their ability to turn grain into liquor.

British general Cornwallis was particularly wary of having these men along his western flank as he marched north in 1780, the prospect of defeating the rebels coming into sharper focus. The two years since Valley Forge had been miserable for the Continental Army, forcing George Washington to write in one letter that "I have almost ceased to hope." Cornwallis, cautious as victory loomed, sent a thousand troops inland under the command of a brash major named Patrick Ferguson to protect his flank against the frontiersmen who threatened his northern advance. Ferguson, sniffing at the group of frontiersmen he called a "set of mongrels," strutted to the base of the Blue Ridge Mountains and told the "backwater men" that if the frontier didn't surrender to the Crown, it would be met with "fire and sword."

Ferguson clearly didn't consider his audience very well, and the threat only could have dredged up bad memories with Americans who had abandoned the Crown on poor terms. The frontiersmen responded by rallying two thousand troops, many reporting for duty with little more than a rifle and a blanket for sleeping outdoors. A Scotch-Irish preacher named Samuel Doak replied that Ferguson's threat would be matched by "the sword of the Lord and of Gideon!"

The sides clashed at Kings Mountain in South Carolina near the North Carolina border. The frontiersmen cornered the British troops on the mountain peak, killing Ferguson with at least eight shots when he refused to surrender. Colonial losses were 28 killed and 62 wounded; Tory casualties were nearly 300 killed, 163 wounded, and almost 700 taken prisoner. The victory greatly boosted American morale, undermined Cornwallis's campaign, and was praised by Thomas Jefferson for helping turn the "tide of success which terminated the Revolutionary War with the seal of independence."

Washington, his morale lifted, was characteristically more reticent than Jefferson, calling the battle proof of the "spirit and resources of the country." The backwoodsmen had given him the boost he needed. Their whiskey—made entirely from homegrown grains and not reliant on imports—increasingly turned into a popular symbol of national unity that helped clear away rum's whiff of colonial rule.

But while Washington was appreciative for now, he'd eventually find himself on the wrong side of the frontiersmen's ferocity a decade later, when he made the same mistake the British had years earlier, of trying to tax their whiskey to pay for a war they had helped win.

. . .

The modern distillery at Mount Vernon is housed in a barn covering an area a little smaller than a basketball court. It holds five stills, just like it did in the 1790s when the distillery, at its peak, produced over eleven thousand gallons per year. Today it is a kind of working museum and the inside is dark and warm, full of scents of smoke and cooking grains. Steven Bashore, who currently manages the distillery and its adjacent gristmill, where grains are ground into flour, shows me around. Whiskey was one of Mount Vernon's most important business ventures and demand from nearby customers was brisk from the beginning, Bashore explains. History books, however, rarely mention this fact, probably because of historically unfavorable opinions of alcohol surrounding the temperance movement, he continues. But as attitudes toward whiskey have improved Mount Vernon has decided to highlight the distillery as part of the nation's heritage, rebuilt in part with funds from the Distilled Spirits Council of the United States (DISCUS), the whiskey industry's biggest lobbying group. As we poke about, Bashore, wearing a full period costume, tells me that the historic site intends to promote the idea of Washington as a businessman as much as a military and political leader.

The distillery makes rye whiskey, based on a recipe from Mount Vernon's records but reengineered for the modern effort by David Pickerell, a former master distiller at Maker's Mark who now consults with numerous craft distilling upstarts, making him a kind of Johnny Appleseed of America's burgeoning craft whiskey movement. Pickerell holds two degrees in chemistry and his knowledge of distilling is legendary. His is a Midas touch to emerging outfits who otherwise would have spent decades struggling to learn a craft with one of the longest learning curves in the food business.

Rye whiskey, made primarily from the grain it takes its name from, was the dominant whiskey of the United States' early decades. The grain grows well where other grains don't, particularly in parts of eastern states like Maryland, New York, Virginia, and Pennsylvania. To be labeled rye whiskey today, the spirit must contain at least 51 percent rye, with the remainder of the grains left up to the distiller. Many of today's rye recipes, though not all, contain at least some corn. The original recipe for Washington's whiskey was about 60 percent rye, 35 percent corn, and 5 percent malted barley (distilleries typically refer to the proportions of grains as the "mash bill"). This approximates what today is often called the Maryland style of rye, including modern brands like Pikesville, which have a considerable amount of corn. Pennsylvania-style mash bills, such as Dad's Hat Rye, generally carry more than 80 percent rye (or are entirely made of it), although neither the Pennsylvania nor Maryland styles is regulated by a strict definition (and there is a minor debate about their origins). No matter the grain makeup, most American whiskies contain at least a little barley because it is a good source of the enzymes that convert grain starches into fermentable sugars.

Think of rye as bourbon's sibling. The majority of modern recipes for each style of whiskey contain the same ingredients, just in different proportions (bourbon's greater portion of corn would become the eventual result of people moving west and settling land where the grain thrived even more than it did back east). Rye whiskey was best described by the American historian and author Bernard DeVoto, who once wrote, "In the heroic ages our forefathers invented self-government, the Constitution, and bourbon, and on the way to them they invented rye."

The rye grain is also an important part of traditional bourbon. The majority of bourbon brands today incorporate rye into their recipes as a "flavor grain" to help balance corn's sweetness with rye's dry spiciness. There are a handful of contemporary bourbon brands, such as Maker's Mark and W.L. Weller, that use wheat as a flavor grain instead, which lends a sweet smoothness in place of rye's kick, but wheat is typically an exception, and the mash bills of most bourbon brands generally use between 10 and 20 percent rye. Some "high-rye" bourbons, such as Bulleit, use 28 percent rye or even more, although there's no official definition of what is "high" or "low" rye content (Old Grand-Dad is another high-rye bourbon, carrying a mash bill that's 30 percent rye). Wild Turkey, with a rye content of about 13 percent, is generally considered a medium-rye bourbon.

The combination of rye and corn in a whiskey forms a whole greater than the sum of its parts. Corn on its own can sometimes taste a little one-note, but rye gives depth in the way that adding a horn section to a band helps bring a song alive. Rye on its own is often flavorful and delicious, but can also have a spiky quality that benefits from the introduction of a smoother corn spirit to mellow its edges. If the grains in bourbon formed a band, corn would be the suave frontman, providing body and mass but not quite able to hold the stage down all by himself. Rye would play bass, giving the ensemble style and soul but a little weird when heard playing alone. You'd still recognize the song without rye, but it wouldn't have near the same groove.

Just as Washington's distillery was being rebuilt, rye whiskey, which largely disappeared from American liquor stores during the later decades of the twentieth century as tastes veered toward different drinks, started making a comeback. Its retro status as a forgotten treasure clicked with drinkers and a cocktail scene looking to the past for nostalgic inspiration. Many new craft distilleries emerging during that time chose to make it in order to create a name for themselves by doing something different from the bourbons that more established distilleries were already doing very well. Rye's relative obscurity gave it the kind of outsider cred that's the currency of cool.

Of course, not everything at Washington's rebuilt distillery is exactly the same as it was two hundred years ago. Bashore and his colleagues, careful not to sugarcoat things, emphasize that slaves were about 75 percent of the distillery's original workforce. Also, Washington wasn't making his whiskey for connoisseurship. He, like other distillers of this time, made it to sell as a bulk commodity—brand names didn't yet exist and producers like Washington therefore had no incentive to spend the time or money to age it. Whiskey was often stored in ceramic crocks owned by the final purchaser, which added nothing to the flavor, and barrels were only used to briefly transport it, which added little.

A book in Mount Vernon's main museum contains Martha Washington's recipes for dressing up young spirits with fruit to make cordials. This was needed in light of the reality that George Washington's whiskey probably tasted hot and harsh, and achieving consistency between batches was almost certainly a problem (nevertheless, the modern unaged version sells for an eye-popping ninety-five dollars per pint in the museum gift shop, no doubt due to its novelty status as "Washington's whiskey"). When I try a sample, it's relatively bright and clean for a white dog, but by no means good enough to enjoy regularly on its own. Bashore hands me another sample that's been aged for two years and it's much better—the wood has contributed notes of light pepper and tangerine, although it could still use a little more time. In any case, it's no doubt better than any of the spirits drunk by the frontier rebels who were about to rise up and threaten the young nation's survival after Washington decided to tax the whiskey that had become an important part of their economy.

. . .

As George Washington slogged through the humid hills of western Pennsylvania on his way to subdue the Whiskey Rebellion during the summer of 1794, all he really wanted was to return home to Mount Vernon. He was barely a year into his second presidential term, which he had originally hoped to avoid, and was feeling the strain of his sixty-two years as the steel parts of his dentures cut into his inflamed gums. Now he had to take care of this mess on the frontier.

Settlers in isolated regions of the countryside had risen up against the unpopular whiskey tax Washington had implemented three years earlier in 1791. Since then, the insurrection had swelled into a debate over the nation's soul. The question of how to best tax whiskey would partially determine how to organize a loose collection of isolated areas into a nation. Would big business or small be the guiding force? The rebellion threatened the young nation's sovereignty, and because Washington had speculatively invested in frontier property, it also threatened his personal fortune.

Two opposing sides were arguing their cases in each of Washington's tired old ears. His response would not only draw the blueprint for the nation's economic future, it would determine how the whiskey industry would operate and decide whether distillers would have a proper environment to refine their craft.

On one side was Alexander Hamilton, Washington's right-hand man since the Revolution and the architect of the hated whiskey tax. Hamilton came from humble beginnings in the Caribbean but had pulled himself up by the proverbial bootstraps to quickly gain acceptance among the elite power brokers of New York finance. During the Revolution, he was assigned to Washington's staff and impressed the general, quickly becoming one of Washington's most trusted advisers. After the war, he was appointed as the first treasury secretary at the age of thirty-two. From that lofty perch he championed industry and big finance and wrote the whiskey tax to promote the advancement of larger, more established distilleries on the East Coast, to the detriment of smaller frontier distilleries. His grave today rests in his adopted city of New York, in a cemetery at the top of Wall Street.

Talking into Washington's other ear was Thomas Jefferson. Jefferson was familiar with the same elite circles as Washington and Hamilton—he had inherited five thousand acres and a full labor force of slaves—but his sympathies ultimately rested with the small farmers operating the thousands of tiny stills puffing away on the frontier. To him, those small farmers were "the chosen people of God" and Jefferson didn't think they should be governed by Hamilton's brand of centralized policies, which he called "a tissue of machinations against the liberty of his country." Whereas Hamilton was a devotee of the economist and philosopher David Hume, who argued that a nation's success relied on wealth controlled by a few powerful individuals who knew how to invest it properly; Jefferson championed local economies. He was a disciple of the writer John Locke, whose hands-off philosophy of laissez-faire economics promoted a decentralized version of capitalism.

Hamilton's justification for the tax, which started at eleven cents per gallon of whiskey, was that it would pay off $45 million worth of debt from the Revolutionary War. The idea that such a little tax could pay off such a huge debt also indicates how much whiskey Americans were drinking by this point. The tax revenue would also help Hamilton fund ambitious national projects like roads, canals, and a central bank. Hamilton ironically took his blueprints for the whiskey tax from England, where small distilleries and government had long clashed, moonshining thrived, and big distilleries helped the British government write tax laws. In return, Parliament offered commercial distilleries tax rebates and banned stills under a certain size. This sort of arrangement had given the small island nation the kind of mighty industrial power and efficiency Hamilton wanted for America. He could only imagine what America, a land of much greater natural wealth, could become if its resources were utilized in the same fashion.

But even though the tax was good for big whiskey producers, it wasn't necessarily good for the development of the product. Just as in England, distillers attempting to avoid the tax would flee into an underground economy. Those making whiskey illegally would be focused on simply getting their product out the door, not refining it, experimenting, or devoting the necessary time to refine their craft.

Hamilton's whiskey tax—the first of its kind on an American-made product—supported larger distillers over smaller ones because of how the tax was collected. In cities, distillers only paid taxes on how much spirits they produced, since tax collectors could easily monitor output and collect accordingly. But in areas the government defined as "the country," distillers paid according to their still capacity, which was assumed to run at full production all the time. The problem was that most frontier distillers used their equipment only when they needed to, meaning they'd theoretically have to pay taxes on spirits they didn't even produce. To smaller distillers, the tax echoed the oppressive government policies that had driven the United States to revolt against Britain.

When small distillers balked, Hamilton responded by giving them a few breaks, such as assigning local courts jurisdiction so tax evaders wouldn't have to travel three hundred miles for their hearings. But, at the same time, he gave large commercial distilleries additional advantages like leakage and shipwreck allowances, which bailed them out of unforeseen disasters. The gestures to small distillers were largely symbolic—the inefficient cottage industry bothered Hamilton. He also thought the tax would be a way for the freeloading frontier to pay for the expensive military protection it required against hostile Indians.

Hamilton also argued for the tax on moral grounds, claiming it was a way to transform intemperance into something productive. It was a "luxury tax" on personal consumption and people would pay based only on how much they drank. The tax, he claimed, would improve sobriety and prevent untimely deaths, and he even enlisted Philadelphia's College of Physicians to argue his case in front of Congress. Opponents in Congress responded by telling the physicians they didn't have the right to tell other Americans how to live.

Ask anyone on the frontier, and they would disagree with Hamilton. To them, whiskey was far more than a luxury. The excise was essentially a selective tax on income, since many on the frontier used whiskey for barter. They were basically being asked to convert an untaxed product into a taxable one. For many, the decision of whether or not to convert grain into spirits wasn't a choice. Spirits used as currency were often more stable than the continental dollar, were easily divided, and were the most efficient way to transport their crops to market in areas with poor infrastructure—a horse could carry six times as much grain in whiskey form. On top of it all, the whiskey tax had to be paid in cash, which was precisely what frontier distillers didn't have.

Then there was the expensive military protection they supposedly required. Those in the backwoods were unimpressed with the government's performance, pointing out their tomahawk wounds.

Both sides had their points. Hamilton's vision could generate revenue to build infrastructure that frontier distillers could use to efficiently get their grain to market and not have to rely on converting it to whiskey. But it also meant control in the hands of a few corporate bosses and efficiency gained at the loss of individual ownership. Some on the frontier argued for a progressive tax allowing them to contribute their part, but not under a tax structure that put them under an inherent disadvantage. Others simply hated the government's taking a cut no matter what the money would be used for.

Whatever the case it made, the frontier was on its own. Jefferson and his political ally James Madison had originally opposed the tax but ceased fighting for it after a bout of political horse trading regarding banking and the location of the nation's new capital. Once the dust settled, Jefferson was out of the conversation, Hamilton had made his case to Washington, and the tax went into effect.

The fighting started in 1791, after the federal government began sending tax collectors into the frontier. One of the first to ride into western Pennsylvania, a man named Robert Johnson, soon found himself confronted in a dark forest by a group of torch-bearing frontiersmen, mainly disillusioned war veterans. They wore women's dresses and blackface makeup that transformed their eyes into angry round moons. The wardrobe was an old tradition inherited from European populist uprisings; it had been used to protest the unpopular whiskey taxes in the Old World and to terrorize neighbors who collected rewards by reporting unregistered stills. It was clear that Johnson was the frontiersmen's enemy. And their prey. They pulled the whiskey tax collector from his horse, sheared him bald, slathered him in hot tar and feathers, then stole his horse and left him in the dark. He almost died before he found his way back home, days later.

Events boiled to a head during the three years following the assault on Johnson. Tempers flared and the rebel attacks got bigger and better organized. Whiskey was much more than the "luxury" Hamilton had called it. The liquid was a way of life, woven into the economic and social fabric of the countryside. It soon became a symbol of dueling ideologies and threatened to spark a civil war.

The West threatened to secede from the East, and some of the voices calling out from the wilderness described an appealing vision. Herman Husband, a frontier preacher, wanted to create a utopian "New Jerusalem" in the forest. He urged a peaceful transition into a place free from slavery, with public support for the arts and sciences, an income tax, progressive wealth taxes, safeguards against nepotism, and a paper currency with a well-tended rate of inflation, limiting the frontier's reliance on whiskey as a form of currency.

Husband's ideas were startlingly sane, but his voice was quickly marginalized by the frontier's other emerging leaders. David Bradford, a wealthy and mouthy lawyer, took greater control of the movement by stoking the frontier's bloodlust. He compared their cause to the ongoing French Revolution, calling himself the Robespierre of the West, after the French terrorist who led mass killings of French citizens during the revolution's Reign of Terror. Some rebels suggested replacing tar and feathers with the guillotine and attacking Pittsburgh, calling it a "Sodom" of merchant cartel operations.

The "Sodom" cry was an extension of what the whiskey tax represented. The measure was another nail in the frontier's coffin as people watched their other fledgling industries—mills, lumber yards, ironworks—taken over by eastern finance men and speculators with little personal investment in these projects. Now whiskey—one of the most profitable businesses they had—was going to be part of the same machine built to enrich the few.

For a symbol of what the tax represented, the rebels need not look any further than General John Neville, the tax inspector in charge of southwest Pennsylvania. Neville had moved there after the Revolution and started the Neville Connection, a business concern dabbling in a number of pursuits, the most lucrative of which was supplying whiskey to army forces fighting the Indians. Neville's business was a Hamiltonian affair attempting to centralize and streamline the army supply process. Under his system, the army would buy whiskey in bulk only from large contractors, who were then responsible for delivering it to army outposts. This gave Neville and other big operators, who had access to more efficient methods of transportation, a way to block small farmer-distillers from the army, their most lucrative market. Neville and his colleagues would then buy the little guys' whiskey cheap and mark it up for their own profit. It was a huge conflict of interest—Neville was in charge of collecting taxes on an industry he was involved in, and had a government-sanctioned tool to undersell smaller producers competing with him. To small distillers, the system was rigged.

In July 1794, Neville was accompanying a federal marshal to issue a court summons when a posse of local militants fired on both men. Neville escaped to his home and prepared for continued violence. Elsewhere, another militia group plotted to take Neville prisoner and try him in what was essentially a kangaroo court. By the time the second militia reached Neville's home, they found the windows boarded up and the government official prepared for battle. Neville's wife, daughters, and slaves reloaded weapons for him as he fought off the small group, leaving four dead on his front lawn. The rebels retreated to gather reinforcements.

In the meantime, eleven soldiers sent from Fort Pitt joined Neville at his home for the looming showdown. Then the rebels returned . . . about six hundred of them.

Neville managed to escape out the back while the soldiers traded shots, killing the rebel commander, another disillusioned war veteran. But there was no way the government forces could win, and soon they surrendered. The army commanders were arrested and the other soldiers sent back to Pittsburgh with news of the defeat. As for Neville's home, the rebels walked inside and drained his private stash of whiskey, according to one account. Then they burned his entire plantation to the ground.

Washington's decision to rally thirteen thousand troops—more than had beaten the British at Yorktown—to quash the rebellion wasn't made without difficulty. Thomas Jefferson and Edmund Randolph, who had recently replaced Jefferson as secretary of state, both argued against using the military against U.S. citizens. Hamilton, on the other hand, told Washington he needed to restore order, and could use the rebellion as an opportunity to show the nation that a strong central government would enforce the law.

For Washington, it was a matter of either provoking civil war or abandoning part of the country. The rebels were his countrymen, but by this point they were also marching on Pittsburgh. Seven thousand of them had already rolled out of the mountains to converge at Braddock's Field, about eight miles outside of the city. They even brought their own flag: six alternating red and white stripes representing the unified counties of western Pennsylvania and northwestern Virginia. They were going to secede.

Washington made the call to suppress the rebellion with troops he would lead to the frontier himself, calculating that articulate radicals such as Bradford had coerced much of the frontier into a frenzy and that cooler heads could prevail. Washington didn't normally drink whiskey, but chose to do so as he rode into Pennsylvania, his aides writing, "As the President will be going . . . into the Country of Whiskey, he proposes to make use of that liquor for his drink."

Washington's assumption was correct. With the federal troops en route, the rebels disbanded and the leaders fled to Spanish Louisiana or other points west. It all ended with a whimper, with just two men sentenced to hang: Philip Wigle and John Mitchell. When Washington met the men, however, he pardoned them after determining that Wigle was "insane" and Mitchell was "simple," demonstrating the kind of compassion for his fellow countrymen that many hoped the president would exhibit. Wigle and Mitchell were just two incompetent pawns the rebellion's leaders had enlisted to do dirty work like commit arson and steal the mail. Nevertheless, in 2012 a new distillery in Pittsburgh would name itself after Wigle, calling him a "good-natured man who was sentenced to hang for his unsinkable love of whiskey," and adopt a noose as its logo.

Wigle and the noose are odd choices no doubt, but a perfect example of the romantic appeal the Whiskey Rebellion still holds for many, even if the history has to be creatively reinterpreted for marketing reasons.

The Whiskey Rebellion failed, but so did the tax. The rebellion cost $1.5 million to suppress, about a third of the amount collected in tax over the next six years, which was how long the tax remained in place before it was abandoned. Washington, however, prospered: the value of his land investments in western Pennsylvania increased by about 50 percent. Hamilton's success was mixed. He had asserted the federal government's authority, but distilling remained a cottage industry as smuggling and moonshining thrived under the tax. His coining of the term "Whiskey Rebellion" was a sly way to diminish the frontier's larger concerns by refocusing attention on a drink that many in his social circle considered vulgar.

As for the farmer-distillers, the rebellion's end only illuminated their concerns. The officers of the federal army were men of the coastal aristocracy, mounted atop fine horses. Many had agreed to join the army only if their demands for splendid uniforms and proper rank were met. They stayed in warm taverns or private homes, drinking Madeira, port, or brandy. The enlisted troops were poor laborers and farmers who weren't very different from the frontiersmen. They slept on the ground or in stables, drinking whiskey.

· · ·

Thomas Jefferson's home at Monticello, in central Virginia, is a portrait of how he wanted the world to see him. His interminable curiosity and pleasure seeking are apparent throughout the interior: books, gardening experiments, maps of Lewis and Clark's expeditions to uncharted wilderness, and other accouterments of the tinkering philosopher are on display. Contraptions abound, including a dumbwaiter designed by Jefferson himself to carry wine from the extensive cellars up through the walls to the dining room. The cellars rest in the foundation of the home, and were the first part of the house built when construction began in 1769.

Jefferson was a wine guy. While serving in France during the 1780s, he even took a vacation, while recuperating from a failed romance, to tour the wine regions of northern Italy and France. He shipped cases of wine home and to his colleagues, including George Washington, and advised other presidents on what wines to serve at state dinners. He also experimented with growing grapes at his home, and invited European winemakers to the United States to promote a domestic wine-making industry in hopes that wine would replace spirits.

Jefferson denounced whiskey as a "poison." He wrote, "No nation is drunken where wine is cheap, and none sober where the dearness of wine substitutes ardent spirits as the common beverage. It is, in truth, the only antidote to the bane of whiskey." Jefferson was merely expressing the attitudes of his social class toward whiskey. He was a friend of the working-man, but didn't care much for the workingman's unrefined drink, although he did occasionally allow his slaves to drink it.

So it's ironic that Jefferson was the one to drastically improve things for whiskey distillers. Two years after winning the presidency and moving into the White House, where he personally curated the wine selection, he eliminated the whiskey tax. Now small distillers no longer had to hide or worry about evading tax collectors—they could take their time, experiment, and refine their craft. Aging would finally get a chance to become a common practice.

. . .

Jefferson's vision of America's economic destiny prevailed in the whiskey industry for the next half century. There was consolidation, for sure, but the picture was largely one of yeoman farmers operating thousands of tiny stills puffing away across the countryside. During the next two centuries, however, that picture would transform into Hamilton's vision. By the year 2000, almost every single drop of whiskey made in America was produced by one of thirteen distilleries owned by just eight companies. Even though there were over one hundred brands on liquor store shelves—different recipes, aged for different amounts of time, bottled at different proofs—almost all of them came from one of those thirteen plants. And even after the craft whiskey boom of the twenty-first century created more than five hundred new distilleries by 2015, tilting the scales back in Jefferson's direction, those thirteen plants were still producing over 95 percent of the nation's whiskey.

By the twenty-first century, whiskey producers had figured out that Jefferson's vision sells: all those small, distinct labels project the romantic image of the independent out on his own. But producers had also figured out something else: Hamilton's vision was a good way to get that whiskey into bottles efficiently and at an affordable cost. Jefferson's vision is on the outside of bottles, but Hamilton's vision often defines the whiskey within. Many brands seem small and distinct, and therefore more personal, which is important for marketing, but much of this is an illusion. The label for Knob Creek bourbon might state "Distilled and Bottled by Knob Creek Distillery, Clermont, Kentucky," making it seem like a freestanding outfit, but it is made at the same plant as many other brands made by Jim Beam. "Knob Creek Distillery" is simply what's called an assumed business name, otherwise known as a DBA, which is the legal shorthand for "doing business as," and is a method that can be used to make one company seem like many. But drinkers who sleuth out the origins of most brands will find their whiskey traced back to one of just a few places.

Almost all of America's dozen or so biggest distilleries also sell whiskey to outsider buyers who market it as something that's entirely independent. One of these distilleries, Midwest Grain Products Ingredients (MGPI), a distillery in Lawrenceburg, Indiana, that used to be owned by Seagram, makes whiskey for outside brands that include labels like Templeton, Bulleit Rye, and some of the High West brands. MGPI's Web site has a drop-down menu featuring the whiskey styles it will make and age for customers wanting to market them as their own. This common industry arrangement is usually called "sourcing" or "contract distilling" and those companies on the receiving end are typically called NDPs, short for "non-distiller producers" (you can tell them apart on the liquor store shelf by tiny print reading "produced by," or some similar variation, rather than "distilled by," since they're not technically distillers and government regulations prevent them from saying otherwise). For many upstart distilleries, sourcing is simply a way to become established while they wait for their own whiskey stocks to age, although most, understandably, don't advertise that fact.

As one might expect, whiskey geeks often scoff at sourced brands. The image of a small, independent producer is hard to resist, and they complain that their notions of authenticity are disrupted when that appearance turns out to be a façade. It's easy to see why, but at the same time it must be pointed out that the practice of sourcing has a long history going back to the nineteenth century, and most of the main suppliers carry reputations for making good whiskey. MGPI is often mocked, but it is actually one of the oldest distilleries in the country, giving it the kind of real heritage that many brands covet. If MGPI had a less severe name and sold whiskey under its own labels, the brands would probably be revered as classics.

Hamilton is the eternal whipping boy of whiskey drinkers. He was an elite power broker, an early embodiment of Wall Street, and a champion of the kind of consolidated industry we rarely associate with personal independence or individuality. Modern Americans probably wouldn't be inclined to share a drink with him. In contrast, the whiskey world fawns over Jefferson. He might have hated whiskey, but his policies helped support its rise and development, all while championing the kind of independent smallholders that remain popular icons even as they become less of a reality. Jefferson's system might have lost out to Hamilton's—something the whiskey world is loath to admit—but Jefferson continues to be revered.

With this in mind, it is greatly ironic that the popular brand named after Jefferson today is sourced. An image of him is literally engraved on the bottle, even though the whiskey within comes from the kind of industry he fought against. The brand was formed in 1997 as an NDP and is headquartered out of New York City, Hamilton's old turf. When I once asked brand proprietor Trey Zoeller why he named his whiskey after the former president, he simply laughed and said, "I had no marketing budget. I simply wanted a recognizable face associated with history and tradition."

But Zoeller is far from using a mere façade—most people buying the small brand probably think they're supporting a modern-day personification of one of Jefferson's smallholders, and in some ways they are, but not in the way they probably expect. Zoeller is a small businessman utilizing the knowledge and efficiency of larger distilleries by co-opting their whiskey. He doesn't actually make his bourbon from scratch, but he does blend bourbons he finds elsewhere to create a unique flavor profile for his own brands. Taken alone, Zoeller explains, none of the separate bourbons he buys is as good as the sum of the parts mixed together, and the strengths and inadequacies of each compensate for each other. For instance, he might purchase stocks of twenty-year-old bourbon that most would find undrinkable after having absorbed too many wood tannins from aging so long. But blended with younger bourbons the older spirit lends the kind of dryness wood tannins offer, helping balance the young bourbon's heavier grain notes. Zoeller doesn't distill, but he does have a refined palate, a quality that shines through in the layered complexity of the whiskies he creates.

Big versus small. That's sometimes how the battle between Hamilton and Jefferson is described. There are benefits and drawbacks to both, and it's a battle cry constantly sounded throughout America's economic history. The respective sides of Jefferson and Hamilton's ideas are still argued among politicians today, and Americans are reminded of it every time they open their wallets and find images of both men emblazoned on U.S. currency. Only Jefferson, however, has his image on a bottle of bourbon.

· CHAPTER THREE ·
DARK AND BLOODY GROUND

Modern distillery visitor centers rumble and shake like revival tents. Stories boil out of them, shouting the creation myths of their brands. In Kentucky, you hear the names of many different early settlers— Elijah Craig, Jacob Boehm, Evan Williams, Basil Hayden—but their tales all follow a similar pattern: once these people arrived at the frontier, they dedicated themselves to the simple principles of making whiskey, establishing the legacy behind whatever bourbon you're drinking today. Every account is a classic American success story, rooted in a fabled past. And even though the tales are often embellished, exchanging mundane reality for serendipity and style, we tend to look past any inconsistencies. This is because the story matters just as much as the facts—it's what we buy into, literally and figuratively.

The stories are also designed to make you believe specifically in Kentucky. The state holds a special connection to bourbon, even though many other places possess the exact same qualities that make Kentucky's whiskey so good: water filtered by limestone, the ability to grow grain, and climates defined by hot summers and cool winters. So what accounts for Kentucky's primacy today? Much of the answer would come after Prohibition, explained by the state's business and lobbying savvy, but that falls later in the tale. Much earlier than that, Kentucky would begin to give its whiskey special prominence with its ability to weave a good story. The frontier didn't keep careful records, and detailed specifics of bourbon's early days—involving questions of why distillers started aging the spirit in charred barrels or how bourbon even got its name—were poorly documented. Kentucky, a colorful state with mythic origins, where history collides with mystery, would soon find creative ways to fill in the gaps. The whiskey industry would later call its marketing efforts "history," but it's this sort of history that the writer Julian Barnes would later describe as "that certainty produced at the point where the imperfections of memory meet the inadequacies of documentation."

Today, the Heaven Hill distillery in Bardstown, Kentucky, makes the Elijah Craig line of bourbon. It is named after the man who for many decades was erroneously credited with making the "first" bourbon. Before Craig moved to Kentucky and began distilling, he was a controversial preacher in Virginia who was jailed in 1768 for sermons so fiery that they enraged the colony's official Episcopalian clergy. Undaunted from his cell, the firebrand pastor continued to preach and draw large crowds, among them a young James Madison, who would later strive to protect religious freedom in the Constitution. Shortly after the American Revolution, Craig decided to start a new life in a freer place. Joining his brother Lewis, he led an exodus of six hundred people to what is present-day Kentucky. The group called itself "the Travelling Church."

The Kentucky they arrived in was a place of transition, new and unknown. To many, even the state's name was a mystery. The Cherokee said it meant "dark and bloody ground," but the Iroquois's interpretation of *Kanta-ke* translated to "meadow-land." The Wyandote interpreted it as "the land of tomorrow," while the Shawnee claimed it meant "at the head of the river." Others said it was simply a name invented by white people.

The frontiersmen who had lived in Kentucky before the arrival of Craig and the Travelling Church were equally confounding. Most were fringe-dwelling loners like the Scotch-Irish distillers who had protected Washington's flank during the war—hunters more than gatherers. They wore buckskin and during their odd visits back east spoke of killing Indians. Hector St. John de Crèvecoeur, a New Yorker who originally hailed from France, described them as "no better than carnivorous animals" that "exhibit the most hideous parts of our society." It would still be decades before a club of writers known as the Knickerbocker Group— including James Fenimore Cooper and Washington Irving—would reimagine these backwoodsmen as a cast of heroic American originals.

The arrival of Craig and the Travelling Church, however, was the result of an earlier phase of Kentucky's image makeover. Crèvecoeur and others had claimed that the frontier needed proper farmers to introduce social bonds and civilization. The idea of Manifest Destiny was in its infancy, and Jefferson's objective to create a rural democracy was just taking root. In 1779, when the future president was governor of Virginia, of which Kentucky was a part until its statehood in 1792, he enticed people like Craig to move by giving away free land if it was used to grow corn.

People started to trickle in, but many were still fearful. What the frontier really needed to attract settlers was the right spokesperson. Enter Daniel Boone, who had moved to the frontier when he was scrappy and poor, then fought Indians there during the Revolution. Later he would win public office and become a Freemason, making Boone the ultimate bootstrapper, embodying the frontier's potential. Then, when he was fifty years old, he became a living legend when the historian John Filson published *The Discovery, Settlement and Present State of Kentucke* in 1784. Filson colorfully chronicled Boone's adventures, glossing over certain details—part of the reason Boone chose to live in the frontier was to avoid debt collectors (which he later repaid)—and often taking spectacular liberties with other parts of Boone's epic and inspiring story.*

It was mythmaking at its best. Other writers with purple pens happily joined Filson's effort to glamorize the frontier and attract quasi-nomadic dreamers like Craig, Elijah Pepper, Henry Wathen, Jacob

---

*Boone's family would eventually establish a distillery on Knob Creek, employing Thomas Lincoln, father of the future president, Abraham.

Boehm (later changed to Beam), and others whose names would, many decades later, eventually lend inspiration to bourbon brands. These writers gushed that Kentucky was a place where a settler only needed to work "scarcely two hours a day to support himself and his family." One writer even called heaven "a Kentucky sort of place." The historian Daniel Blake later wrote that Boone's Kentucky was "first and perhaps foremost, an idea. It was an idea born of need and hope."

Once Craig and his Travelling Church arrived in Kentucky, they founded a town called Lebanon, borrowing the name for what the Old Testament called the "land of milk and honey" (in 1790, the name was changed to Georgetown, to honor the first U.S. president). The group soon learned that the region was also a perfect kitchen for making whiskey. Each hill on the Kentucky horizon was a paler blue echo of the one before, the rolling topography resisting erosion and creating bottomlands with soil so rich that one settler compared it to black butter. From the very beginning, the bottomlands were legendary for growing corn. Hierosme Lalemant, a Jesuit missionary living in Wisconsin a century before whites first started moving into Kentucky, was told by Indians that Kentucky's cornstalks were bigger than trees, the ears were two feet long, and the kernels were bigger than grapes.

That, of course, was just the kind of exaggerated storytelling that seems to be part of Kentucky's DNA. Nevertheless, the corn did grow well there, and was a practical choice for planting in the state's newly settled rough acreage because it didn't need as much plowing as smaller grains and could grow faster than the weeds. It exploded out of Kentucky's legendary soil like fireworks. Whereas Maryland farmland typically produced ten bushels of corn per acre, Kentucky land yielded forty. This was more corn than any single family could consume, leaving surpluses to be distilled into whiskey that wouldn't spoil and could be used for barter or the inevitable drinking. It must have seemed impossible that the land could ever be exhausted.

The layer of limestone underneath Kentucky's rich topsoil was also important to the whiskey. Water bubbled through it to springs, which native Shawnees believed were entrances to the underworld. Shawnee warriors sprinkled tobacco around the springs and asked the spirits for a safe return from hunting missions. Farmer-distillers like Craig found the water a valuable medium to a different variety of spirits. The limestone filtered iron salts from the water and added calcium, which helped yeast thrive during fermentation.

The land and its economics dictated a whiskey that increasingly resembled modern bourbon: primarily corn, with some rye and a little malted barley. The grain combination was perfect from both a technical standpoint and a flavor perspective. Corn was inexpensive and yielded a relatively high amount of alcohol per bushel, an asset that also made it smart from a business perspective. Rye added flavor and presented a way to use a grain that sometimes struggled to find another purpose (wheat is better for making bread and barley is better for beer). Potential grains outside this trio presented other difficulties. Wheat was relatively expensive, buckwheat becomes gummy and easily scorches, and oats are difficult to work with due to their high bran content—if not fermented fully before beginning distillation, they can boil up into the worm and blow up the still.

Recipes from the era are rare, but the ones that do exist often indicate mash bills reflecting bourbon.* One distillation manual from the early nineteenth century explained that "if the proportion of one fourth part of rye can be obtained, it is enough."† The account also indicates that distillers used whatever was at hand and that proportions were rarely standardized, meaning that any modern claims by companies that they are adhering to a strict and ancient "family recipe" from the era are highly questionable. Whiskey still was sold primarily as a bulk commodity and brand names didn't exist, meaning that consistent flavor as part of a brand's identity wasn't an issue. In 1819, Anthony Boucherie published a distilling manual confirming that recipes were

---

* The diary of Union County resident Jonathan Taylor, likely written around 1795, contains corn whiskey recipes both with and without rye. Louisville's Hope Distillery was established in 1816–17, and its later purchases of corn, barley, and rye reflect proportions similar to modern bourbons.

† This mash bill is in the general neighborhood of Basil Hayden's, a bourbon brand that would be created in 1992 by Jim Beam Brands to honor a farmer-distiller who arrived in Kentucky from Maryland around the same time as Craig.

basically free-for-alls, writing that "whiskey is made either with rye, barley, or Indian corn. One, or all those kinds of grains is used, as they are more or less abundant in the country."

Regardless of the recipe, quality probably varied. The clear, unaged spirit emerging from most stills was quickly nicknamed "paleface." It served its practical purpose, but likely didn't serve the taste buds or the soul. Flavor was improved with fruit, herbs, or oils from clove, anise, or juniper, just as it was with Washington's rye whiskey. Cherry bounce was one popular recipe made by adding syrup and cherries or bark from the root of a cherry tree steeped in hot water.

A more sophisticated way to improve the taste involved filtering the spirits through charcoal. This removed the unpleasant flavor of excessive fusel oils and helped give the spirit sweetness by neutralizing acids found in the raw alcohol. The process usually involved a tub with a false bottom punctured with holes: flannel was placed over the bottom and covered with a pile of charcoal made from green wood such as sugar maple or hickory, and raw spirits were poured through.

But charcoal filtering was only a quick fix for smoothing out the liquor's rough edges. Kentucky still hadn't earned its legendary reputation for producing particularly tasty whiskey.

And this is where today's marketing comes in, fantastically but erroneously crediting Craig with the idea of aging bourbon in charred oak barrels. As the story goes, once Craig was settled in Kentucky he continued preaching but devoted an increasing amount of time to distilling (other Baptists started criticizing his entrepreneurship, claiming it was impossible to serve God and Mammon both). The legend as it's told by Heaven Hill today is that a barn fire was responsible for accidentally charring the insides of barrels Craig had intended to use to store and ship his whiskey. The frugal frontiersman addressed this problem by using the barrels anyway, serendipitously discovering the unique flavor their charred interiors gave his whiskey.

And, so the legend goes, bourbon was born.

But it's not true. The Elijah Craig brand has existed since 1986, and Heaven Hill was first established in 1934. Naming the brand after a firebrand historical figure gives it an instant heritage anchored in a romanticized past.

The Craig myth first appeared in 1874, when the historian Richard Collins claimed that Craig made the "first" bourbon. He didn't use Craig's name, but he wrote under a list of "Kentucky Firsts" in his sixteen-hundred-page *History of Kentucky*—which for decades was standard in Kentucky classrooms—that "the first Bourbon Whiskey was made in 1789, at Georgetown, at the fulling mill at Royal Spring," which identified Craig by the location of his distillery. Collins, of course, provided no evidence that Craig's whiskey was different from any of the other whiskies that had already begun flowing out of Kentucky at that time. Modern historians speculate that the Craig story was a way for Collins to defend the reputation of whiskey, which was under attack by the temperance movement when he made his claim.

It is no mystery why Heaven Hill would run with the Craig tale— it's far more exciting than a dry explanation that the rise of bourbon was an organic affair, emerging from the collective efforts of thousands of nameless farmer-distillers who, over time, adopted a succession of good practices after word spread over the countryside. The distillery understands that great tales can't have a flock of heroes, they can only have one, and Craig won the casting call.

In bourbon marketing, stories like Craig's are the rule rather than the exception. For many years, the companies behind the brands were the only sources explaining the history of the industry, and there is no advantage whatsoever in telling the boring version of the story. Don't believe 90 percent of the tales you read on whiskey bottles, but don't forget to enjoy them either. The stories are just like the whiskey itself. They start as a vapor, condense, and then sit unseen in a barrel for years. Finally they emerge, transformed into something entirely different and enchanting.

· · ·

Every whiskey barrel is a sort of medieval alchemist's laboratory, a dark and sooty place from which a clear spirit poured inside emerges years later, golden and transformed. Barrels first started as humble shipping containers for whiskey, but over the centuries were promoted into something else: an ingredient as well as a vessel.

Barrels have been used to transport all matter of goods—whale oil, fish, nails—since at least the first century AD, when Pliny the Elder noticed their use in the Alps. As a shipping tool, barrels have been compared in importance to the wheel, the simplicity of their design so obvious yet brilliant. They bow in the middle where wooden staves connect the top and bottom, buttressed against each other. The result is maximum ruggedness. If a barrel were to tumble off a rack or gangway it is less likely to break because all the staves supporting each other absorb the impact. Barrels are pieced together like puzzles and held by a few metal bands that don't touch the liquid. They require no nails, which could rust if touched by liquid and are often made of iron, which would react with the whiskey and ruin it.

The bowed design of a barrel weighing hundreds of pounds enables an average-sized person to handle it with relative ease. If stored upright, it is easily tilted onto its edge and rolled to wherever it needs to go. Since only a small part of the barrel touches the ground, it can pivot in any direction, its immense weight maneuvered with a light shove. Barrel sizes varied greatly, but were typically forty-eight gallons for much of the nineteenth century when the biggest buyers were beer brewers and oil companies (whale, then petroleum). When those industries moved to steel barrels after World War II and the whiskey industry became the primary customer of wooden barrels, the standard size was increased to around fifty-three gallons because that was the maximum that would fit on the racks installed in most aging warehouses. When full of liquid, barrels that size weigh about five hundred pounds, roughly the maximum weight safely handled by the average dockworker.

Even the early Romans knew that water and wine stored in charred barrels stayed fresher longer, and by the fifteenth century the French used barrels like this to mellow brandy and give it flavor and color. In America, drinkers in the early nineteenth century also noticed that spirits transported in charred oak—which is often used for liquids because the wood's tight grain prevents leakage—tasted better after long voyages. It was a short step from using a barrel as a mere transport device for whiskey to treating it instead as an ingredient.

Most bourbon makers today estimate that somewhere between 50 and 80 percent of the spirit's final flavor comes from the barrel. Alcohol is a solvent that over time breaks down elements found in the wood such as cellulose, hemicellulose, and lignin, which are responsible for the vanilla, mint, and anise notes found in bourbon. White oak in particular is loaded with these compounds, which vary depending on the age of the wood, where it was grown, and a host of other factors. These elements are responsible for the swirling platter of flavors reminiscent of butterscotch, vanilla, cinnamon, coconut, and citrus that are found in whiskey.

When the barrel is charred, the inside looks like burnt toast, but what you don't see is the layer of wood just beneath the char, where natural sugars are baked and caramelized. Think of a toasted marshmallow, with a blackened outside skin covering the toasted brown patches of crunchy sugar bits hiding just beneath. During warm weather, pressure inside the barrel rises, pushing the bourbon through the char—which filters impurities—and into the toasted layer. When the weather cools, the bourbon contracts out of the wood, taking with it a bouquet of aromas and flavors. If you look at a cross section of a piece of wood from a whiskey barrel, you can see a mark—sort of like a high-water mark on a riverbank—where the whiskey soaked into the wood grain. The whiskey ebbs and flows like a tide, driven by tiny fluctuations in temperature between night and day, melting into larger cycles occurring between the seasons. In the American Midwest and South, where winters are cold and summers are hot, relatively extreme temperature swings can speed up the aging process by causing the whiskey to move in and out of the wood more aggressively. In places where temperature swings are much less dramatic, such as Scotland, whiskey generally requires more time to age.

Since greatness always involves a lot of luck, a barrel size in the neighborhood of fifty gallons of capacity, although it was designed for transport, also turned out to be ideal for aging whiskey. Distillers sometimes attempt to rush the aging process by using smaller barrels—producing whiskey in a matter of months rather than years—but the results don't always impress. Small barrels increase the surface-to-volume ratio of wood to liquid, speeding up the extractive process by quickly adding coloring and flavor, but shortchange other parts of the aging process that require more time.

Those other factors include oxidation, evaporation, and esterification, all of which reach their peaks according to different rates that are altered by the barrel size. You can hurry along the extractive process by using a smaller barrel, but that step will finish before the others have had a chance to catch up—this is the difference between simply flavoring a whiskey with wood and "maturing" it. With large barrels, distillers are better able to bring all these different factors in synch. The greater volume allows more time for evaporation to occur, which helps concentrate flavors, while the slower extraction of wood flavors—due to a lesser surface-to-volume ratio—prevents the whiskey from becoming bitter and overpowered after absorbing too many wood tannins.

During oxidation and evaporation, the barrel of whiskey breathes as if it were a lung, driven by alternating cycles of hot and cold temperatures. When the liquid cools and contracts out of the wood, it "inhales" by pulling in outside air through the barrel walls. Oxygen is introduced and slowly absorbed into the liquid, helping develop and mellow its flavor. When the temperature warms, the whiskey expands and the barrel "exhales" air, alongside a small amount of evaporated liquid that is nicknamed "the angels' share," an artful term referring to the amount of whiskey lost as vapor.* The oxidation that occurs while the barrel is breathing is accompanied by a chemical reaction called esterification, where the long, complex molecules found in raw distillate break down and reconfigure. These molecular chains react differently with the wood

---

* Evaporation in warm midwestern climates averages around 4 percent per year but can go as high as 8 percent, depending on the temperature.

each time they come in contact with it, evolving to add even more depth and additional flavors.

Maturing whiskey—balancing all these different factors against each other—requires perfect timing and controlled speed, just like cooking barbecue, another process where perfection calls for patience. When cooking meat, you can speed the process by upping the heat for a shorter time—technically it is cooked—but the proteins and fats don't break down as perfectly as they do with barbecue cooked slowly with low heat. In the case of bourbon, using a large barrel to age whiskey is the equivalent of barbecuing "low and slow." The results will usually take at least three years to be worth drinking and the better part of a decade to be worth remembering. Distillers who are unable to afford this kind of time rely on small barrels for aging, the equivalent of cooking meat in a microwave—it's still edible, if not as enjoyable.

Of course, since taste is ultimately subjective, there is inevitably debate about whether or not small barrels are really inferior. Drinkers with a taste for whiskey aged traditionally with large barrels tend not to like the resinous, spiky qualities of small-barrel-aged whiskey. Distillers who use small barrels typically reply that they're not going for tradition, that they're attempting to make something that tastes different and unique. Fair enough, although the subjectivity of taste still doesn't mean that all whiskey is created equal. In any case, it's the honest and fiery debates about such matters that make it fun to be a whiskey geek.

Scientists are still working to understand the swarm of factors involved in the aging process. The Buffalo Trace Distillery in Frankfort, Kentucky, has a facility it calls "Warehouse X," dedicated to aging experiments. Different chambers within the warehouse vary conditions like temperature, natural light, and humidity, all with an eye toward better understanding the maturation process. Chemists at the distillery have found three hundred different wood compounds that contribute to flavor, but have only specifically identified about two hundred of them. All those different compounds affect whiskey differently, and become part of a vast equation of other variables (time, heat, oxidation, esterification, extraction) that distillers must carefully balance. Of course, there are occasionally exceptions to every rule, which make whiskey production a blend of both art and science. Our understanding is still evolving, but when Americans first started aging spirits in barrels, they understood only one element—wood—and that it made the whiskey taste better, especially when it was burned a little bit.

. . .

Some liquor companies today claim that Kentucky's whiskey industry was sparked by fallout from the Whiskey Rebellion, when Pennsylvania's fiercest rebels—those distillers most strongly opposed to the whiskey tax—settled west because it was farther removed from the strong arm of authority. As a modern marketing tool, this reimagining of history helps infuse bourbon with a powerful sense of independence and strong ideals. But the truth is that the roots of Kentucky's whiskey industry were already established when the rebellion erupted, more in thanks to the savvy efforts of Thomas Jefferson the policymaker, John Filson the mythmaker, Daniel Boone the spokesperson, and people like the prickly dreamer Elijah Craig. Because of them, the population of Kentucky would grow from 73,677 in 1790 to 687,917 by 1830, including many more farmer-distillers as well as middleman merchants. It was this latter group—the salespeople—who turned out to be the unsung heroes of bourbon. They were the ones who established the use of the barrel and likely gave bourbon its name (as always, there is no better embodiment of capitalism than bourbon).

In the early twenty-first century, historians such as Dr. Michael Veach of Louisville's Filson Historical Society, one of a scarce handful of people to closely study the history of bourbon, began focusing their attention on these salespeople to better understand bourbon's murky origins. Two brothers were particularly interesting: Louis and John Tarascon, who were born in France and who fled to the United States shortly after the French Revolution started in 1789. By 1807, the brothers were traders between Louisville and New Orleans and had a warehouse in Shippingport, Kentucky, which sits on an island in the Ohio River just west of Louisville. The Tarascons had recruited a group of

French immigrants from New Orleans to Shippingport, where they were perfectly placed to purchase whiskey coming down the river and improve it the best way they knew how: by aging it in charred barrels like many of their fellow Frenchmen had done back home in Cognac, a region known for its legendary brandy. Then they sent it on to other French traders in New Orleans.

Pablo Picasso once claimed, "Good artists borrow, great artists steal." He stole the quote from the composer Igor Stravinsky, who apparently stole it from the poet T. S. Eliot, who almost certainly stole it from somebody else. Merchants like the Tarascons were familiar with the concept as well, stealing inspiration from abroad that would influence bourbon's evolution. America certainly didn't pine for the old continent's way of life, but it did yearn for its drinks. Counterfeits of foreign spirits abounded, prompting one Philadelphia distiller, Harrison Hall, to write in 1811, "The ingenuity of man was stimulated to obtain a substitute for foreign spirits by the distillation of grain, and, such was the influence of patriotism, or rather, the desire of making money, that a single still put up in a shed, with a worm made of gun barrels, was all the apparatus at this time employed in many places making whiskey."

Then as now, status and prestige ruled the drinking world, and copying exotic foreign drinks gave distillers access to the deep pockets of those willing to pay for them. Brandies such as cognac already had a storied reputation among the upper class. The drink was a symbol of wealth and luxury, and was considered the apotheosis of the distiller's art. Aged for long periods in oak barrels—*charred* oak barrels—cognac embodied sophisticated drinking. That was important to those drinking it; what was important to those making it was that they could charge a higher price for the same reason.

Importing cognac from France was expensive, however. For a certain type of frontier entrepreneur, counterfeiting was the answer. Americans excelled at distilling "foreign spirits" able to "deceive very good judges," Hall wrote. Kentucky grocers were soon selling "Irish Whiskey" alongside "Holland Gin," "Jamaica Rum," "Old Scotch," and "Cognac Brandy," according to one grocery advertisement from 1817. In a world of lax trademark laws and without today's international labeling protections, these spirits were probably those things in name only.

Whiskey made primarily from corn, which is relatively sweet compared to other spirits, gained even more sweetness and flavor from the wood during the long voyages to distant markets. This would have made it all the more appealing to drinkers of brandies like cognac, which is also relatively sweet and mellow. The port of New Orleans quickly noticed that whiskey shipped from Kentucky and other environs of the Ohio River Valley, a lengthy endeavor, gained many of the smoother qualities of sophisticated brandies like cognac.*

A sample of this new kind of western whiskey made its way, via New Orleans, to Philadelphia, where Harrison Hall first tasted it. Some easterners sneered at the frontier spirit, but Hall championed it and criticized his counterparts' "common prejudice against using corn." He noted the round warmth contributed by the wood, as well as western distillers' tendency to barrel the best parts of the distilling run, discarding the lesser-quality heads and feints. Most important, these steps increased the whiskey's value. There was no profit from selling unaged or minimally aged whiskey—prices for it were the same in local markets of the Ohio River Valley as they were in distant ones, which would have translated into financial losses after accounting for shipping costs. During the first decades of the nineteenth century, whiskey aged somewhere between six and twenty-four months regularly sold for 60 percent more than unaged spirits. A journey downriver by flatboat was a lengthy ordeal, making a trip from Kentucky worth the additional shipping expense only if the whiskey tasted special.

Cognac's influence has always remained on the periphery of bourbon's story—what kind of modern red-blooded American would really want to admit that blue-collar bourbon took any cues from blue-blooded cognac? Nevertheless, signs surfacing in modern-day New Orleans and

---

*The earliest *written* record of using charred barrels to age Kentucky whiskey comes from 1826, when a Lexington grocer told a distiller named John Corlis, "It is suggested to me that if the barrels should be burnt upon the inside, say only a 16th of an inch, that it will much improve it." Of course, the fact that somebody else had mentioned charring to the grocer indicates that the method was already in use.

Louisville reveal faded historical links of the French connection shared by the two cities. Each place is one of the oldest cities in its respective region, has a French namesake, and is festooned with the ever-present fleur-de-lis. Both cities also have the most shotgun houses of any cities in the United States. These elongated homes resting on small city plots were built out of dismantled ramshackle flatboats that traded goods between the two towns but were unable to make the return voyage.

Empires don't become great through agriculture but through trade, which was what would eventually make bourbon great as well. The queen of North American commerce was New Orleans, by far the biggest market for whiskey shipped through the important regional trading hub of Louisville.* Before the railroads, more than 95 percent of whiskey exported from the western states through the middle of the century went through New Orleans, according to trade data from the era. Once there, spirits generally weren't reexported elsewhere, as were most other goods, but were consumed within a city that was one of the heaviest-drinking places in the world.†

New Orleans demanded whiskey, but what were they calling it? In the first decades of the nineteenth century, the term "bourbon" wasn't common. The first known case of anyone in Kentucky calling the whiskey bourbon was in 1821, but that was a rare instance. Three years later, France's Marquis de Lafayette visited Kentucky, but his hosts didn't offer him bourbon. Instead, they presented him with a "wiski," according to one journal account. Lafayette had helped arrange the financial assistance that France had sent to America during the Revolution, after which Bourbon County was named in its honor. If Kentuckians had been calling their whiskey by the same name, they surely would have let Lafayette know.

---

* Louisville still enjoys its status as a trading hub. Worldport, the UPS shipping center located there, is the largest of its kind in the world, and is within a four-hour flight of 95 percent of the U.S. population, meaning a bevy of other companies have also established distribution facilities near the city.

† At the time, New Orleans dwarfed most other American cities, a fact that has been forgotten during a modern era that has seen the city's population fall. For most of the nineteenth century it was one of the largest cities in the nation.

Up until the 1840s, whiskey was typically referred to generically—simply as "whiskey"—or was given the name of the closest town or village: "Bardstown whiskey" or "Loretto whiskey." Almost all of it was consumed locally. In 1812, Kentucky alone had two thousand registered distilleries, and probably many more unregistered ones. The only places that imported whiskey—and thus might have cared about the name or origins—were large cities. Grocers and middlemen such as the Tarascon brothers would have needed a way to make their whiskey stand out in these far-off places, especially in New Orleans, their biggest market. More modern theories speculate that a name like "bourbon" would have been a perfect marketing tool, appealing to the city's large French-speaking population.

But the explanation for bourbon's name as it's often told today is that the spirit was named after Bourbon County in Kentucky after liquor dealers in New Orleans started asking for whiskey shipped from the port at "Limestone, Bourbon County, Kentucky." Unfortunately, this explanation isn't backed by a paper trail, as historians such as Michael Veach and Charles Cowdery have pointed out. Limestone, Kentucky, which is today called Maysville, was only briefly part of Bourbon County before Kentucky became a state in 1792. When that happened, Bourbon County shrank drastically as it was divided into many smaller counties. The port at Limestone, to which the name is so often attributed, became part of Mason County. People continued calling the port "Old Bourbon" for about twenty years after the name change, but that habit ended well before the term came into common usage for the whiskey. During the period when "Old Bourbon" was still a widely used moniker for the port at Limestone, trade with New Orleans was still limited, and it's highly unlikely that liquor dealers in New Orleans would have noticed a spirit by that name.*

The most interesting theory about the origins of bourbon's name is

---

* Kentuckians living in or near Maysville, which is a two-and-a-half-hour drive east of Louisville, today sometimes bristle when this theory is disregarded. There are few modern distilleries in this region, and not having the title of "Bourbon's Bethlehem" has cut them out of the tourist trade that Kentucky promotes around its bourbon industry, which from a logistical standpoint makes sense to center around a bustling city like Louisville.

that it was likely a shrewd marketing ploy cooked up by middlemen merchants like the Tarascon brothers. The French population living alongside the Tarascon brothers around the shipping hub of Louisville would have been well aware of the affiliation the name once had in the region and its suitability to their biggest market. Many French residents moving to New Orleans in the early nineteenth century were royalists fleeing the Revolution and would have appreciated the name. For any revolutionaries taking offense at it, the term could simply be linked back to the Bourbon County that had been named in honor of France's support of the American Revolution. "Bourbon" was a perfect marketing tool—it meant different things to different consumers and didn't offend anyone. It also had the perfect sound: a word full of round vowels that rolls off the tongue with the same easy warmth as the spirit itself.

Thus the name got its foothold, although not until the Civil War would it take hold nationwide. Even so, the aged whiskey coming from the Ohio River Valley was making a name for itself—not as a brand, but as a distinctive style—and a national drink was born. Hall, an early champion of what he himself called "western whiskey," wrote, "The French sip brandy; the Hollanders swallow gin; the Irish glory in their whiskey; surely John Bull finds 'meat and drink' in his porter—and why should not our countrymen have a national beverage?"

· CHAPTER FOUR ·

BY WHISKEY GROG
HE LOST HIS BREATH

America was astonishingly drunk. This was the assessment of many foreigners visiting the young nation during the early to mid-nineteenth century. The roster of guests included luminaries such as Charles Dickens, Alexis de Tocqueville, Frances Trollope, and Harriet Martineau, all arriving with diaries and journals in hand to observe this new country and discover what made it tick. They all noted the whiskey: a binding force that knitted together the economy, infused political life, accompanied America's strange diet, and was on everyone's breath. In 1825, the French epicure Jean Brillat-Savarin wrote in his groundbreaking *The Physiology of Taste,* published after his own visit to the United States, that "the destiny of nations depends upon the manner in which they nourish themselves." America was nourishing itself with whiskey, which was fast becoming a powerful symbol of the young nation's psyche and forming important parts of an image the drink continues to hold today.

These foreign guests weren't necessarily harping on Americans or insulting them with their observations. In fact, most of what they said about the new country was complimentary. They praised America's sense of independence, self-sufficiency, work ethic, and egalitarian ideals. John Stuart Mill in 1840 wrote that every book written by travelers returning to England from America became a party pamphlet, used to urge positive political and economic change back home. One of the few common points attracting criticism rather than praise, however, was the subject of whiskey. The foreigners who criticized it often considered themselves the Americans' friends—and indeed, their perspective as impartial outsiders allowed them to appreciate and point out qualities, as good friends do, about the United States that went unnoticed or underappreciated by Americans themselves. Mark Twain would return the favor several decades later when he published *The Innocents Abroad*, detailing his own travels in Europe and observing the sometimes unflattering qualities about his hosts that they themselves were unlikely to notice or admit to.

The reasons for Americans' heavy drinking were many. Whiskey was cheap, abundant, and by now firmly established as a patriotic workingman's drink, an attitude held over from the American Revolution. Drinking it was a way to express national unity and one's egalitarian credentials. The foreign journalists also noted, somewhat fretfully, that Americans seemed to use whiskey as a way to battle the difficulties of their unique environment: greater numbers of people were moving into a scattered and expanding frontier that was lonely and stressful. During the first third of the nineteenth century, an average of about one in seven Americans lived outside of established communities, creating the highest level of isolation experienced in U.S. history, according to contemporary historian W. J. Rorabaugh. These vast stretches of isolated land also produced most of the nation's whiskey. Drinking roughly three to five times more than they do today, Americans, Rorabaugh noted, drank from "the break of dawn to the break of dawn."

. . .

Just as modern critics of the American diet complain that corn is in everything, with high-fructose corn syrup composing a large part of so many manufactured food products, America's nineteenth-century visitors noticed the same thing. The entire American diet seemed to have a common origin: cornbread, corn-fed meat, and corn-based drink were an American's "common necessaries," one English traveler noted. The

English writer Frances Trollope, whose book *Domestic Manners of the Americans* was an enormous best seller, claimed that what little culinary creativity America had was reserved for inventing new ways to serve corn. If not converted into whiskey, it was often served in some sort of mush or pancake form. "All bad," Trollope sniffed.

Corn that wasn't eaten or distilled was fed to pigs. In the 1820s, foreign visitors nicknamed Cincinnati "Porkopolis" because of all the corn-fed meat slaughtered there (the city was also a leading whiskey stronghold). When Trollope visited Cincinnati she commented on the "extraordinary quantity of bacon" consumed by Americans living in the Ohio River Valley, and was shocked at the number of pigs wandering the streets. She soon decided that she liked the pigs—in cities with scarce public services, they ate the trash out of the gutters. Once the pigs were done eating the trash, Americans ate the pigs, consuming an estimated pound of meat per person each day, certainly one of the highest proportions in the world. Much of the pork was preserved with salt, adding to the great thirst for whiskey, which helped cut through all the starch and fat.

Americans certainly could have had a more varied and interesting diet, but they seemed to actively reject it, the foreigners noted. Even when fresh vegetables were in season, many Americans chose their salted pork and spirits instead. "The luxury of whiskey is more appreciated by the men than all the green delicacies from the garden," Trollope observed. When Prince Maximilian of Wied visited Missouri, he also was startled to find garden foods ignored in favor of "salt pork, biscuits, and whiskey."

The Europeans quickly learned that the American diet was an act of defiance. It was simple fare and nonfussy, emblematic of how the Americans wanted to be seen. Meals stood in stark contrast to what many of these Europeans, who tended to hail from society's upper crust, were accustomed to eating. To Americans, "Obsession with the delights of the palate was considered a symptom of Old World decadence," the historian Daniel Boorstin would write of American eating habits many years later.

Americans took great pride in drinking the whiskey that helped distance them from the Old World's cultural protocols. Many of these wealthy European visitors, alongside their prosperous American counterparts, looked down on whiskey, including those styles made on their home continent (this attitude would eventually change, but not until later in the century). Many preferred wine instead, leading some Americans to associate it with the snobbish elite. Nor was wine's reputation helped by the fact that it regularly cost roughly four times as much as whiskey because the drink needed to be imported (Thomas Jefferson's attempts to establish a domestic wine industry had failed). Thus the subtle pleasures of wine were often mocked in favor of inexpensive everyman favorites like whiskey and cider. Just as Americans had thrown off political and economic colonialism in the preceding century, they rejected it once again in its culinary form. Frenchman Barthélemi Tardiveau noted that Kentuckians hostile to foreign ideas and drinks had pledged to "drink no other strong liquor than whiskey."

Not only was whiskey an expression of egalitarian credentials and national unity, it also complemented the fast, intense hustle of America's work ethic. A quick shot of whiskey versus a leisurely mug of ale was the choice of fast over slow food. British writer Archibald Maxwell observed that America's national motto could have been "Gobble, gulp, and go." As soon as food landed on the table, diners would "fall upon it like wolves on an unguarded herd," he wrote. To Americans, it was an honor to finish meals before everyone else and then move to the bar for a "cock-tail," wrote Trollope, which "receives its highest relish from the absence of all restraint whatever."

People increasingly turned to whiskey as a remedy for the massive cases of dyspepsia caused by this fast-and-furious diet. The French philosopher Constantin François de Chasseboeuf noted that Americans ate by "heaping indigestions on one another; and to give tone to the poor, relaxed and wearied stomach, they drink . . . which completes the ruin of the nervous system." Charles Dickens used the character Martin Chuzzlewit to describe his American dining companions. They were "dyspeptic individuals" who "bolted their food in wedges; feeding, not themselves, but broods of nightmares."

These "broods of nightmares" point to America's anxiety. The experiment in democracy was still young, and the entire world was watching for signs of failure. Americans were self-conscious and aware of the world's scrutiny. As a result, they obsessed over the tiniest political matters, Trollope noted. They got their news from taverns or groceries that doubled as liquor stores, meaning that being informed often meant getting drunk. Trollope asked one country interlocutor if it was "from a sense of duty, then, that you all go to the liquor store to read the papers?"

"To be sure it is," he replied, "and he'd be no true born American as didn't. I don't say that the father of a family should always be after liquor, but I do say that I'd rather have my son drunk three times in a week, than not look after the affairs of the country."

. . .

Foreign visitors noting Americans' intemperance were sometimes only noting a trend they had observed in their own countries, where economic conditions similar to America's had also led to drinking binges. Drunkenness and gluts of cheap spirits are common in countries on the brink of industrialization. England guzzled gin before its Industrial Revolution in the eighteenth century, just as Sweden, Prussia, and Russia all overindulged in spirits before their economies shifted away from agrarian pursuits. America was no different. As a cottage industry attached to farming, America's surplus of cheap spirits was the result of too much manpower pooling in one part of the economy.

Western farmer-distillers were most vulnerable to the coming economic upheaval. Eastern farmers could get their grain to distant markets more easily, meaning they were less reliant on converting it into spirits to preserve its value. America's distilling strongholds thus became the remote parts of the Ohio River Valley—upstate New York, western Pennsylvania, Ohio, Tennessee, and Kentucky—where farmers still used liquor for currency and as a way to preserve the value of their crops. By 1810, the Ohio River Valley produced more than half the nation's spirits, although relatively few people lived there. Many of those moving in were distillers, pushing the number of distilleries from fourteen thousand in 1810 to twenty thousand by 1830.

The economics of whiskey were volatile. After the First Bank of the United States died in 1811, the economic link between East and West relied primarily on commodity exchanges, which in the West meant considerable amounts of whiskey. However, surpluses of the spirit drove down prices, undermining the West's trading relationship with the coast. The western economy stagnated in the 1820s, in part due to a whiskey glut that now flooded the struggling West with a large surplus of an inexpensive depressant. Alexander Hamilton, who had been shot dead by Aaron Burr in a duel in 1804, must have been rolling over in his grave. He had championed the national bank, and his whiskey tax had been intended to prevent this sort of thing from happening—it would have helped build infrastructure to allow farmers get their grain to market. Nevertheless, the tax was poorly designed and executed, and the West's overreliance on whiskey as currency almost guaranteed resistance against its taxation.

When Frances Trollope visited the besotted West, she was impressed by the independence and rugged individualism of its people, if not with their drinking. The strong character of Americans, however, was accompanied by "something awful and almost unnatural in their loneliness," she wrote. The disruptive land speculation driving Americans' western migration meant a continuous cycle of pulling up stakes to move where living was cheaper. People remained isolated from one another, preventing the kind of social institutions from taking hold that help limit heavy drinking. The United States was unencumbered by oppressive authority, but that freedom came with a cost, Trollope noted. The Americans "will live and die without hearing or uttering the dreadful words, 'God save the king,'" she wrote. But their graves would occupy lonely spots in the forest where "the wind that whispers through the boughs will be their only requiem." In America's most remote outposts she constantly found "reeking forth the fumes of whiskey."

Americans generally weren't as introspective about their drinking as Trollope was. They were too busy working, dismissing such ponderous matters with cavalier cheer. Kentuckian Tom Johnson responded to European worries about his drinking with a wisecrack, emblazoning his tombstone with the words:

> *By whiskey grog he lost his breath,*
> *Who would not die so sweet a death.*

· · ·

In the drinking world, wine has long carried an elitist reputation that some say dates to ancient times, when sophisticated Romans drunk on wine scoffed at beer-drinking Huns. This perception isn't necessarily fair; in many places—Southern Europe, parts of South America—wine is a staunchly working-class drink. Nevertheless, Americans don't typically see it that way. The attitude is traced back to the nation's coming of age, when the wine drinkers of the old colonial powers came to visit the upstart nation and sniffed at its rough whiskey. They were the Romans and Americans were the Huns. In matters of taste and style, Europeans set the tone.

Even though New World cities such as New York would eventually rival their Old World counterparts as centers for art and fashion, some Americans still occasionally look to Europe for guidance in matters of style. It is this way with wine, which inevitably remains the drinking world's tastemaker. And as American whiskey undergoes its twenty-first-century renaissance, it finds itself pulled into wine's sphere. The same thing happened to beer during the 1990s when the craft beer boom suddenly found that drink paired with cheese and sold in 750-milliliter wine bottles. Now the inevitable food and whiskey pairings are shepherded by whiskey sommeliers, a new breed of food industry professional born in America's glitzy coastal enclaves around 2012. You know your drink has arrived when somebody with a fanciful title from the wine world starts telling you how to drink it.

But wine's rules occasionally need to be defied, the way Americans once joyfully defied those who dismissed their whiskey. The partnership between whiskey and food is often clumsy and awkward, the high proof of whiskey overpowering the food rather than enhancing it the way that beer and wine do. Diluting whiskey with ice or water is one way to overcome this problem and there are a few whiskey and food pairings that work well, but the pairings nevertheless often seem designed to make whiskey more credible by dressing it up like wine. Whiskey, however, yearns to be governed by its own natural style, much like the frontier from which it hails. Perfect before or after dinner, it seems determined to be left alone, in line with its natural character.*

Then there are purists who claim that whiskey should only be had neat or with just a few drops of water to "open it up," but their advice is tiresome and dull. Whiskey is a drink of independent adaptability and does whatever it wants, even if that means pairing itself in cocktails or with soda, plain water, or ice (or food, if you like). Whatever suits the season and the time, whiskey doesn't care about being judged. It is a drink of Americans who once used it to defy the arbitrary social protocols of those who deemed it unsophisticated and rough.

But even though wine and whiskey are separate and distinct, wine has nevertheless created the rules of connoisseurship by which whiskey is often evaluated. In its role as a tastemaker, wine is responsible for the sensory approach—describing drinks based on their phenolic compounds—typically used to evaluate whiskey and other spirits today (comparisons like "hibiscus," "sandalwood," "nougat," or "saddle leather"). Whiskey, like wine, shares specific phenolic compounds with seemingly unrelated items, which people can train their palates to detect, heightening their ability to enjoy the subtleties both kinds of drinks can offer.

---

*Lew Bryson, managing editor of *Whisky Advocate*, once told me that whiskey and food pairings are "a little like going to church: more people talk about doing it than actually do it."

Appreciating and detecting these things can sometimes seem like a high art, the province only of sommeliers and other members of some kind of culinary priesthood. But this isn't the case at all. In fact, having ordinary senses is perhaps better than having exceptional ones. "Supertasters"—people who are genetically more sensitive to smells and flavors—oftentimes aren't particularly adventurous eaters, shying away from spicy or bitter flavors because of their acute sensitivity, according to some studies. And just as having sensitive hearing doesn't make somebody a better music critic, an acute sense of smell or taste doesn't automatically make somebody better at judging wine and spirits. "Tasters are created, not born," Hildegarde Heymann, a professor and enologist at the University of California at Davis, told me. She and other sensory scientists stress that learning to taste just takes a little practice and attention to detail. They recommend that tasters simply keep notebooks and write down flavors and aromas they detect. Compare the notes to others reviewing the same whiskey but don't worry if they don't perfectly match up—tasting notes almost never do. For this reason, *Whisky Magazine* has two separate critics review the same whiskey, usually with notable differences. Most experienced tasters will readily admit that their ability was developed through simple practice, not because they have mastered some kind of occult knowledge.*

We evaluate with our minds as much as the nose or the tongue. In nineteenth-century America, wine gained its snobbish reputation because of whom it was associated with and because the economics of trade gave it a relatively higher price. Outside associations like price and status continue to dictate our appreciation, and are tools that marketers have mastered. When tastings are blind, expectations are always confounded. In blind wine tastings, cheap castoffs are often named as favorites and cherished vintages from prestigious vineyards are disregarded. At the Judgment of Paris, held in 1976, wines from California's burgeoning wine industry were chosen by French critics over their French counterparts.

---

*For those seeking a guide on developing their palates, with recommendations on in-depth tastings, both Lew Bryson's *Tasting Whiskey: An Insider's Guide to the Unique Pleasures of the World's Finest Spirits* and Heather Greene's *Whisk(e)y Distilled: A Populist Guide to the Water of Life* are excellent resources.

Francophiles were horrified and embarrassed; if the tasters had known, national pride almost certainly would have prevented them from choosing the American upstarts.

Price also warps perceptions of quality, even if it has nothing to do with the liquid in the bottle. In the 1930s the wine baron Ernest Gallo made a sales call on a New York customer and offered him two glasses of wine—one from a five-cent bottle and one from a ten-cent bottle. The wines were identical, but "they always buy the ten-cent wine," Gallo said. Customers were preoccupied with not looking like cheapskates rather than just trusting their gut about which wine was better.

As the rules of connoisseurship have developed over time, appreciation, a thing that was originally considered an art, has become an industry. As you might expect, wine blazed the path that whiskey now follows. During the nineteenth and early twentieth centuries, the style of wine-tasting notes was literary rather than sensory. In 1932, the wine critic and classical scholar H. Warner Allen described the Latour 1869 this way: "The palate recognized a heroic wine, such a drink as might refresh the warring archangels, and the perfection of its beauty called up the noble phrase 'terrible as an army with banners.'"

As the wine industry developed in America, and as more people began making a living by offering advice, either as sommeliers or in magazines like *Wine Enthusiast,* the need arose for a system that seemed more legitimate and less fanciful than writing about flavors and aromas as if they were "warring archangels." The idea of tasting notes gained in popularity during the latter half of the twentieth century. In 1990, Ann Noble, a chemist at the University of California at Davis, invented the "Wine Aroma Wheel," which attempted to standardize tasting conventions. Pineapple was an example of "tropical fruit," while fig and raisin represented "dried fruits," all of which were categorized under a "fruity" family of aromas. "Sulfur flavors" such as burnt match described another family of aromas. The wheel described almost a hundred different scents. While far from being a perfect science, the approach nevertheless gave professional tasting a sense of legitimacy.

The studied approach to tasting inevitably led to an increased emphasis on scoring, which helps humans fulfill our almost compulsive desire to rank things. After experimenting with a few different approaches during the twentieth century, the wine industry eventually settled on the hundred-point rating system devised by the wine critic Robert Parker Jr. in the 1980s. This system—or a ten-point scale extended out to one decimal place, which is essentially the same thing—was later adopted by many spirits publications.

The very precision of these systems casts doubt on their validity—how can there really be a meaningful distinction between a 92 and a 93? Thoughtful industry watchers often argue that these numbers, which appear meticulously deduced, give ratings an aura of authority because they *seem* scientifically evaluated, but are really just ways to capitalize financially on something that is in fact highly subjective (by making it seem more specialized or precious than it really is). Many of the organizations that provide the ratings, such as the official-sounding Beverage Testing Institute, are likewise named so they seem more credible and unassailable.

Among the sharpest critics of modern ratings systems is Charles Cowdery, the author of numerous guides to appreciating whiskey and a regular contributor to magazines like *Whisky Advocate*. In his book *Bourbon, Straight,* Cowdery points out that very few whiskies ever score below 80 on what is admittedly a lopsided scale. This is because wine and whiskey publications are pushed by advertisers to do ratings because "they know lazy consumers buy from them," he writes. Like field day at an elementary school, everybody is made to look like a winner. The lopsided scales are designed as much to avoid offending liquor companies—which advertise in the magazines and sponsor tasting events—as they are to give drinkers accurate evaluations. The San Francisco World Spirits Competition, for instance, uses a rating scale of double gold, gold, silver, and bronze. Even if a brand scores in the bottom half of entries, it still gets a medal that looks good to the average customer. But because almost *all* the ratings look good at first glance due to the way the scales are inflated, it's hard not to conclude that their primary purpose is simply to sell more booze. The business of ranking spirits is essentially an industry within a wider industry, and it understandably wants to protect what can be a pretty sweet gig by not offending the hand that feeds it. Spirits critics have a fun time—and some even make a good living—by offering advice to people who are unsure of their palates. That advice is sometimes worth seeking out, but never without a grain of salt.*

Ultimately, the best advice for evaluating and appreciating whiskey can be linked back to what impressed wine-drinking Europeans about their American hosts two centuries ago. The Europeans were sometimes critical, but their praise usually far outweighed their complaints. Almost all of them extolled the whiskey-drenched republic's independence, self-sufficiency, and aversion to arbitrary rules.

* Rating guides that regularly use the full scope of their scale are rare but generally provide more trustworthy advice. This includes Clay Risen's *American Whiskey, Bourbon, and Rye: A Guide to the Nation's Favorite Spirit,* which uses a four-star scale and regularly gives whiskies one or zero stars, thus more clearly expressing what the author and his tasting panel thought were truly exceptional whiskies versus those that were just mediocre.

· CHAPTER FIVE ·

THE ICE KING

Save for quarrels about how to make proper barbecue or martinis, no American culinary tradition is more debated than the julep, the most famous of the bourbon cocktails. Juleps have only four ingredients—bourbon, mint, sugar, ice—but the combination of those ingredients is dictated by a million rules. The debate—about proportions, technique, presentation—started in the nineteenth century and is still awaiting its day in front of the Supreme Court. Nevertheless, there is one undeniable truth of a proper mint julep: it is the most luxurious of all cocktails. Served in a silver cup, it requires a glacier's worth of ice and a good five ounces of liquor, more than double the size of the average cocktail. Shaving the ice demands an eternity of time, as does drinking something so boozy and large.

The julep's difficulty and the commitment it requires are part of its appeal. One cool gulp of the minty sweet liquid on a hot day makes up for everything the drink demands. Anticipation is part of the julep's genius—like Miles Davis playing trumpet on "All Blues," coming into the song when he's good and ready, knowing that waiting is just as important to the music as the next phrase. Juleps epitomize the concept of patience.

But the julep is also defined by its contradictions. The unhurried leisure of the southern lifestyle defined by the julep was made possible only by slavery; the drink is a simple pleasure but requires a lot of work; and it's the most famous of the bourbon cocktails, but is rarely ever consumed—people today mainly drink juleps as a nostalgic nod to the past while watching the Kentucky Derby. But the julep's most important contradiction is that, despite all its overtones of ritual and custom, the drink actually embodies change. The same industry and invention leading to its creation during the nineteenth century revolutionized how bourbon was made and consumed. Today the bourbon industry constantly trumpets tradition, but before it could get to this point it would require innovation. Two men, Frederic "the Ice King" Tudor and James Crow, otherwise known as "the father of modern bourbon," were the ones to provide it.

. . .

The julep's rise in America followed a similar path to many other cocktails. It has old roots—"julep" is a French word derived from the Arabic *julab*, meaning rosewater, and ancient juleps were nonalcoholic concoctions containing crushed rose petals to help medicine taste better. The rose petals were replaced by mint once the drink migrated to the Mediterranean, and once it drifted across the Atlantic, Americans added booze. The first American versions of it poked up around 1800 in Virginia and were spiked with brandy or rum but still no ice, which was a scarce luxury.

As the julep migrated west across the United States, whiskey came into play. In the South, political candidates in antebellum elections plied voters with rudimentary versions of juleps (which were still iceless). Battered tin cups hung from the sides of barrels of free whiskey sitting outside polling centers. Candidates' names were stenciled on the side of the barrels and a bouquet of mint and a few pounds of sugar were tossed inside. It was primitive but effective.

These lukewarm juleps were an extension of the days during the late eighteenth and early nineteenth centuries when cocktails were generally served hot. This was a holdover from British drinking culture that used warm drinks to ward off damp chills. The British had long been making punches involving spirits mixed with citrus juice and other flavorings, but Americans, as is their nature, soon reimagined and reinvented the process. Established hierarchies between wine, spirits, and other ingredients were shattered, and anything and everything was mixed together, *e pluribus unum*.

And then everything got put on ice. Cold drinks suited the warmer American climate, prompting one English observer to write, "Ice is an American institution—the use of it an American luxury—the abuse of it an American failing." The presence of ice marked an increase in Americans' standard of living and the trickle-down process of converting luxuries into necessities. Like many stories of American ingenuity, it also involved a pigheaded and stubborn businessman whom early potential investors didn't take seriously. Nevertheless, he eventually became one of the nation's first millionaires by creating an industry around providing year-round ice that most Americans today take for granted. Along the way, he revolutionized cocktails like the julep.

During the early nineteenth century, ice was a luxury. It could be kept year round in insulated icehouses, but access to these was often limited to the wealthy, particularly in warmer southern states. This all changed, however, when Boston businessman Frederic Tudor revolutionized the ice trade. It all started in 1806 when his brother remarked that they could probably make a lot of money by selling frozen water cut from Massachusetts lakes and ponds.

Tudor wasn't the first to notice the value of ice, of course. The ancient Greeks, Romans, Persians, and Chinese all harvested and stored it during winter to chill their food and drinks in summer. Tudor's ice trade stood apart because of its sheer ambition. He saw untapped markets scattered across the globe and believed that cutting ice and shipping it across the world to the tropics, where it would provide relief from the oppressive heat, would make him "inevitably and unavoidably rich," he wrote.

Most potential investors saw nothing inevitable or unavoidable about the riches expressed in Tudor's vision. Instead, with their flinty New England gazes, they saw what Daniel Boorstin described as Tudor's "flamboyant, defiant, energetic, and sometimes reckless spirit." Yes, the market for luxurious ice was growing in the United States, but wouldn't it just melt during a long voyage to the tropics? Their understanding of the science was accurate, and much of the ice Tudor shipped to Martinique and Cuba between 1806 and 1810 melted into large financial losses.

Besides that, potential customers in those markets didn't really know what to do with the frozen stuff once it arrived.

Tudor solved the melting problem by packing his ice tighter and insulating it with sawdust. He solved the second problem—demand from customers—with cocktails. Tudor's initial customers bought ice to preserve food and medicine, but he later branched out by selling ice to cafés and wealthy households so they could chill their drinks.

Tudor sold his ice utilizing the same business strategy as a shrewd drug dealer: give the first hit away for free and then charge once customers are hooked. Customers were enticed, compliments of the house, with slushy cocktails that offered relief from the sun's glaring heat. Then the bill came when they asked for a second round. After people tried their drinks cold, they could "never be presented with them warm again," Tudor wrote. He then anchored himself in his various markets by bribing local officials to let him build a monopoly of icehouses.

Tudor made his first profits by 1810, only to be swindled by a business partner and land in debtor's prison. After he was released, he secured a loan enabling him to continue with his obsession, but significant profits were still another fifteen years away.

Those profits eventually came, however, and Tudor's increased success led to the hiring of a new foreman named Nathaniel Wyeth to help meet growing demand. At that point, ice was laboriously cut by hand with saws. Wyeth developed a horse-drawn ice plow and a system in which frozen bodies of water could be divided into chessboard patterns and cut into ice blocks about two feet square. This mass-produced ice was easier to transport and store, reducing Tudor's costs by two-thirds and enabling him to sell more.

Tudor's most ambitious plan came in 1833, when he set out to deliver ice to Calcutta, a voyage of fourteen thousand miles that involved crossing the equator twice. Tudor and his investors wondered if the ice would even sell, but their concerns were put to rest by his extraordinary profits. In an editorial, the *India Gazette* thanked him for making "this luxury accessible, by its abundance and cheapness."

By that point, Tudor's success had drawn competition to the ice trade, and Americans across the country were becoming accustomed to the luxury. Henry David Thoreau chronicled the growing industry near his Walden outpost, describing one stack of ice as "an obelisk designed to pierce the clouds." The ice symbolized an increasingly complicated world breaking from its preindustrial past, and a luxurious counterpoint to Thoreau's experiment in simplicity. Besides, Thoreau didn't appreciate having his peace disrupted. He couldn't help but marvel, however, that "the pure Walden water is mingled with the sacred water of the Ganges."

By that time, Thoreau's fellow Americans were developing a taste for slushy cocktails such as the julep, as well as ice cream and other frozen delicacies. Ice was becoming integral to daily life, and newspapers followed the trade closely. Unseasonably warm winters prompted newspapers to issue warnings about "ice famines," and ice harvesters would sail to the Arctic and make up the shortfall by chopping up icebergs. The benefits of ice spread well beyond cocktails. Fishermen stayed at sea longer with their catches packed in ice, and its ability to preserve fresh vegetables also meant that food could be sold in the distant markets of growing cities.

Alongside transportation improvements, ice helped push more fresh fruits and vegetables into America's turgid diet of salt pork and corn mush, helping decrease the whiskey binge that had so alarmed foreign visitors. During the late eighteenth century, the Philadelphia physician Benjamin Rush had called for Americans to substitute vegetables for salt pork in their diets as a way to reduce the intake of spirits, which he noted were drunk at an alarming rate. His idea gathered momentum as reformers like Sylvester Graham promoted diets that rejected whiskey, coffee, meat, and other items they claimed "stimulated" the emotions and exacerbated domestic abuse and other forms of violence caused by insobriety. In 1829, Graham, a vegetarian and temperance advocate, created the graham cracker as a wholesome way to promote the more healthful mind-set, and he advised Americans to wash it down with water, not whiskey. Spirits consumption peaked around 1830 but then started to slowly decline, although it was still considerable.

Technology and innovation were changing how Americans drank whiskey, transforming ice from a luxury into a necessity, and enabling other social changes. Soon they would also revolutionize the whiskey itself.

. . .

Just as Frederic Tudor's ice business was becoming a profitable success, the Kentuckian James Crow began bringing bourbon into the modern age, implementing scientific production standards and creating the kind of whiskey modern drinkers would recognize. The modern brand named after him, Old Crow, is only a husk of the legend it once was—the same in name only—but the legacy of its creator is found in every other bottle of bourbon for sale today. Crow was the Steve Jobs of bourbon: he didn't invent anything but took methods and practices others had discovered and perfected them. The whiskey landscape of the 1830s was a random patchwork of clunky old ways and promising new technologies and methodologies begging for integration. Bourbon needed a coherent force to collect and streamline all the stray bits of knowledge.

A Scottish native educated in chemistry and medicine, Crow moved to Kentucky via Philadelphia in the 1820s. As a physician, he mainly practiced for free, spending the remainder of his time working for a handful of distilleries in Woodford County before eventually landing at a distillery owned by Oscar Pepper by the side of Glenns Creek on land where the Woodford Reserve Distillery sits today. Distilling first began on the spot around 1812 when Elijah and Sarah Pepper, Oscar's parents, built a grain mill next to the water. Elijah died in 1825 and Oscar took over, building many of the stone buildings—still in use at the distillery today—between 1838 and 1840. At this time, he hired Crow.

In the decades before Crow started at the Pepper distillery, distilling equipment improved technologically. In 1810, Phares Bernard of New York patented a still using steam that allowed him to cut his labor by a third and his fuel by half. Other innovations followed—the nation's most popular magazines regularly published articles about distilling technology, and between 1802 and 1815 more than a hundred patents were issued for distilling equipment, a number amounting to more than 5 percent of all patents granted in the United States.

Of all the innovations, the landmark achievement was the invention in the 1820s of the continuous still, also called a column still, which allowed production of higher-proof liquor. In 1831, Irish inventor Aeneas Coffey patented an even more efficient version of the column still. The stills themselves were large—up to five feet wide and a few stories tall—and allowed the liquid to be pumped through in a continuous flow, meaning distillers no longer needed to empty or clean pot stills after single batches. The beer was poured in at the top, then trickled down through a series of plates perforated by holes. Steam was pumped into the still from the bottom and rose up to meet the beer as it trickled down. The steam stripped the alcohol from the beer and carried it away as vapor. It condensed back into a liquid in the coiled piece of tubing known as the worm. Column stills devoured beer when they ran at full capacity, producing volumes unimaginable to small distillers using traditional pot stills.

Distilleries using these new technologies required far less labor, leading to the first wave of industry consolidation and a tilt away from the Jeffersonian vision of a cottage industry toward the Hamiltonian vision. Although the number of distilleries in America had increased from fourteen thousand to twenty thousand between 1810 and 1830, that number fell by half between 1830 and 1840.

Even though consolidation today is often viewed as a steamroller of brutal efficiency, leaving a vicious wake of lost jobs and sacrificed freedom, during the 1830s it allowed for changes that many farmer-distillers surely welcomed. Industrialization in growing urban centers in the Ohio and Mississippi valleys absorbed excess labor from the agrarian sector, allowing previously nomadic families to establish roots in their communities and create social institutions that helped limit excessive drinking. An expanding system of canals, steamboats, and transportation infrastructure helped create a national grain market that made farmer-distillers less dependent on whiskey sales. For those continuing to make whiskey, the shipping revolution helped create new markets and expand old ones. Price differences between commodities became less drastic and many western farmers discovered they had more economic opportunities aside from just whiskey production.

For James Crow, however, the achievements in efficiency weren't matched by gains in quality. Any diaries Crow might have kept are lost, but letters written by those who knew him indicate a refined intellect and an obsession with improving his whiskey. He produced volumes of notes recording the particulars of fermentation, distillation, hygiene, and temperature. He constantly asked why things happened as they did and recorded both his successes and failures so that his methods could be improved upon. For Crow, God was in the details.

Crow was a wizard of tools ending with the suffix -ometer—saccharometers for sugar, hydrometers for alcohol, thermometers for temperature—and used them to solve problems others considered mysteries. Crow scrutinized the particular qualities of limestone-filtered water and was the first to realize that the limestone removed iron salts that can ruin distilled spirits. He also recorded the different temperatures involved in the fermentation process, which affects the development of different chemical compounds. Controlling temperature allows a distiller to influence how many chemicals and impurities are included in the spirit. Just enough lend whiskey complexity and nuance; too many and it's undrinkable. For instance, diacetyl is a chemical compound with an intensely buttery flavor that is produced during fermentation; distillers attempt to remove most of it by limiting how much of the foreshots they allow into the middle portion of the run. Trace amounts of diacetyl give whiskey a pleasingly rich and oily mouthfeel tasting faintly of butterscotch; but too much diacetyl reeks unpleasantly of movie theater popcorn. Crow realized that balance and control were needed as he navigated his whiskey through a tangled jungle of factors and effects. Distilling wasn't just a straight line—beer in, alcohol out— it was a quilt stitched together in interconnected webs. You pull on one tiny part, and the whole thing shifts. Crow wanted to know how everything was connected.

But he couldn't start until his work environment was clean. The first thing Crow did at Pepper's distillery was to improve sanitation by moving hog and cattle pens away from the distillery. For most distilleries at the time, a side business of fattening hogs and cattle on spent mash was lucrative but introduced a fuming mix of bacteria, microorganisms, wild yeast, and other biological invaders that destroyed consistency between batches.

Up to that time, contamination and bacterial infections often wreaked havoc on whiskey. In the early 1820s some distillers had begun guarding against these setbacks by implementing the sour mash process, which is how almost all bourbon today is made. In the sweet mash process, used by Thorpe and other early distillers, yeast is simply added to the cooked grain to begin fermentation. The sour mash process, however, involves adding spent mash that has already been fermented and distilled during a previous run. The spent mash is more acidic, and adding it to a new batch helps prevent bacterial infections, maintains consistency, and helps yeast thrive. "Sour Mash Whiskey" isn't a separate style of whiskey, as is sometimes thought, it simply refers to the methodology used to make almost all American whiskey on store shelves today. Crow didn't invent the technique, although he is sometimes credited, but he studied it, improved upon it, and promoted it until it became a widely implemented standard.

Crow didn't keep his methods a secret (even though all of his original records are lost, he gladly passed his discoveries on to his colleagues). He warned others against trying to get too much alcohol from a single bushel of grain, and that doing so would undermine its quality. For the best whiskey, Crow claimed that no more than two and a half gallons of whiskey should come out of one bushel. He also aged his own whiskey, an uncommon practice that helped him ensure quality. Most distillers of his day sold their unaged whiskey immediately, leaving aging to be accomplished by retailers who weren't always trustworthy.

Crow's boss, Oscar Pepper, charged almost double the going rate for Crow's whiskey, which was increasingly known among drinkers as Crow or Old Crow, and was recognized for its higher quality. Slowly other distillers followed suit and during the 1830s began branding the distillery name on the end of the barrel, helping give rise to the term "brand name." Saloons displayed the barrels over the bar so that customers could see them. Among this early crop of nationally recognized brands, Old Crow was an exemplary producer, attracting specific praise from the likes of Andrew Jackson, Daniel Webster, William Henry Harrison, and Henry Clay.

As Crow was helping build bourbon's reputation, use of the term "bourbon" continued to gain prominence. During the 1840s, a variety of colloquial names were still used to describe bourbonlike spirits. In *Moby-Dick,* published in 1851, New Yorker Herman Melville compared the gushing blood of a whale to the reddish color of aged whiskey, but he didn't call it bourbon. Instead, he mentioned "old Orleans whiskey, or old Ohio, or unspeakable old Monongahela!" "Old Monongahela" referred to the style of rye whiskey common from Pennsylvania, but "Orleans whiskey" and "old Ohio" likely referred to whiskey shipped from the western Ohio River Valley down the Ohio and Mississippi rivers to New Orleans. This was probably bourbon.

In the same way that regional dialects merge together as nations form from fiefdoms, colloquial names were eventually abandoned as "bourbon" became the accepted designation for the Ohio River Valley's corn-heavy style of whiskey. Around 1861, Napoleon Joseph Charles Paul Bonaparte (who played up his family ties to Napoleon Bonaparte I by calling himself Prince Napoleon) was given a glass of whiskey while visiting New York from France and was told that it was called "Old Bourbon." Considering that his namesake had supplanted the Bourbon dynasty for a period, Prince Napoleon replied, "Old Bourbon, indeed. I did not think I would like anything with that name so well."

Even though brand names were still rare, bourbon was in a sense branding itself. Melville and Napoleon's hosts were making distinctions between different styles. In Thorpe's time, terms like "aqua vitae" and the Gaelic *uisge* were often used as catchalls to describe any type of spirit. Then whiskey became the accepted norm for any type of grain spirit. Then terms like "old Monongahela" and "bourbon" began to define specific styles of that grain spirit, just as Crow's brand name was used to distinguish single exemplary producers.

Crow died suddenly in 1856, and for a short time Pepper controlled the fledgling brand. But he too soon died, and ownership of the brand passed between a series of investors and other distilleries, all of whom maintained its reputation well into the twentieth century. During the second half of the twentieth century, however, Old Crow's recipe changed and its reputation crumbled. The brand remains drinkable but it is no longer a legend, occupying a space near the bottom shelf of most liquor stores. No known portraits of James Crow have ever been found, and the image on bottles carrying his name today is just a bird. A crow, to be exact.

· · ·

The Woodford Reserve Distillery today makes a mint julep enshrining the legacy of both Frederic Tudor and James Crow. The company once invited me to witness Chris Morris, the brand's master distiller, create a mint julep designed to reestablish the sense of extravagant luxury that once characterized the drink. Only a small handful of these special juleps are sold every year at the Kentucky Derby. They cost $1,000 a pop, and each is so decadent that even Marie Antoinette would covet a sip.*

First, Woodford has upgraded the ice, just as much of the ice used in high-end cocktails today has been upgraded. In the century following Tudor's death in 1864, ice became routine, even boring. Artificial refrigeration eventually replaced Tudor's ice-harvesting empire and put what was once a luxury into the hands of the masses. This prompted Mark Twain to compare ice to jewelry previously available only to the rich, but now worn by everybody.

---

* Part of this price tag is funneled to local charity causes.

Ice had become commonplace, and by the twenty-first century it had declined in quality. The thick, dense ice cut from Tudor's giant blocks—able to cool a drink without overly diluting it—was replaced by those crescent-shaped shards from ice machines that are foamy and white and full of air. This kind of fast-melting ice instantly converts a cocktail into an insipid puddle.

But with the revival of cocktail culture that has accompanied this century's whiskey renaissance, ice's glory has been restored. High-end bars like the Aviary in Chicago hire full-time icemakers who use Clinebell machines to produce three-hundred-pound blocks of clear, dense ice like those Tudor cut from Massachusetts ponds. Bartenders at these kinds of places often resemble an expedition sent up the side of Mount Everest: a blur of Alpine tools (imported from Japan, exquisite and expensive) whacking and chopping away. Chunks of ice are tailored to the drink—shaped into spears, cones, or globes—so they melt at an ideal rate. The Aviary even offers one cocktail called "In the Rocks" that features a drink held inside an ice shell that explodes when struck by a slingshot, releasing the liquid and evoking the same sense of wonder enjoyed by Tudor's tropical customers when they first tried their cocktails cold. Bars with fancy ice programs usually charge accordingly, borrowing another page from Tudor's playbook by translating luxury into profits.

The juleps made by Woodford Reserve take ice one step further. For the 2013 Kentucky Derby the distillery imported blocks of ice made from water that had permeated geologic formations in Nova Scotia containing gold veins (every year the Derby juleps have a different theme, and in 2013 the theme was "gold"). Past themes for Woodford's Derby juleps have required ice chopped from Arctic glaciers, mint imported from Morocco, and sugar grown in the South Pacific.

On the day I witnessed the construction of one of the Woodford juleps, Morris set himself to the task of shaving the giant block of ice. It took him nearly ten minutes to finish. Afterward, he resembled someone who has just shoveled his driveway after a snowstorm. He then assembled the julep in a traditional silver cup that was gilded in gold and included a gold-plated sipping straw. The bourbon used in the drink was Woodford Distiller's Select, a bottling that "has won a gold medal in every major spirits competition," Morris bragged. Ready for his finale, he sprinkled the julep with a bit of gold dust, his fingers quivering over the drink as if he were conducting a tiny orchestra.

Morris called this last step the "Midas touch."

· CHAPTER SIX ·

COFFIN VARNISH

The whiskey-soaked bones of dead Civil War soldiers fill the National Museum of Health and Medicine in Silver Spring, Maryland. They no longer smell like the booze that surgeons used as a preservative, but most still contain shell fragments. They also carry pebbled scars, like those on the nose of a heavy drinker, from where the bone tried to fight off infection. Other body parts that were originally preserved in whiskey are displayed throughout the museum. A brain resting in one case resembles a little moon and features a crater in the left lobe, as if a tiny asteroid had crashed into it. A sign beneath it reads, "Gunshot wound."

The museum was founded during the war by army surgeon Major John Brinton, and the amount of whiskey he needed to preserve the war's carnage was astounding. All of the liquor that was confiscated in Washington during the war was funneled to him, and a giant still built on the museum's original grounds clattered nonstop. Make no mistake, the liquor used on the bones was rarely the refined bourbon of producers like James Crow or the other fledgling name brands with a growing reputation. When nectar like that came into the museum's possession, Brinton usually traded it for favors that made his job easier, like procuring good horses for trips out to the battlefield. The bones resting here were instead drenched in the venomous dreck of a war that later reshaped the whiskey industry the same way that it reshaped the nation.

In the days leading up to the war, John Brinton wasn't sure if he should fight. He was thirty years old, a respected doctor and only son from a prominent Philadelphia family, and worried about what his mother would think of his joining the army. But after shots were fired on Fort Sumter in April 1861 and Abraham Lincoln issued a call to arms, he and his friends realized they were all going to war.

Many would join as officers and were required to supply their own uniforms, but tailors in the city were swamped with orders. Brinton soon took a commission as a brigade surgeon, and as he waited for his uniform to be tailored he joined a swarm of men buying pistols for the fighting. Firearms were scarce, but Brinton finally got his hands on a "discreditable looking affair," he wrote in his memoirs. He later traded it for a more reliable Colt revolver, but it wouldn't matter—except for target practice, he never shot it.

Exactly one year after joining the army, Brinton was ordered by Surgeon General William Hammond to establish an Army Medical Museum in Washington, D.C. There, he and a group of doctors would collect and study battlefield specimens in order to improve military medicine. The specimens arrived in casks of whiskey diluted to an appropriate strength, and Brinton was authorized to buy as much whiskey as he needed, despite strict rationing measures on spirits. The army had discontinued daily whiskey rations in 1830 to limit the rowdy behavior of drunken soldiers, although commanders could still issue it to troops at their own discretion. Officers were authorized to purchase their own liquor, but the biggest bartenders in most army camps were the doctors, who were permitted to prescribe whiskey for ailments including rheumatism, measles, and sexually transmitted diseases.

Brinton's medical colleagues used whiskey as a cure-all. Medical understanding of the day still considered it a stimulant rather than a depressant, probably for the simple reason that it often made people belligerent and rowdy. Unfortunately, it also created more problems than it cured. For instance, because whiskey was considered a stimulant, it was used to treat patients suffering from the cold. But alcohol only makes people *feel* warmer, while actually causing their body temperatures to drop. Alcohol causes blood vessels to dilate, moving warm blood closer to the skin where heat escapes the body, exacerbating the problem.

But that's just the beginning of a carnival of errors. *The Medical and Surgical History of the War of the Rebellion,* which kept a running account of how soldiers were treated, is full of prescriptions like "quinine, opium, and whiskey." Another popular cure was "whiskey and morphine," which sounds better suited for the title of a heavy metal album than a medical prescription. Many patients were prescribed a pint a day; others were given "as much whiskey as [they] could take," according to the *History.*

When not drinking it, soldiers were washed in it. One man had an inflammation on his leg bathed daily with a mixture of "turpentine, with carbonate of ammonia, and whiskey." But because bacterial infections were poorly understood, whiskey wasn't often used as a disinfectant, where it might have been more beneficial. Doctors used it instead as a wash for its so-called mystical "stimulating" properties.

Surprisingly, the stereotype that soldiers often drank a manly slug of whiskey before going under the knife for surgery isn't true. During the Civil War, opinion on the use of anesthetics varied, and a few surgeons used whiskey instead of ether or chloroform, but the majority knew better. With the copious amount of blood lost during amputations, abandoning proper anesthesia for whiskey, which thins the blood, would only have wreaked havoc.

The museum's most famous specimen is the whiskey-preserved leg of Union general Daniel Sickles. It was shattered into a dozen pieces by a cannonball, and the museum staff has carefully reconstructed the bone shards, a fitting symbol of the man who used the loss of his leg to reconstruct his failing political career.

Before the war, Sickles was a Tammany Hall politician and U.S. congressman. In 1859, he killed the exceedingly handsome Philip Barton Key, son of national anthem scribe Francis Scott Key and the district attorney of Washington, D.C., when he learned that Key was having an affair with his wife. The shooting happened across the street from the White House, and Sickles was acquitted with the nation's first successful plea of "temporary insanity." Unsurprisingly, the murder dampened Sickles's political prospects and sent him looking for other career options. When the Civil War began, he joined the army as a colonel and soon found himself promoted to general.

At Gettysburg, a twelve-pound cannonball tore through Sickles's lower leg after he defied the orders of his boss, Major General George G. Meade, in a stupid tactical move of his own devising. As he was carried to the field hospital in a stretcher to have his leg amputated, Sickles calmly lit a cigar and told his men to stand firm. Under most circumstances he would have been court-martialed, but his political connections and the fact that he was effectively removed from fighting by the cannonball spared him.

Sickles was aware of orders from the surgeon general that his leg should be sent to Brinton at the medical museum. He had it wrapped in whiskey-soaked cloth and placed in a coffin-shaped box, which he sent with a note reading, "With the compliments of Major General D.E.S." For years afterward, on the anniversary of the amputation Sickles would visit his leg at the museum to remind everyone of his heroic sacrifice, using it to revive a political career that lasted until he died at the age of ninety-four. Though he learned to use an artificial leg, he relied on a crutch during political events. In 1897, he convinced the War Department to issue him a Medal of Honor even though military historians consider his battlefield tactics appalling. Meeting Sickles in later years, the writer Mark Twain concluded that he "valued the leg he lost more than the one he's got."

Sickles had made it easy for Brinton by gift-wrapping his own leg. When the museum first opened, however, Brinton often found himself toting his own whiskey to battlefields to show field surgeons how specimens should be collected. After hearing about unusual injuries that warranted study, he would head to the field and slosh into swampy pits of human meat and fluid. He later wrote, "Many and many a putrid heap have I had dug out of trenches where they had been buried in the supposition of an everlasting rest, and ghoul-like work have I done, amid surrounding gatherings of wondering surgeons."

After Brinton educated his colleagues about how specimens should be collected, the museum began shipping the preservative whiskey to battlefield surgeons by rail, where railroad workers often drank it and caused shortages in the field. To prevent the theft, Brinton chose particularly good barrels of whiskey and added tartar emetic to induce vomiting. Problem solved.

The museum itself became a kind of whiskey depot after the secretary of war ordered that confiscated liquor go directly to Brinton. A side lot next to the museum soon swelled with "kegs, bottles, demijohns and cases, to say nothing of an infinite variety of tins, made so as to fit unperceived on the body, and thus permit the wearer to smuggle liquor," Brinton later wrote. The contents ran from "champagne to the commonest rum," and wines or other lower-proof alcohol were dumped together into the still, which ran nonstop, to increase the proof. The still occasionally blew up, but "never caused any active harm," Brinton wrote. When not engaged in making liquor, it was used to redistill sulfuric ether for cleaning bones.

Brinton's problems finding whiskey were minor compared to those faced by the troops. Demand was still strong for liquor that could numb the pain of war, but grain was needed for food, farmers were off fighting, and supply lines from whiskey-producing regions were often severed. Shortages were particularly bad in the South, where most of the war's fighting occurred and where the government had confiscated copper stills and melted them down to produce war materiel. Southern states ordered strict prohibition for civilians in order to preserve grain. In 1860, whiskey in the South cost twenty-five cents per gallon, but by 1863, as the fighting raged, shortages caused it to spike to thirty-five dollars.

Brinton's medical colleagues on the Confederate side were often accused of stealing quality liquor and foods donated by civilians to recovering troops. One southern newspaper even claimed that medical staff regularly ordered troops to raid private cellars in search of the best spirits. The doctors were also accused of killing patients while operating drunk. One surgeon defended his malpractice by claiming he was so overworked that he needed the so-called stimulants.

Before Brinton established the museum he occasionally met his Confederate medical counterparts in neutral territories where both were treating patients. He even befriended a few of them, noting in his memoirs that they were more confident in their fighting abilities, but also more poorly outfitted, largely due to the agrarian nature of the southern economy versus the manufacturing-focused north. "The uniforms of the Confederate officers were generally of a shabby dirty gray, with a good deal of tinsel and cheap gold ornamentation," and "their arms were poor," he wrote.

The quality of whiskey that Confederates drank followed suit. The rebels famously made do with substitutes like cleaning solvent, and their whiskey was given nicknames like "coffin varnish," "chain-lightning," and "tangleleg." They got it from back-alley bootleggers who used other soldiers as middlemen. Containers were sometimes so scarce that a soldier from a Tennessee regiment was once seen drinking whiskey straight from the barrel of his gun. One newspaper claimed that a single drop of Confederate whiskey "falling on the cobblestones would sound like a peal of thunder as it rent asunder the earth's surface for a quarter of a mile around."

Within the Confederacy during the war, distilling whiskey became a matter of states' rights—it was like a mini civil war within the larger Civil War. Most southern state legislatures tightened restrictions and invoked their sovereignty whenever the Confederate government attempted to seize whiskey. Virginia imposed stiff penalties on distillers who fulfilled contracts with the Confederate government. Even as Union general William Tecumseh Sherman galloped through Atlanta at the war's close, Georgia's legislature was bickering about its prohibition laws.

Union soldiers drank better than their southern counterparts. The North had more money, troops were regularly stationed near cities, commanders were more likely to issue alcohol as a part of rations, and the Federal government had better supply lines. Moreover, distilling strongholds in Pennsylvania, Maryland, Ohio, and Illinois—all Union states—didn't suffer as much fighting as the South.

Some distillers even found fortune in the war. Kentucky was neutral during the beginning of the conflict and sold whiskey to both sides. The Bluegrass State eventually sided with the North, but many Kentuckians continued to fight for and sympathize with the South. Jim Beam, born in 1864, was given the middle name Beauregard in honor of the Confederate general who captured Fort Sumter. The Samuels family, which would go on to found Maker's Mark, operated a distillery where Quantrill's Raiders, a rogue guerrilla unit fighting for the South, became the last Confederate militia to surrender.

Union general Ulysses S. Grant finally took control of most of Kentucky in 1862. The move helped ensure supplies of that state's whiskey for the Union, and apparently of Old Crow for Grant personally. Grant had been known as a heavy drinker since his days as a junior officer at frontier outposts in California, but officers close to him claimed it never hampered his performance. This included Brinton, who became close with the general while serving on his staff. The doctor's memoirs are carefully circumspect about Grant's drinking, probably to protect the general's reputation amidst all the rumors, and claim that Brinton was the only staff officer authorized to carry liquor for medicinal purposes, per Grant's order.

Regardless, after Grant suffered heavy losses at the battle of Shiloh in 1862, even though he technically won the battle, his critics blamed the carnage on his drinking. When Missouri congressman Henry Blow complained directly to Lincoln, the president famously replied, "I wish I knew what brand of whiskey he drinks. I would send a barrel to all my other generals."

There was a lot of speculation about Grant's preferred brand. Twenty years after the war ended, Union colonel Isaac Stewart claimed it was Old Crow. According to Stewart, he was with the general on a steamboat several months before the Union took Vicksburg in 1863. Grant proposed a nightcap among the officer staff, claiming, "Stewart has got some prime Old Crow whiskey around here somewhere." Grant allegedly downed a brimming goblet of the bourbon in one gulp.

As for Kentucky, the war put the state's whiskey industry in a precarious position. By that point, its natural advantages were obvious: it was well placed for distribution, its reputation was growing, and it was strongly associated with the catchy name that was increasingly used for a distinctive style of whiskey. However, three years of raiding and battle had reduced the number of distilleries in the state by half, down to about 150, according to some estimates.

Nevertheless, the thinned-out competition during a period when large producers were already pushing aside smaller ones helped ease the way for the "bourbon aristocracy" of names and successful brands that would come after the war—Dant, Pepper, Pogue, Taylor, and Wathen. The fortunes of those families, however, would forever be subject to a new whiskey tax that Lincoln revived in 1862 to pay for the war. Such taxes had been overturned by Jefferson in 1802 and were briefly reinstated between 1813 and 1817 to pay debts caused by the War of 1812. Lincoln's tax started at twenty cents per proof gallon (a gallon of 100-proof whiskey). As the cost of war increased, however, so did the tax, climbing by steady increments until it reached two dollars by 1865. Once the southern states returned to the Union after the war, they were also subject to the levy.

Thus was born the moonshiner, a new kind of war, and bourbon's black sheep cousin.

. . .

When Confederate soldier Amos Owens returned to North Carolina after the war and learned that his only slave had been freed, he vowed never to pay the whiskey tax. Owens had nearly died in a Union prison camp and harbored a lingering resentment of Yankees. Returning to a broken South back under Federal control, he was confronted by this new whiskey tax, as well as other new legislation Congress had passed during the absence of obstructive southern delegations: a transcontinental railroad, higher-education support, the abolition of slavery, a national currency, and the Homestead Act. The war was over, but not all the fighting, and Owens "registered a blood red oath that this tax he'd never pay."

Owens's life as a moonshiner and his battles with law enforcement would become the stuff of legend. His court appearances were dramatic affairs, covered widely in the press, and he would create the archetype of the backwoods moonshiner. The newly established Bureau of Internal Revenue Service enforced the whiskey tax and, with four thousand employees, was instantly the largest single department in the U.S. government. Agents were deputized to find and punish tax evaders like Owens, relative smallholders dwarfed by an expanding segment of the whiskey industry that was growing more consolidated and industrial (and thus easier to tax).

Distilling in the isolated hollows of Appalachia and other rural areas had changed little since the days of the Whiskey Rebellion. The "benefits" of economic, cultural, and technological shifts often arrive at such places last, while the disadvantages of those same changes unfortunately arrive there first. In the hills, older methods of making whiskey continued: small stills, sweet mashes, minimal or no aging.

Even though the quality of these spirits no doubt varied widely, genius occasionally made an appearance. A few moonshiners earned legendary reputations as master craftsmen whose "white lightning" inspired the noble traditions of country life. They made spirits for their personal circles, caring more about the quality of their product than a farmer-distiller selling whiskey as a bulk commodity to a wholesaler might. Even though an exceptional unaged whiskey is a difficult endeavor, a few were able to pull it off—a fleeting miracle of the woods.

But many others, preoccupied with evading the law and turning a profit, quickly turned to cheap shortcuts. They abandoned pricey copper pot stills for sheet metal, which doesn't remove sulfur compounds as well as copper does. Copper bonds with the sulfur, limiting compounds like hydrogen sulfide (which makes rotten eggs smell) and dimethyl trisulfide (which tastes like rotten vegetables). Moonshiners would mimic the effects of aging by adding charcoal to the jug and shaking it.

Or they'd just put sawdust in a tobacco pouch—like a hillbilly tea bag—and place it in the whiskey. Some aged their hooch in small three-gallon pickle barrels.

Ingredients also suffered. Moonshiners quickly began swapping grain for cheap sugarjack, a low-quality grade of sugar, which produces a high yield of very low-quality alcohol. Some used hog feed, a cheaper grain more likely to be infected with things like ergot, a parasitic fungus that can cause hallucinations and seizures.

Cities had their own moonshining problems, often worse than the rural enclaves more frequently but erroneously associated with moonshine culture. In 1867, a detachment of marines was sent to Philadelphia to smash illegal distilleries. And in 1869, marines sent to Brooklyn to dismantle illegal distilleries were beaten off by a mob. But regardless of bootlegging's urban infestations, the image of rural moonshiners stuck in the nation's mind. For some it was simply a way of life—they were dirt poor and just trying to get along as they always had. But for others, like Amos Owens, moonshining was also an act of defiance. He came from a line of Scotch-Irish distillers dating back to a grandfather who had fought at the battle of Kings Mountain, and the tax no doubt dredged up comparisons to Ireland's whiskey wars and America's Whiskey Rebellion. Owens, a former slave owner, declared with no self-reflection whatsoever that his freedom was hampered by a federal government denying his right to turn crops into "legal tender." To him, moonshining was just carrying on the proud tradition of his blockading ancestors practicing their "inalienable right" to make a living from their land.

Point taken, but moonshining in another sense was also defiance for the sake of defending the status quo, resisting the inescapable changes of a war that would transform America. During the early 1870s, a North Carolina division of the Ku Klux Klan, another group dedicated to preserving the status quo, teamed up with moonshiners—united in their hatred of the government—to intimidate revenue collectors and government informants. In Pickens County, Georgia, twenty-seven moonshiners formed an order called "the Honest Man's Friend and Protector." They adopted the same hoods and gowns of the KKK, only in black instead of white, and would occasionally set fire to the homes of their neighbors. The period of moonshiner resistance to government in postbellum Georgia is sometimes called the "Georgia Moonshine Wars," and by some estimates was responsible for more than three-quarters of federal court cases. It was the fallout of a nation in transition.

. . .

There are few more compelling portraits of the Civil War's aftermath than those provided by today's whiskey bottles: their labels, how they are arranged at the liquor store, who owns them, and their marketing. They are a collective symbol that can be interpreted to reveal the rifts that once divided a nation, and how those injuries continue to heal. They show how we remember, and how we forget.

An age-old hierarchy at the liquor store is determined by what shelf a brand occupies. The choicest brands are on top—the position of dominance and prestige—and from there everything else trickles down. Like all pecking orders, this arrangement is not always fair. Today's bottom shelf is the home of the moonshine, or "white whiskey," as it's sometimes called. It's often sold in Mason jars or ceramic crocks, as if a bootlegger running from the law just delivered it by moonlight. Of course, this isn't real moonshine—it is made by legitimate, taxpaying companies. Much of it is just a gimmick, inexpensive vodka dressed up with a different label to capitalize on moonshine's romantic outlaw appeal. This Disney-esque marketing simply gives faux-moonshine's façade the same feel as a Confederate flag bumper sticker or those T-shirts featuring Che Guevara as a mascot for World Revolution, Inc. What isn't vodka is usually white dog: unaged whiskey made from quality grains instead of the cheap sugarjack used in most real moonshine. White whiskey is mostly sold by young, cash-strapped distilleries hungry for quick revenue without accruing any additional aging expenses. Surprisingly, white whiskey often costs more than superior aged whiskies—hillbilly heritage sold for *Beverly Hillbillies* prices. This is because young distilleries have relatively higher overhead costs and smaller economies of scale than their more established counterparts. In a way, the high price tags are aspirational—the white whiskey will support the young distilleries' eventual transition to aged whiskey as they emerge from their isolated backwaters and climb to higher rungs of the liquor store's social ladder.

Sitting above the faux-moonshine is Jack Daniel's, a brand symbolic of a long-running interstate rift. Jasper Newton "Jack" Daniel was from Tennessee, a state that once wasted no love for its northern Kentucky neighbor that originally supported the Confederacy but pragmatically reversed course and joined the Union. As a brand today, Jack Daniel's emphatically asserts that it is *not* bourbon. It technically qualifies, and could be labeled as bourbon if it wanted, but proudly uses the label "Tennessee Whiskey" instead. The term is broadcast on the label in huge letters trumpeting the brand's state pride.

While the taste of Jack is very similar to bourbon, and the methods and ingredients used to make it are nearly identical, there is one big difference between the two whiskey styles. Before Tennessee whiskey is put in the barrel, it is filtered through a column of charred sugar maple to remove the young spirit's rough edges. The practice is known as the Lincoln County Process, and it gives the whiskey a slightly smoky flavor alongside a glass-smooth texture and round sweetness. Contrary to popular belief, the Lincoln County Process doesn't disqualify whiskey from being labeled as bourbon, but nonetheless helps set Tennessee whiskey apart since spirits labeled as bourbon tend not to use it.*

Jack Daniel was born around 1850 (historians are unsure of the exact date) and for much of his career was known as a kind of wunderkind "boy distiller," a reputation largely owing to the fact that he was barely five feet tall. He boosted both his height and his ego with high-heeled boots and commonly dressed to the nines in colorful vests, frock coats, and a wide-brimmed planter's hat. When Daniel began his distilling career after the Civil War, his native Tennessee lay in ruins—only Virginia had seen more battles—and animosity toward the North ran high.

---

*In order to be called a Tennessee whiskey, the spirit has to be made in Tennessee, although it doesn't have to use the Lincoln County Process. Prichard's, a craft outfit in Tennessee, makes a non-charcoal-filtered "Tennessee" whiskey. As of early 2015, regulations to further define whiskey were under debate.

Kentucky's relatively quick success in rebuilding its postwar whiskey industry could only have been watched by its southern neighbor with a mix of scorn and envy. Tennessee's distillers considered the Kentuckians "proud, almost arrogant, about their whiskey," according to Jack Daniel biographer Peter Krass. They increasingly used a snooty name associated with French royalty to describe their whiskey and were beginning to develop "the tradition and the name recognition Jack wanted for himself," Krass writes. For an ambitious distiller like Daniel, the goal would be to build an equal reputation with something called Tennessee whiskey, not bourbon.

Jack Daniel's today is often seen as a bit downmarket, the quaff of biker bars and a prop of Guns N' Roses band photos. This is likely because the brand isn't particularly expensive and its relative sweetness and low proof help it go down easy, just right for a shot. Critics today sometimes complain that its overpowering sweetness makes the drink one-dimensional and a little boring—this is perhaps a result of the Lincoln County Process adding sugars to the spirit while stripping it of certain chemical compounds and neutralizing acids that, if left in the distillate, might evolve into more nuanced flavors. But despite these critiques, Jack Daniel made respectable whiskey for his era. In his time he wasn't always competing with whiskies that matched modern standards—the Lincoln County Process would have quickly given his whiskey a welcome smoothness and distinguished it from competing brands.

As Daniel built his company in the postwar years, sales of his brand slowly increased as the relationship between North and South improved. It wasn't a huge brand back then, as it is often described today, but it was successful enough to afford Daniel a comfortable lifestyle. After Daniel's death in 1911, the distillery fell under the control of his business partner, Lem Motlow, who successfully restarted it after Prohibition. Until the 1950s, however, the distillery spent very little money on advertising and was virtually unknown outside of Tennessee, aside from a small cult following that included luminaries such as William Faulkner and Winston Churchill (Churchill's mother was American, and he greatly annoyed the Scots when he divulged his enjoyment of Jack instead of scotch).

Then, in 1956, Louisville's Brown-Forman, the spirits company that still owns it today, bought Jack Daniel's. *Time* magazine claimed it was the "ultimate compliment" that the bourbon titan, from a place many Tennesseans still scorned, could pay to the small distillery. The *Nashville Tennessean* was less happy about the acquisition, dredging up the bad blood between the border states by writing that Jack Daniel's "never again will seem quite the same now that it has fallen into the hands of Kentuckians."

But regardless of any lingering interstate resentment, Brown-Forman catapulted the brand's success into the stratosphere. After the acquisition, it hired a man named Angelo Lucchesi as Jack Daniel's first marketing agent. Lucchesi, who accidentally lost an arm in his dad's sausage grinder as a youngster, was friends with Frank Sinatra and kept the singer supplied with the brand. One day while onstage, Sinatra raised a glass of the drink before his audience and called it "the nectar of the gods." (When he died, the singer was even buried with a flask of it for his trip into the afterlife.) After the Brown-Forman acquisition, a bigger advertising budget—and no doubt Sinatra's celebrity endorsement—boosted sales by 10 percent annually for two decades and then tripled them the decade after that. Although Jack Daniel's might secretly envy the pedigree of bourbon, its staggering sales numbers—far beyond Jim Beam, the best-selling bourbon—probably help take the salt out of any lingering wounds.

Nevertheless, the shelves above Jack Daniel's are owned by bourbon. Among them is a popular brand called Rebel Yell, which was created in the 1940s amid a flare-up of southern nationalism that preceded the civil rights movement. The label was the brainchild of Kentucky congressman Charlie P. Farnsley, who convinced his uncle, Stitzel-Weller Distillery co-owner Alex Farnsley, to create a bourbon brand specifically for southerners (the distillery's other co-owner was Julian "Pappy" Van Winkle, who typically handled marketing).* Rebel Yell

---

* Since its creation, Rebel Yell has had many owners, but currently is made by Heaven Hill under contract for another company that owns it.

uses wheat instead of rye as the flavor grain and has a refreshing citrusy quality that is particularly suitable to the steamy southern states where it was exclusively marketed after its creation. The original label read, "Especially for the Deep South" and featured a Confederate soldier—sword drawn, the taste of Yankee blood in his mouth—riding a galloping horse into battle. Almost a century after the Civil War ended, its iconography still resonated deeply with southerners.

But after Rebel Yell was expanded into national markets in 1984 and international markets shortly thereafter, the provocative label was toned down, presumably so it wouldn't offend its new and larger customer base. The soldier's sword became a little smaller and the bright Confederate gray tones of his uniform became more muted (although the brash logo did play well in Japan, where it apparently clicked with customers holding romanticized notions of violent American subcultures). A few years later, as the war's wounds continued to fade and the message carried by Rebel Yell's original marketing became less politically acceptable, the brand's label was sanitized further when the soldier was replaced by the silhouette of a cowboy. By 2014, the marketing was fully scrubbed as the phrase "Rebel Yell," which remained offensive to some, was shortened to just "RY." In brand advertisements today, the "rebel" has been converted into something far more palatable to modern consumers: a musician with a scruffy beard and sunglasses, strumming a guitar.

· CHAPTER SEVEN ·

THE RING AND THE OCTOPUS

Throughout the summer of 1875, a cascade of headlines, full of political scandal soaked in corruption, sex, and whiskey, swamped the nation. Newspapers reported how Republicans had diverted tax revenue from a giant network of whiskey distilleries into illicit political slush funds used to buy elections and bury opponents. The politicos who faced charges all attempted to backstab and bribe their way out of trouble. The group was quickly nicknamed the Whiskey Ring, and investigators traced it all the way up to a little room just off the Oval Office, occupied by Orville Babcock, personal secretary to President Ulysses S. Grant.

Whiskey had entered the Gilded Age, the period lasting from the end of the Civil War to the early twentieth century. Also nicknamed "the Great Barbecue" and "the Saturnalia of Plunder," it was the most corrupt era in U.S. history and a time of great transition as a relatively invisible prewar federal government transformed into a powerful postwar government. These complicated new institutions were largely reliant on alcohol taxes (including both domestic excise taxes and tariffs on imported liquor), which gave the government nearly half its revenue and were its biggest cash source until the income tax was introduced in 1913. As the nation figured out how that kind of power and money should be organized, public office became a regular tool for private gain. The railroad mogul Collis Huntington showed up at each new Congress with a cash-filled trunk to buy votes, lobbyists sold stock certificates outside the House and Senate chambers, Boss Tweed ruled New York, western lands were seized with fraudulent grants, and the financier Jay Gould created his own fortune while masterminding stock schemes that created enormous losses for his own investors. The generation of men who had fought to save the Union—and were likewise turned numb by an excruciating war—all scrambled to get their cut of the action.

Whiskey producers were deeply involved in all the corruption, and the quality of the whiskey itself often reflected that fact. They were a casualty of an industry with too few regulations or protections against copyright infringements, truth-in-packaging laws, and labeling requirements. Good whiskey in the league of Old Crow and other fledgling brands was less than 5 percent of the market because it was expensive and time-consuming to make. With almost no government oversight or accountability, outfits called "rectifiers," specializing in high volumes of cheap spirits, grew to dominate the trade. Even today, the whiskey industry struggles to reverse negative parts of its image rooted in this era. But the Gilded Age wasn't all gloom for the whiskey industry. Working to scrape its way out of the muck and adapt to an increasingly industrialized business model, bourbon managed to make some bold strides during this period that continue to be part of its modern legacy.

. . .

For an industry that peddles a drug, maintaining a good image is crucial. The Gilded Age years provided a wellspring of ammunition—on a variety of fronts spanning political, economic, and cultural matters— for Prohibition advocates who would begin making their strongest case during this period. Whiskey's image was given no favors by the fact that at the beginning of the era it was also the lifeblood of the era's most outrageous political scandal.

The Whiskey Ring had a simple design: more whiskey was made than reported, and the additional profits from the untaxed overage were pocketed when the whiskey was sold for the same price as its taxed counterparts. But the simple design included logistics that were a criminal's worst nightmare—a blizzard of bogus accounting, false serial numbers, and counterfeit labels all managed by crooks who were paid different amounts according to their rank in an unequal pecking order. It's a testament to the times that the scheme lasted as many years as it did.

Ever since whiskey taxes were invented, people have broken laws to dodge them. During the first whiskey tax—the one that caused the Whiskey Rebellion and was eliminated after Thomas Jefferson became president—the government ordered tax collectors to use hydrometers to accurately measure a spirit's alcoholic proof. Without a hydrometer, measuring proof was a slapdash affair: distillers would "prove" (hence the origin of the term) a spirit's strength by mixing it with gunpowder and lighting it on fire. If the flame sputtered because the alcohol content was low, the liquor was "under proof." If it flared up like a bonfire, it was "over proof." A steady and even flame, which occurs when whiskey is about 50 percent alcohol by volume, meant it was "100 percent proved" (which is why liquor that's 100 proof is 50 percent alcohol). By 1868, with the whiskey tax back in place, the government further clarified the definition of a proof gallon as 50 percent alcohol by volume at 68 degrees Fahrenheit in order to foil tax evaders. Alcohol contracts at cooler temperatures, and distillers were chilling their vats at tax time in order to lower the amount of measurable alcohol.

After the war, the government assigned revenue agents called "gaugers" to guard whiskey that sat aging in warehouses and prevent any tampering before taxes were assessed. In many cases, if gaugers weren't actually in charge of profit-skimming plots, they were soon bribed or bullied into them. Redundant serial numbers were written on barrels and paperwork was doctored. Tax evasion became so lucrative that some distillers were able to transport grain from the Midwest to New Orleans, turn it into whiskey, ship it back upriver, and still undersell competitors who were running legitimate businesses. The Whiskey

Ring was created as hundreds of individual tax dodges snowballed into one giant scandal. Various officials, increasingly higher up the food chain, began noticing gaps between revenues and volumes on the paperwork turned in by their subordinates. They assumed, correctly, that profits were being skimmed, and soon began demanding their cut of the action.

The Whiskey Ring's nerve center was John McDonald, a former brigadier general who was close friends with Orville Babcock, Grant's personal secretary. Before establishing the ring, McDonald had narrowly missed getting pinched in another scheme to rob the federal treasury by cashing bogus war claims on property that had been destroyed during the fighting. The plan failed, and McDonald soon turned to his friend Babcock for a job. Babcock convinced the president to give McDonald a position at the Bureau of Internal Revenue, effectively placing a wolf in the henhouse.

McDonald was assigned to St. Louis as the head revenue collector for a large part of the Midwest. Once he arrived at his post he soon noticed the bizarre accounting at the whiskey warehouse and seized on the lucrative opportunity. The ring of McDonald's devising had five principal members—including himself and Babcock—who each received between $45,000 and $60,000 per year, roughly the same amount paid to participating distilleries. Babcock, serving as the inside man in Washington, kept his boss Grant only selectively apprised of matters.*

In 1871, the ring earned $1.5 million, an amount that turned McDonald's St. Louis office into the de facto headquarters for Republican Party politics. Party members facing tough campaigns would telegraph the former general asking for new duties on distilleries in order to raise cash that would prevent a close election from slipping to the Democrats. In 1872, Grant, perhaps coincidentally, won reelection.

The Whiskey Ring continued collecting $1.5 million each year until

---

* Grant was never directly implicated in the scandal and is typically described by most historians as a trusting sort, elected to the White House on the reputation of his battlefield heroics rather than his abilities as an administrator.

1875. Meanwhile, ring members were buying elections, lavish homes, and nights with exclusive call girls. The men dripped with diamond jewelry, which was easy to hide during bankruptcy proceedings or stash away during quick getaways. Babcock's appetites in particular "for clothing, drink, and fornication—all to be satisfied at the cost of the public Treasury—led him to ever more brazen adventures and needless risks," according to *The Politicos*, Matthew Josephson's seminal 1938 book on corruption during the era.

By 1874, the ring's wake of saturnalia caught the eye of treasury secretary Benjamin Bristow, one of the era's few honest operators. Suspicious of the tax evasion scheme, Bristow recruited Myron Colony, a business reporter with the *St. Louis Dispatch*, for an undercover operation. The reporter, who regularly hung around distilleries and grain depots collecting information for the paper, would secretly record incoming and outgoing shipments of grain and spirits. Within a month he collected enough evidence to arrest three hundred ring members and implicate thirty-two distilleries in every major distilling center across the nation. Bristow estimated that only one-third of the total taxes due on whiskey in the United States were being collected.

The ensuing investigation quickly led to the White House. When Bristow approached the president to tell him, Grant, famously oblivious to many of the working parts of his administration, replied, "There is at least one honest man in St. Louis on whom we can rely—John McDonald. I know that because he is an intimate acquaintance and confidential friend of Babcock's."

"Mr. President," Bristow said with a grimace, "McDonald is the head and center of all the frauds." Babcock was also fingered.

Even so, Grant was fiercely loyal to his friend Babcock and insisted that he testify on his behalf, just barely earning him an acquittal. McDonald, with no similar favor from the president, did prison time. Nevertheless, the era's suffocating corruption soon found Babcock involved in another scandal, involving the planting of fake evidence on a man who had helped the ring's prosecutors. Grant, still faithful to his friend, removed Babcock from Washington and set him up with a plummy gig as the chief inspector of lighthouses. Babcock loved the job, which allowed him to use his engineering degree from West Point and spend time near beautiful beaches. Seven years later, however, tragedy struck when a boat ferrying him from a schooner to shore near Florida's Mosquito Inlet capsized. A few days later, Babcock became an unfortunate symbol of the era when his body washed up on a scrubby patch of beach, nibbled on by sharks.

. . .

Most of the distilleries involved in the Whiskey Ring scandal resembled sawmills or factories. They were a far cry from the small distilleries that had defined the whiskey industry just several decades earlier: a single pot still in a shed or a barn, located near a creek. America was shifting from an agrarian economy to an industrial one, a trend that whiskey—a product that is both agrarian and industrial—represented well. Of the many small farmer-distillers who were still making tiny amounts of whiskey, most sold their spirits to larger distilleries. The bigger operations souped together this random mix of unaged spirits and redistilled it to an eye-popping proof with their own equipment, giving it consistency but removing much of the character.

The industrial efficiency of this new type of large distillery came from towering column stills. These were the stills patented by Aeneas Coffey in 1831 that by now had come to replace many pot stills. Today, pot stills are seen as beautiful relics of a bygone era—they were never the most productive pieces of equipment, but there was a beauty to their inefficiency. Slow and sputtering, they produced spirits at a lower proof, thus preserving the liquor's heavier, richer flavors. A handful of distillers still use them, but their numbers are few. Column stills dominate the industry today, but are often misunderstood because they can do both great and terrible things to whiskey.

Column stills specialize in efficiency and volume. They hold the ability to strip almost pure alcohol (ethanol) from a liquid and leave behind all the trace elements that lend a beverage spirit its character and flavor. This brazenly sterile product is known as "grain neutral spirits," and it is produced at well over 190 proof (something like that is sold as Everclear or as vodka—with vodka, the proof is lowered with water before it is bottled). You can age neutral spirits, but coaxing life from them is like trying to grow a vegetable garden on the surface of the moon—they will chew away at the wood for years but the barrel will typically spit out something medicinal and unpleasant. Outside of the spirits industry, column stills are used to produce industrial solvents, furniture polish, and torpedo fuel. The mechanics behind them are similar to those found in distillation columns at oil refineries.

But despite their industrial nature, column stills also produce some of the most renowned spirits in the world, as well as the vast majority of bourbon on store shelves today. If a distiller shows restraint with a column still, aiming for a lower proof that preserves the oils and compounds that give a spirit nuance and character, the same flavor richness of a pot can still be achieved. That's how bourbon makers today use column stills. The different kinds of stills do produce slightly different flavors because their mechanics are different, but they are simply just that: *different.** One kind isn't necessarily better or worse than the other—it simply depends on how they are used.

But this point is fiercely debated by modern whiskey geeks, a group that will admittedly find a way to argue everything to death. The romanticism of the pot still—harkening back to a simpler time before everything got so big and intimidating—is hard to resist. Today, Woodford Reserve uses large pot stills where visitors see them during tours of its facilities, but the brand is primarily made with column stills located at a different facility (the spirits are mixed together afterward). Despite this marketing ruse, Woodford's decision to use column stills arguably results in a better whiskey. Many modern distillers find that column stills give them greater control over corn and rye's relatively high lipid levels, which can foul a spirit's flavor. (This isn't as much of an issue for the malt used

---

* For instance the shape of a pot still's neck affects flavor. A thin, long neck favors the passage of lighter compounds that carry floral and fruity notes. A short neck allows heavier compounds to make it into the spirit, leading to a richer, nuttier taste.

in scotch, an industry for which pot stills are often more prevalent.) Even though Matt Hofmann, master distiller at Seattle's Westland Distillery, uses pot stills to make the company's single-malt whiskies, he once told me that if he were to make a corn or rye-heavy spirit he would probably use a column still, for the control it would give him over lipids. The choice would be made entirely on what he thought would result in the best flavor, not the mystique associated with the equipment.

Many modern distilleries claim they use pot stills but are actually using hybrid stills, equipment shaped like a pot still at the bottom but possessing a small rectification column on top. In marketing, the pot still's old-fashioned, romantic appeal is emphasized, but the column portion of the hybrid equipment allows distilleries the benefits of the modern technology, which is ultimately best for the whiskey (or any type of spirit). In the scotch world, the romance around pot stills is far more extreme than in America, and often plays a major role in brand marketing. Nevertheless, Jim McEwan, master distiller of Bruichladdich, a Scottish distillery that uses pot stills, once admitted to a reporter from the *New Yorker* that much of the marketing arguing for the superiority of one kind of still over another was little more than "a kind of fairy story." What really mattered in terms of the quality and flavor wasn't the equipment as much as it was "the artisanal skills of the whiskymaker," he said.* Ultimately, the final judgment of a whiskey depends on one simple question: how does it taste?

During the Gilded Age, many distilleries dispensed with the kind of "artisanal skills" referred to by McEwan and used their column stills to make extremely high-proof spirits, which are more profitable because they can be stretched further. The quality of their whiskies varied

---

* Christopher Williams of Coppersea Distilling in upstate New York, which uses pot stills, once described the difference to me in a more poetic way: "A lot of the most elaborate German stills—with their elaborately piped/ windowed/ plated hybrid columns—look a lot like shiny tenor saxophones. Whereas our simple pot stills are like a little Marine Band diatonic harmonica. If you're John Coltrane, you can really make magic happen on a tenor sax, but you better have a comprehensive grasp of music theory and scales. Meanwhile, a badass blues harp player typically has absolutely no understanding of theory, but intuitively understands how to play and can even bend notes to create sounds that the harmonica was not designed to make. So in this sense we're more like Little Walter or even Howlin' Wolf in our approach to distilling."

greatly. In some cases the flavorless neutral spirits were mixed with a small amount of aged whiskey to add aroma and character, producing a kind of pale echo of something better. Burnt sugar, prune juice, or other additives gave these whiskies color and sweetness—they were relatively harmless, if not exactly tasty. In the worst cases, ingredients like sulfuric acid or sulfate of ammonia—two items commonly found today in insecticides and bombs—were added in an attempt to mimic the effects of proper aging. Distilling manuals of the era that described how to make charlatan whiskies sold well. Pierre Lacour's *The Manufacture of Liquors, Wines, and Cordials without the Aid of Distillation*, published in 1863, advised rectifiers to make "Old Bourbon Whiskey" by mixing four gallons of neutral spirits with three pounds of sugar, one pint of decoction of tea, oil of wintergreen, tincture made with cochineal (a red dye made from the crushed and dried bodies of insects), and burnt sugar. The whiskey probably wasn't good, but it was profitable.

. . .

Whiskey flavored with harmful additives and insect parts seems a perfect reflection of Gilded Age politics and business. Eventually, some of those lobbying the corridors of power lobbied on behalf of bourbon for changes to government regulations that would improve the spirit's quality.

Kentucky Democrat John Carlisle wasn't a particularly good poker player, but he did play cards with presidents and congressmen, meaning that whatever he lost at the table he often recouped by gaining legislative support for the whiskey industry. Serving in both the House and Senate and as treasury secretary, Carlisle, over a thirty-year career, lobbied for changes that improved whiskey by altering tax codes. This allowed distillers to age their product longer and not have to pay as much tax on spirits that evaporated during the maturation process. Drinkers no doubt appreciated his measure but Republicans, who enjoyed increased support from the temperance movement after the war, began using liquor for political attacks. They called whiskey the "national beverage" of Democrats. The term "Bourbon Democrat" drew on the word's old political meaning, rather than as a drink, to mock conservative but classically liberal Democrats such as Carlisle, Grover Cleveland, and a very young Woodrow Wilson—in Louisiana, the term was primarily used to associate Democrats with old-fashioned thinking, linking them with royalists who had opposed the French Revolution nearly a century earlier. A valuable marketing tool on one hand, a political insult on the other, the word "bourbon" was again proving that its protean nature endured.

As federal regulations began growing around the spirits industry, Carlisle and politicians from other whiskey strongholds, such as Pennsylvania senator James Cameron, ensured that their states fared well. In 1879, Carlisle lobbied to increase the bonding period on spirits—the amount of time whiskey can sit and age before it is taxed—from one to three years, which gave distillers an incentive to age their whiskey longer because they wouldn't have to pay taxes on the evaporated portion. Considering the smoldering fallout from the Whiskey Ring scandal a few years earlier, it was a significant achievement. Then, in 1894, the bonding period was extended to eight years, giving most bourbon the time needed to find its sweet spot.

The whiskey industry and government were setting important precedents by learning how to work together, but missteps invariably occurred. For instance, whenever Congress raised taxes on whiskey, it never made the tax increases retroactive for spirits already aging in bonding warehouses, a move supported by distillers. If rumors of a looming tax increase drifted out of Washington, distillers responded by drastically boosting output to get whiskey into storage and take advantage of the old tax rate. The result was vast whiskey surpluses that far outstripped demand. When the bonding period ended and the tax was due, distillers were forced to sell at a loss or go out of business if the market wasn't in a good mood. When prices went back up, entrepreneurs rushed back into the business, exacerbating an impulsive cycle.

The precarious supply gluts were aggravated on the trading floor. Almost every major newspaper in the country covered the whiskey industry in detail and the *Wall Street Journal* reported whiskey prices daily, the same as for coal, steel, and pork bellies. In 1883, almost half the whiskey in Kentucky was actually owned by bankers in Boston, New York, and Cincinnati who purchased bonded whiskey receipts from distillers for immediate cash, giving distillers another reason to boost production without considering demand constraints. As a result, whiskey in storage went from about fourteen million gallons in 1879 to ninety million in 1882, almost six times the estimated amount people were actually drinking. The huge gluts caused volatile price drops, prompting banks to lobby for increases to the bonding period to protect their investments in what they called "Kentucky gold." In 1883, the House Ways and Means Committee supported the proposal, but the Senate rejected it (the measure wouldn't get approval for another decade). Angry at the government's failure to increase the whiskey bonding period, one banker made a "too big to fail" case for the banks, claiming that Washington's insistence on getting its "pound of flesh" would "ruin many banks, and incidentally cripple every branch of industry and every line of trade," he told the *Boston Daily Globe*.

Some drinkers might think that price swings aren't a bad thing, especially if they occasionally translate into cheap whiskey. But what if parts of the industry fold as a result of the volatility? Distilling was a huge industry spread throughout the country, woven into many different parts of the economy. Wherever distilleries opened, other businesses bloomed, such as cattle-feeding operations utilizing the distilleries' spent mash. Shocks to the whiskey trade amplified other regional economic woes subject to a fickle Gilded Age economy that was prone to drastic and repeated recessions.

Chaotic boom-and-bust cycles made the whiskey trade a huge gamble, but the payoff was worth the risk. Whiskey made up close to 70 percent of America's alcohol business in the decades after the Civil War. Beer, enjoyed by a midcentury influx of German immigrants, was gaining in popularity but still didn't quite match whiskey sales (beer consumption increased fourfold between 1880 and 1913, the year when it finally edged out whiskey in popularity). Like any good gamblers, distillers looked for ways to improve their chances. This required bringing order to the industry, which in true Gilded Age fashion meant price fixing and blocking competition by any means necessary. It meant forming a cartel.

. . .

After Standard Oil Company founder John D. Rockefeller became the richest man in the world, he offered gardening advice to a group of young men at a Brown University Bible study. He told his admiring audience, "The American Beauty Rose can be produced in the splendor and fragrance which bring cheer to its beholder only by sacrificing the early buds which grow up around it. This is not an evil tendency in business. It is merely the working-out of a law of nature and a law of God."

Rockefeller's audacious winner-take-all metaphor about the American Beauty rose was a description of how Standard Oil had bested its competitors. The clumsy reference to God at the end of the remarks was a meager attempt to morally sanction the ideas of philosopher Herbert Spencer, who had recently seduced the robber baron community by adapting scientific ideas like "survival of the fittest" into a loose form of Social Darwinism that defined Gilded Age business.

So when a few powerful whiskey distillers decided to organize their own cartel in 1887, it surprised nobody when they modeled themselves directly after the most successful monopoly in the world: Rockefeller's Standard Oil trust, which had been formed five years earlier. The Whiskey Trust, officially known as the Distillers and Cattle Feeders Trust, copied Standard Oil's charter almost word for word. (Standard's business model of creating a monopoly wasn't yet technically illegal, but would be the impetus behind the Sherman Antitrust Act that was passed in 1890 to make it so.)

Reporters soon gave the Whiskey Trust a nickname: "the Octopus."*

---

* This same nickname was sometimes used for the railroad trust.

At its helm was Joseph B. Greenhut, the biggest distiller in America during the Gilded Age. Today, Greenhut's legacy stands in stark contrast to his counterparts in the beer world—names like Anheuser, Pabst, Busch, and Schlitz—which still grace countless neon signs in bars and ballparks. Greenhut's name, in contrast, is nearly forgotten, partly because he defined a whiskey industry far different from that of today. The big names in modern American whiskey—Beam, Samuels, Daniel—were relatively small during Greenhut's era, gaining prominence only after sweeping regulations enacted in the twentieth century would enable their rise. Jim Beam's home in Bardstown, Kentucky—which remains in the family—was a humble affair. Greenhut's home in Peoria, Illinois, however, was a thirty-five-room mansion graced with turrets and a glass conservatory. In 1899, he entertained President William McKinley there, and in 1916 he lent another of his homes at the New Jersey shore to Woodrow Wilson to use as a summer White House. Today, his Peoria mansion, at the end of High Street at Sheridan Road, has been converted into condos that look like they could use a little maintenance.

But in his time, Greenhut was a giant whose importance was evident to anyone standing near him. He was handsome, with a bulldog's stout build and the kind of bushy mustache you might find on a Prussian field marshal. People turned in his wake when he walked into a room, and he avoided making small talk and apologies. Born in Austria in 1843, Greenhut had immigrated to Chicago with his family in 1852. As a teenager he traveled to Mobile, Alabama, to find work as a coppersmith, a profession that led many people into the whiskey business for their ability to work on stills. A highly decorated Civil War veteran, he landed back in Chicago after the war but eventually struck out for Peoria in 1878.

Not only was the Peoria that Greenhut arrived in a whiskey town, it was *the* whiskey town. Between the Civil War and Prohibition, Peoria made more spirits than any other place in the United States. The city was the largest purchaser of corn in the world and produced 185,000 gallons of spirits per day, contributing more alcohol-related taxes to the government than any other place in the country (next in line were Chicago and Cincinnati, the other two biggest distilling centers). Peoria's former primacy, however, was quietly forgotten after the whiskey industry later consolidated in Kentucky and Tennessee, the winners that ultimately got to write history. Much to Peoria's chagrin, the city could never quite capture the same reputation as Kentucky, a perceived slight that various writers periodically tried to correct with frustrated editorials in trade magazines like *Bonfort's Wine and Spirit Circular*. Nevertheless, Peoria was once America's spirits capital, and Greenhut was its king.

In 1881, Greenhut founded the Great Western Distillery. It was the polar opposite of the kind of farm-based outfit Thomas Jefferson would have championed, the no-nonsense predecessor of a future corporate age where every detail was scrutinized. At Great Western decimal points were taken out a few notches and consultants specializing in matters like fermentation were brought in from as far away as Japan. Whereas the average distiller of the time coaxed around 4.24 gallons of alcohol from a bushel of grain, Greenhut knew that his operations were getting 4.535 gallons per bushel, that tiny extra fraction translating into more additional yearly income for him than smaller distillers might earn in a lifetime.

Greenhut corralled together sixty-five distilleries and some eighty industrial alcohol plants spread throughout the country to form the Whiskey Trust. These outfits were largely responsible for making industrial alcohol and the kind of grain neutral spirits many rectifiers and blenders used as a base to make their whiskey brands.* Each distillery that joined agreed to turn control of its business over to nine trustees. If a distillery refused to join, the trust lowered prices to undercut its business and force it in. Once the rebel holdout was brought into the fold, the trust would increase prices, which it controlled by offering rebates to wholesalers who agreed not to carry competing brands. Straight

---

* For this reason, the trust was sometimes called the "Highwine Trust," referring to the kind of high-proof spirits it specialized in.

bourbon and rye producers—those generally making a quality, unrectified product—were explicitly excluded, which put them at loggerheads with the trust because their straight whiskies would be in direct competition. Insufficient labeling and trademark laws also made it difficult for customers to know exactly what they were buying, giving the trust and the companies it supplied with cheap imitations a distinct advantage with their invariably lower prices.

Greenhut shut down most of the distilleries that joined his organization, often against their will. Thus he eliminated his competition by cannibalizing it, a strategy that also allowed him to control the kind of surplus output that threatened the industry's health. All but twelve of the distilleries brought into the trust were closed, the survivors selected according to how close they were located to plummy markets or who could get the cheapest shipping rates. Most of the survivors were located in Peoria, a railroad and waterway hub with good access to water, coal, and grain markets.

Distilleries that fought the Octopus faced warfare. Stubborn holdouts were burned to the ground after their insurance companies received anonymous messages to cancel their policies (distillery fires were common, making it an easy crime to hide). In one instance, explosives were thrown onto the roof of Chicago's H. H. Shufeldt and Company but failed to destroy it completely. George Gibson, the trust's secretary, was later arrested when he attempted to pay an undercover Internal Revenue agent $25,000 to finish the job at the Shufeldt distillery by planting a contraption designed to shoot a torpedo through a vat of alcohol, which would explode in a fireball. Gibson was miraculously acquitted (the trust never even bothered to take him off its payroll). When another distiller attempted to publish a book detailing the trust's methods, the trust paid him $50,000 for the manuscript, which never saw the light of day.

Straight bourbon and rye producers soon found their business with small, upscale markets threatened as cheap imitations became invasive. They responded by forming their own trusts. The Kentucky Distilleries and Warehouse Company was a combination of fifty-nine distilleries that controlled about 135 brands. Alongside the Kentucky cartel, many regional distilling centers in places like Pennsylvania and New York organized, working together to manipulate markets by coordinating stoppages and boosting prices.

But no group of distillers, including Greenhut's trust, was able to successfully create a monopoly for very long or control the market with the success of their counterparts in other industries. Standard Oil was able to establish its dominance because oil is a notoriously hard industry to break into, requiring staggering amounts of capital and specialized knowledge.* Whiskey didn't have the same intense barriers, and the Whiskey Trust, despite what control it did achieve, could never eliminate competitors the way it wanted. In fact, its success and profits actually helped attract competitors to the industry.

Many members of the Whiskey Trust also failed to see where the market was headed and the rising importance of brand names. These industrial big wheels were typically wholesalers selling their cheap spirits to marketers who used them as the base for their own brands. Over time, these brand owners would increasingly want to control the entire process, owning their own distilleries and vertically integrating all their operations under one roof. Beer brewers and other food manufacturers were already building their respective industries this way, operating in streamlined, closed systems that boosted revenues.

The U.S. government eventually pursued the trust, claiming it was restricting trade under the provisions of the Sherman Antitrust Act. The trust also faced constant scrutiny from a public that was increasingly worried about the excesses of the Gilded Age. Newspapers, for their part, loved stories about independent distilleries standing their ground against the cartel. The *National Tribune* ran one such story that involved the Green Mountain Distillery in Kansas City, Missouri. In

---

*This remains true today. In 2014, when Diageo announced it would build a new plant in Kentucky for $115 million, the project was hailed as huge for the whiskey industry. This amount of money, however, is the cost to build a *single* deep offshore oil well, putting into context the kind of capital required for each of these different businesses.

prose gilded to match the age the paper editorialized, "Of all the nefarious combinations of capital which control, or try to control the necessities of existence and to crush out legitimate competition, there is none so far reaching in its scope, so grasping in its methods, so rapacious in its exhibitions of greed and so thoroughly unscrupulous and unrelenting in its purpose to throttle the independent distillers as that prince of monopolies known as the WHISKEY TRUST."

· CHAPTER EIGHT ·

THE HARD SELL

There's a fine art to naming a liquor brand. The choice should appeal to a drinker's sense of heritage and legacy, but most important, it should sell the booze. Today, most brands have their formulas pretty well figured out: rum is named after pirates or tropical islands (think Captain Morgan or Mount Gay); scotch brands enshrine beautiful but unpronounceable places in Scotland (Laphroaig, Bruichladdich, Auchentoshan); gin brands conjure up images of the British Empire sending adventurous men to India clad in jodhpurs and pith helmets (Bombay Sapphire, Old Raj). Vodka labels emphasize luxury so people can forget that they paid too much.

Bourbon brands are a different breed. They often celebrate individuals. Sometimes the labels honor the specific tastes of master craftsmen like Elmer T. Lee, Albert Blanton, Booker Noe, or Jimmy Russell, distillers whose namesake labels reflect taste profiles they loved. Other bourbons are named after individuals on name alone: Elijah Craig, Evan Williams, Thomas Jefferson, or Basil Hayden.

But choosing a singular iconic personality is a bold move because it can invite embarrassing and unwanted scrutiny, especially when certain facts are revealed after a brand is established. Today, bottles of Evan Williams claim that their namesake became Kentucky's "first distiller" in 1783. This claim, which is false, is based on the writings of historian

Reuben Durrett, who declared Williams the "first" in 1892. But like Richard Collins and the Elijah Craig myth, Durrett was shooting from the hip with his facts, creating a nugget of incorrect information that would filter down through the ages as received wisdom. Truth is, Williams didn't even arrive in America, first landing in Pennsylvania, until 1784. When he finally made his way to Kentucky, distilling was long under way by countless others. What the bottles also fail to mention is that Williams's neighbors in Louisville thought his whiskey so bad that his distillery was declared a nuisance and he was indicted for selling without a license.

Regardless, when Heaven Hill created the brand in 1957 it ran with the incorrect information anyway. It's a curious thing—why not just choose a more truthful story? There are plenty of frontier icons resonating with powerful myths to choose from, so why pick that one, however harmless it might seem? It begs the question of what other information on the labels we shouldn't believe. What are the real legacies here? And what, exactly, is in those names on the bottles?

· · ·

For years, a questionable rumor floated around bourbon circles that Old Forester was named after Nathan Bedford Forrest, the Confederate cavalry leader who helped found the first Ku Klux Klan. Forrest's picture never appeared on the bottle—with deep-set eyes, hollow cheeks, and a pointy beard, he physically resembled "the very devil" that Union general William Tecumseh Sherman described him as. Born into poverty, Forrest created a fortune for himself as a slave trader. During the Civil War, his exploits as a cavalryman were so fierce that they would later inspire the blitzkrieg tactics of Nazi field marshal Erwin Rommel. At Fort Pillow, Forrest slaughtered scores of Federal African-American troops attempting to surrender. He has remained a symbol of southern resistance, held in esteem by a sliver of southerners who cite antiquated notions of cunning and daring as reasons to honor him.

Old Forester, on the other hand, is a legendary whiskey brand, regularly touted as the town favorite of Louisville, bourbon capital of the world. Old Forester was created in 1870 by George Garvin Brown, the cofounder of the Brown-Forman Corporation, one of today's most successful liquor companies. For bourbon, Old Forester is about as "classic" as it gets: a solid foundation of corn flavored with enough rye to make it interesting and add just enough spice to mature the corn's honeyed sweetness. Aged between four and six years, Old Forester holds the different flavors from grain, wood, and yeast in careful balance. It's affordable and timeless, achieving an ideal that other brands strive to match.* For these reasons alone it is one of the last bourbons you want to see tarnished by an association to a man like Forrest.

Brown-Forman today emphatically claims that the brand is "in no way shape or form associated with Nathan Bedford Forrest," according to one company spokesperson in a letter to me. Instead, the company claims that Old Forester is actually named after William Forrester, a physician friend of George Garvin Brown, since doctors regularly prescribed whiskey as medicine when the brand was created. Old Forester was originally spelled with two *r*'s, just like the names of both William and Nathan Bedford, and Brown-Forman claims the spelling was changed after Dr. Forrester retired, since his signature endorsement no longer would have been valid. But despite this explanation, the company admits there is reasonable doubt behind the name and that ultimately "the inspiration and origin of the Old Forrester brand name died with George Garvin Brown."

Other explanations for the brand's name only add to the confusion. One account claims the brand was linked to the nineteenth century's logging industry, and indeed, at one point the label featured an oak leaf cluster. All things considered—the spelling changes, the old labels indicating different explanations—the brand's true heritage may never be

---

* Other brands in this category—workhorses that helped build successful companies and offer far more than their low price tags suggest—include Wild Turkey 101, Buffalo Trace, Four Roses Yellow Label, Old Grand-Dad, Evan Williams, Ancient Age, Heaven Hill, and Weller Antique. Appreciating the complexity of expensive and super-premium whiskies is one thing, but seeing past the hype and recognizing the true quality and relative value of everyday bourbons is when you know that your palate has reached a higher level of appreciation.

certain. The Nathan Bedford Forrest explanation can be found in author Gerald Carson's *The Social History of Bourbon*, a book written in 1963 by a social historian who documented most of his sources, with the exception of his claim that the Klansman was the brand's namesake. One historian familiar with the book's publishing history told me that Carson acquired his information directly from Brown-Forman. But since Brown-Forman so emphatically denied any connection with Nathan Bedford, this suggests that the William Forrester explanation could be a marketing cover-up to protect the brand's reputation.

But there is another reason why Carson claimed Old Forester was named after the KKK founder, and it ultimately saves the brand's legacy while illustrating the perils of modifying a brand's marketing to fit a faddish moment in history. When Carson wrote his book, the Civil War's centennial was looming, war kitsch flooded American advertising, and Rebel Yell bourbon was successfully making money from a resurgent wave of southern nationalism, tempting Brown-Forman to join in the fun. The company had never widely advertised the brand's real origins and figured it could "generate some interest" by making up a story that Old Forester was named after the controversial Confederate war figure, another company spokesperson eventually told me. The strategy didn't catch fire, but the story has lingered the way one would expect it might. Brown-Forman has since backtracked from the explanation that one of its most famous brands was named after a Klansman. It's one of the few cases where a bourbon brand, surrounded by a handful of colorful creation myths, emphatically endorses the most boring one. Fortunately, it's still a good tale.

· · ·

Created in 1870, Old Forester was the first bourbon sold exclusively in sealed bottles. This was a break from the traditional practice of selling whiskey straight from the barrel, poured into reusable containers—crocks, vases, other bottles—brought to the store by customers. It was a bold strategy—individual bottles were still handmade and expensive, often more valuable than the liquor served in them. Not until 1903 did distilleries bottle their own liquor on a wider scale, after Michael Joseph Owens created a glassmaking machine to engineer consistently sized bottles at a rate of 240 per minute, reducing labor costs by 80 percent. Distillers in Kentucky were only bottling four hundred thousand gallons a year in 1903; by 1913, the figure had risen to nine million gallons.

Old Forester also sat at the cusp of a new era of whiskey advertising. In the years following the Civil War, markets grew less local and more regional, and a few labels, Old Forester and Old Crow included, gained national attention. Improved transportation meant individual brands could cheaply travel greater distances, increased magazine advertising meant word could spread faster, and industrial advances in distilling meant larger volumes could meet the increased demand brought by clever advertising.

Before he joined the whiskey industry, George Garvin Brown was a pharmaceutical salesman who frequently called on his friend Dr. William Forrester. The job brought him into the whiskey industry's orbit because the spirit remained popular as a medicine. It was in this market—whiskey as medicine—that Brown saw opportunity. Doctors complained that the whiskey they bought was inconsistent, often adulterated by middlemen and of questionable quality. Brown responded by marketing Old Forester directly to physicians in sealed bottles tagged with the slogan "Nothing Better in the Market." The bottle prevented tampering, acted as built-in advertising, and set the brand apart. The reason for the name's later spelling change—from Old Forrester to Old Forester—to this day remains unclear. Some accounts say it was because of Forrester's retirement, but it's just as likely that other doctors didn't want to prescribe something bearing a competitor's name. Another account claims that the nation's expanding temperance movement made Forrester squeamish about having his name on a whiskey bottle.

Over the following decades, Brown's approach became common in the industry. Advertising focused less on price alone, and more on the person paying it. Customers, for their part, were learning to value ineffable things like powerful backstories, thus easing the way for the rise of modern brands. In 1870, only 121 trademarks of any kind were registered under the U.S. Trademark Act, but alongside Old Forester other future icons for goods that were formerly considered generic commodities would soon emerge: Campbell's Soup (1869), Levi Strauss's Overalls (1873), Quaker Oats (1878), and Ivory Soap (1879).

Relative to today, few whiskey brands emerging in the decades after the Civil War were marketed by the distilleries that actually produced the liquor. Most distillers remained content to let wholesalers create brands targeted to customers. Thus for a time power was in the hands of marketers rather than makers. As brand names became more prevalent, many brokers found they had become industry heavyweights, purchasing distilleries and trading them among each other. The most powerful brokers were in large cities like New York and Chicago, although smaller versions of this model still dominated local markets, creating house brands for saloons and catering to regional sensibilities—"Alligator Bait" was a popular brand in Florida, while "Jeff Davis" was a favorite in the Deep South.

Along with his brother, Brown entered the whiskey industry as a broker and a blender. He made Old Forester by purchasing quality stocks of aged whiskey from outside suppliers and blending them to achieve a unique flavor profile (this made him an NDP). By 1902, however, his company had begun distilling and aging the brand itself.* By that point, many distilleries had realized that marketing liquor held just as much if not more power than producing the actual liquid being marketed. Brokers continued to play a big role—and still do today—but men like Brown realized that commanding the entire process was more efficient. As his counterparts in the oil, steel, and beer industries had already learned, power was gained by vertically integrating.

"Drummer" was the whiskey industry's term for the traveling salesmen who sold whiskey brands to bars or other distributors. These men

---

* During its first decades, Brown's company cycled through many different names, accounting for various business partners. It became Brown-Forman in 1890, Forman being the name of the company accountant.

filtered in and out of bars praising the virtues of whatever they were hawking. Sometimes they slipped nails into the barrels of competing brands because the iron would turn the whiskey black. Another drummer trick was to offer customers a comparative taste test, pouring their own whiskey first, then giving a long speech about it. As the whiskey sat, certain undesirable flavors and compounds would evaporate, giving it an advantage when the two competitors were compared.

Drummers were expert at modifying their pitches. If their brand was unknown, it became an exclusive gem that was hard to find because other customers had snatched it up. When aged stocks were on hand, drummers emphasized how old their whiskey was. When young whiskey was all they had, the subject of age was dropped. In this way, history repeats itself. When liquor companies "educate" customers today, it's usually an exercise in guiding people's tastes toward the particular whiskey they're selling. Age became a huge selling point after the 1970s when slow sales kept bourbon surpluses in the barrel longer, even though many in the industry thought the whiskey was ruined from having absorbed excessive wood tannins. The strategy nonetheless worked, particularly in foreign markets that were unfamiliar with bourbon and reflexively associated age with quality.

But by the early decades of the twenty-first century the opposite would be true. Whiskey would be popular again and some distilleries struggled to meet demand. Reliant on sales of younger whiskies, many began to increasingly praise the hotter "bite" or grainier flavors of such spirits (one producer even promoted its faux-moonshine on the merit that it was "unpretentious," even though the spirit came from a boutique distillery in a recently gentrified urban zone and cost nearly four times more than many well-aged competing brands). Distillers also began dodging the subject of age by claiming that their whiskies were "aged to taste," "artfully aged," or by using other nonspecific expressions as a way to avoid giving specific age statements. Older brands that had been created when demand was weak and companies needed to use age statements as marketing tools would drop their age statements entirely, giving themselves the option of blending younger whiskies into their products and moving them out the door faster. An age statement on a bottle must reflect the *youngest* whiskey used in a blend, and even though many younger whiskies are preferable to their older counterparts their youth is rarely considered a marketing advantage. Nevertheless, instead of denying customers information, companies should just list the younger age, alongside an explanation of why older whiskey isn't necessarily better, thus giving drinkers valuable information they can use to help develop their palates. In any case, if a company isn't completely forthcoming about what's in the bottle—divulging mash bill, age, entry proof, size of the barrel used, where the liquid was actually distilled, or any other technical detail, either on the label, Web site, or after a phone call—it might be downplaying a trait it considers undesirable. If a brand doesn't divulge this information, be careful. In the history of whiskey marketing, it has ever been thus.

· · ·

In the nineteenth century, White Protestant and a few odd Catholic distillers looked to their frontier forebears for bourbon brand names. Whiskey had provided an economic toehold in America for these Western European immigrants and their legacies were enshrined accordingly. Whiskey would provide the same economic opportunities for many Jewish immigrants fleeing Europe for America later in the century, but their names rarely made it onto bottles.

One such American, Isaac Wolfe Bernheim, immigrated to the United States in 1867 with no particular plans to join the whiskey trade. Nor did he plan on becoming a "bourbon aristocrat," the term used for Kentucky's most successful distillers during the late nineteenth century. However, by the time he died in 1945, Bernheim had started many brands, although none with his name, save for the I.W. Harper brand, which Bernheim created in 1879 but only gave his first two initials. The surname likely came from John Harper, his horse trainer (there is a minor debate about this). Bernheim, like many Jewish distillers of his era, probably feared that his ethnic name wouldn't sell well. But after World

War II, I.W. Harper was famous, sold in 110 countries. It's still popular today, although export-only and unavailable in the United States.*

After arriving in the United States from Germany and making his way to Paducah, Kentucky, where he had an uncle, Bernheim was invited to join a distillery owned by Moses Bloom and Reuben Loeb after they noticed the young man's bookkeeping abilities. He earned enough money to bring over his brother Bernard, and the two siblings opened up the Bernheim Brothers Distillery in 1872, which they moved to Louisville in 1888.

In the Louisville occupied by the Bernheims, Jews comprised roughly a quarter of those involved in the whiskey trade, even though they were only about 3 percent of the local population. Other cities showed a similar pattern. In Cincinnati, one of America's top three distilling centers, Jews owned five of the fifteen biggest whiskey operations in town in 1875. In Canada, where the Seagram empire would eventually flourish and for a time become the biggest liquor company in the world, the name of the Bronfman family who started the business means "distiller" in Yiddish.

The increase in Jewish liquor entrepreneurs in these places reflected the unique advantages whiskey offered to America's new arrivals. Historically, the liquor trade had helped Jews skirt oppression. The need to ensure that wine used in religious rituals was kosher had long resulted in Jewish involvement in every step of the alcohol trade, from manufacture to distribution. In medieval and early modern Europe, when Jews were banned from owning land for crops, many transitioned to intermediary market roles, including alcohol importing and exporting. After Russia grabbed hold of many Eastern European enclaves, the liquor business in those places was often one of the few jobs where Jews weren't restricted. Those same countries later launched waves of Jewish immigrants like Bernheim and Greenhut to the United States.

Jews arriving in America during the nineteenth century were familiar with many parts of the alcohol trade, but often focused their efforts on

---

*The brand is currently owned by Diageo.

whiskey. Wine was too small a market to seriously entertain, and even though beer offered sizable business, owing to the midcentury influx of Germans, many breweries only hired Protestant immigrants from Germany. This was a remnant, perhaps, of the ban on Jews held by many European brewing guilds. Breweries also tended to run "tied-house" saloon systems, with direct supply lines between brewers and retailers that removed intermediary positions offering entry points for Jewish immigrants without cultural or family ties to brewing.

Whiskey, on the other hand, wasn't vertically integrated like the beer trade and didn't have a direct distribution system, creating more opportunities for aspiring entrepreneurs. Local clusters blossomed around immigrant groups who drew on family ties for manpower. One advertisement in a Louisville Jewish publication read, "WANTED: Three Jewish young men to represent a leading whiskey house. Need have no experience but must be first class, tiptop salesmen and come well recommended." Solomon Levi and Julius Freiberg, two of Cincinnati's foremost distillers and liquor wholesalers, made a point of hiring younger Jews as traveling salesman and clerks, a common practice throughout the industry.

American whiskey's Jewish heritage is largely unknown, and Isaac Wolfe Bernheim wouldn't get his name on a bottle until nearly a half century after his death, when the Heaven Hill distillery introduced Bernheim Original wheat whiskey in 2000.* It was a fitting tribute from a distillery started in 1934 by the Shapira family, itself the progeny of Russian Jewish immigrants. Like Bernheim, the name Shapira has never been enshrined on a label. Instead, Heaven Hill built much of its success with brands like Elijah Craig and Evan Williams—two labels named after bourbon's favorite fairy tales rather than the people actually behind them. Even so, Heaven Hill today quietly honors bourbon's lesser-known Jewish legacy in one other way. Built into the very architecture of the distillery's visitor center the wooden beams above the tasting bar are held up by iron supports shaped like the Star of Da-

---

* It is technically named after the Bernheim Brothers Distillery.

vid. You have to look carefully for them—the gesture is subtle, carrying the weight of bourbon's most famous names.

. . .

As brands like Old Forester, I.W. Harper, Campbell's Soup, and Coca-Cola grew, companies obsessed over how to best grab customers' attention. What made people tick? What do most people spend their time thinking about, and how do you get inside those thoughts? Today, companies employ teams of psychologists and market analysts dedicated to that sole task. Icons, heroes, and other symbols of national greatness resonate with the nation's collective psyche and sell lots of booze. The other ways to grab people's attention were easy to figure out: sports and sex.

The first Kentucky Derby was held in 1875, the same year that two brothers from the Chapeze family introduced Old Charter bourbon.* For years after its Derby debut, Old Charter boasted of its horse-racing connection. Drinking and gambling are allies as natural as bourbon and mint, and juleps from day one have been a part of the race's culture. At Churchill Downs in Louisville, where the race is held, juleps became the event's official drink in 1938. They were first sold in "official" souvenir glasses for seventy-five cents a piece. Today, while spectators wait for the race—which takes less than two minutes to run—Churchill Downs goes through 150 bushels of mint and 60 tons of ice.

The roots of Kentucky's legendary horse-racing culture are entwined with its bourbon industry. A tiny sculpture of a horse sits on stoppers of Blanton's, and Rock Hill Farms features a picture of a thoroughbred in a field. W.L. Weller used to advertise itself as "The Thoroughbred of Bourbons," and Green River, the most advertised brand before Prohibition, had a lucky horseshoe logo. Hundreds of now-extinct labels from before Prohibition had horses as mascots and names like Kentucky Champ, Old Sport, and Trotter. Many of the sprawling mansions and horse stables in Woodford County were once owned by bourbon

---

*Old Charter still exists as a brand, but in the years since its creation has drifted between nearly a half dozen different owners and is currently made by Buffalo Trace.

aristocrats, and this was where Isaac Wolfe Bernheim stabled Ten Broeck, one of the most successful racehorses of the nineteenth century. According to Kentucky lore, the first barrels of whiskey shipped to New Orleans were even traded for horses. The animals needed to be fast, as the legend goes, to provide quick getaways for whiskey merchants attacked by robbers along remote stretches of the Mississippi River during their return. Once the horses reached their new home in Kentucky, they thrived by munching on bluegrass, which helped their bones grow strong because it grew in soil enriched by the same calcium deposits that makes bourbon sweet by removing iron salts.

Of course, historians of horse racing tell the story differently, countering that Kentucky's famous reputation for the sport really started when uptight Yankees banned gambling in eastern states during the 1890s and 1900s, including betting on horses. There was no such ban in Kentucky, and Louisville businessman Matthew Winn took advantage of the situation by lowering minimum wagers and eliminating the role of bookies by initiating a form of gambling called parimutuel betting. This drove up profits, allowed more people to participate, and allowed horse racing in the state to become financially successful. After that, millionaire gamblers and big-wheel thoroughbred breeders from all over the country began building their mansions in the same Woodford County where James Crow had brought bourbon into the modern age a half century earlier.

Today, the Woodford Reserve Distillery, situated on Crow's old stomping ground, makes the "official" bourbon of the Kentucky Derby. Since the brand has only been around since the 1990s, it's an unlikely choice for such a historic event. It is a "classy" brand, however, and the association is likely related to Churchill Downs' attempts in recent years to clean up the Derby's image. It's always been known as an extravagant society event, marked by southern belles and Colonel Sanders doppelgängers wearing seersucker and fancy hats. But as Hunter S. Thompson famously pointed out in a 1970 article titled "The Kentucky Derby Is Decadent and Depraved," the event can also resemble a blurry carnival of besotted jackasses braying at each other while gulping mint juleps and gambling away their kids' college funds. Making a business-class drink like Woodford Reserve the Derby's official bourbon helps offset that image.

As an "upgraded" brand, Woodford also offers a valuable lesson in brand marketing. It is made by the same company that makes Old Forester, and even though its price is higher, the two share the same mash bill and yeast—the Woodford is simply aged a little longer, and in heated warehouses that prod the aging process along a little bit. Woodford Reserve's flavor is a little more round and rich, with less of the brighter grain notes of Old Forester. Using similar mash bills among different brands owned by the same company is a common practice in the whiskey industry, although the similarities between labels that are marketed to different demographics are almost never advertised—Old Forester is marketed for its good value, whereas Woodford is usually sold as something fancier. Buffalo Trace's W.L. Weller 12-Year Bourbon is very similar to the lauded Pappy Van Winkle, which the distillery also makes from the same recipe, but whereas Pappy sells for astronomical prices reaching into the four-figure range, the Weller sells for much less. Because Buffalo Trace markets and names the two products differently, most drinkers are unaware of just how similar the two are.

· · ·

When James Pepper, the most flamboyant of the bourbon aristocrats, considered how he should brand his bourbon, the choice was easy: he named it after himself. As the grandson of Elijah Pepper and son of Oscar Pepper (the man who had employed James Crow), James Pepper was bourbon royalty. He continued his family's respected distilling legacy but was a trailblazer in another important aspect of whiskey marketing: much of the history he advertised was made up. The truth of his claims and the veracity of the dates he put on his bottles were all extremely questionable. Today that point is easy to forget, since the simple passage of time has turned Pepper's artificial history into actual history. But in another way, he was also helping to establish an industry tradition.

Like so many other iconic brands, James E. Pepper Whisky (he spelled it without the *e*) has faded from existence. It folded in 1960, its last decades spent as an asset traded between different corporate conglomerates. But during this century the Pepper trademark was revived by a businessman named Amir Peay, who sources the brand from an outside supplier. Bourbon's resurgent popularity has made this practice with defunct brands common, as companies attempt to resurrect the lost glories of once-famous labels in an industry that thrives on heritage. Peay is a whiskey geek's whiskey geek, and rents a private storage unit dedicated entirely to Pepper memorabilia (bottles, titles, advertisements, office paperwork).* The whiskey sold under the Pepper brand name today might not be identical to what it once was, but it is still quite good, and if not for Peay the memory of this bourbon icon would be entirely lost.

Even though Pepper was the offspring of a trailblazing distiller, his parents died when he was young, and the boy was adopted by Edmund H. Taylor Jr., the éminence grise of bourbon. Taylor had purchased the rights to the Old Crow brand shortly after Oscar Pepper died, and around the same time he agreed to be James Pepper's legal guardian. Pepper eventually inherited the Old Crow brand, selling it in 1867 to Gaines, Berry, and Co. (his distillery continued to make it for them). In 1879, he opened the Henry Clay Distillery in Lexington, which, like many distilleries, made brands for outside wholesalers.

By 1890, Pepper had tired of making whiskey for outside blenders who used it however they saw fit. Like his contemporary George Garvin Brown, he saw the value of owning the entire process. When he created his own brand he claimed that it was "Born with the Republic 1776"† and that it used his grandfather Elijah's Revolutionary War–era recipe. Of course, 1776 was the year his grandfather Elijah was actually *born*, not the year he started making whiskey. When Elijah started making whiskey in 1810, it certainly didn't taste like his grandson's product.

---

* Before Peay acquired the brand, its resurrection had been stifled by Dr Pepper, for obvious reasons.

† The James E. Pepper brand would have a number of slogans related to this theme, including "Born with the Revolution," some of which were created by other marketers of the brand following Pepper's death.

Pepper had backdated things by 114 years in order to exaggerate his brand's legacy.

But no matter: Pepper's marketing bravado simply helped blaze a trail that many have followed. Few, however, have done it with his panache. He also managed to get himself credited as the person who introduced the cocktail known as the old-fashioned from the Pendennis Club in Louisville to New York. Of course, people were talking about the old-fashioned before the Pendennis Club even existed, and nobody knows for sure where the cocktail came from. Peay, who shoulders the duty of reviving the legacy of somebody who often invented many parts of his own "legacy" out of thin air, has decided to keep the exaggerated claims about such things on the brand's current labeling. His move is tongue-in-cheek, honoring a history of bourbon marketing that has often played fast and loose with actual history.

When Pepper built his distillery in Lexington, the era's engineers were impressed, noting the high quality of the remarkable volumes it produced. The plant earned him enough money that he could afford to spend much of his time living in New York City's Waldorf Astoria hotel, traveling between Manhattan and Lexington in a private railcar. In December 1895, Pepper was invited to join America's most famous business leaders for a banquet at Delmonico's in New York to celebrate the centennial of the Jay Treaty, which had prevented another war with England shortly after the American Revolution. Each man took turns at the lectern to speak about his respective industry, Pepper discussing whiskey alongside John Jacob Astor (real estate), John D. Rockefeller (oil), Cornelius Vanderbilt (shipping), Charles Pillsbury (baking), Frederick Pabst (brewing), Charles Tiffany (jewelry), William Steinway (pianos), Francis du Pont (gunpowder), Levi Morton (banking), Pierre Lorillard (tobacco), Thomas Eckert (Western Union), and Philip Armour (meatpacking).

Some of Pepper's racehorses were as well known as his whiskey, and many had names like The Bourbon and Pure Rye. The African American jockey Isaac Burns Murphy, a three-time Kentucky Derby winner and arguably one of the greatest jockeys of all time, rode his horse Mirage in one Derby race, and the society pages of the *New York Times* detailed Pepper's many successes at the track. The paper also recorded his considerable losses—he was good at making whiskey and money, but he wasn't very good at managing the latter. Bankruptcy had prompted the sale of his family's distillery years earlier but Pepper always found a way to recover from such financial disasters, often by relying on the family fortune of his wife, Ella Offut Kean. He probably should have worked her into the business—during one financial low point that forced him to sell off a stable full of prize horses, Ella bought the horses cheap, restored their reputations by running and winning them, then sold them for a tidy profit.

Even after Pepper died in 1906, after taking a bad fall, his brand's promotional flair lived on. In 1910, James E. Pepper Whisky was the backdrop of one of the twentieth century's greatest sporting events. On July 4 of that year the boxer Jack Johnson fought Jim Jeffries in Reno, Nevada, in a match famously known as the "Fight of the Century." Johnson was the heavyweight champion of the world, the most famous athlete in the country, and highly controversial. He flaunted the era's prejudices by bragging of his many relationships with white women (he married and divorced seven of them), and for a brief period he even had a white midget in his entourage.

When Johnson fought the formerly undefeated heavyweight champion Jeffries, the entire nation watched, at the peak of the Jim Crow era, as this African American battled a man whom many were calling the "Great White Hope." James E. Pepper Whisky helped sponsor the fight, and old photos show "Born with the Republic" banners all over Reno.* Perhaps sensing a promotional flair that rivaled its own, the Pepper brand backed the controversial Johnson, and in one advertisement, Johnson sits in a suit while surrounded by fans. He's grinning broadly, with a bottle of James E. Pepper sitting next to him, raising his glass toward the photographer right before he went out to win the match and make history.

---

* Even in original photos from the time of the fight, some of the banners look like they were painted into the advertisements after the fact, which somehow seems oddly appropriate to Pepper's legacy.

. . .

The prominence of white men on bourbon bottles speaks to patriarchy. It's not that women or minorities didn't contribute to the history, they just don't get the credit they deserve. Old photos of distilleries often show women and African Americans working on the bottling lines and stirring the mash tubs—they were the people actually *making* the whiskey, though rarely the ones who held the capital backing it. When their images did make it onto bottles, it was rarely flattering.

Sex sells, and the level of finesse with which it was employed in liquor advertising ran the gamut. Gin was still widely associated with the gutter life of the urban poor, and brands like Black Cock Vigor Gin, distributed by Lee Levy & Co., out of St. Louis, didn't help the spirit's image. A bottle of it cost only fifty cents, marked up from the twenty-seven cents it cost to make. The label featured a mostly nude white woman and one magazine described the flavor as having a "brief wave of heat as from a match, then a flash of sweetish, pungent, bitter vapor, which seemed to leave all the membranes of the throat covered with a lingering, nauseating mustiness."

Today, the Distilled Spirits Council of the United States (DISCUS, the whiskey industry's main lobbying organ) organizes an industry code of responsible practices that liquor companies can voluntarily follow. Black Cock Vigor Gin almost certainly wouldn't pass muster. When a company breaks the code today, it is scolded by its own, helping the industry police itself and avoid marketing missteps that erode its image, and therefore everybody's bottom line.

But no such holds were barred at the intersection of the free-for-all Gilded Age and the dawn of modern advertising. Union Distilling Company's Tippecanoe Kentucky Whiskey brand featured a voluptuous bare-breasted Indian maiden in a canoe. Another of the most popular advertisements of the 1890s came courtesy of Cincinnati's Mayer Brothers & Co. Distillery. It featured a naked woman in a Middle Eastern harem, robed men hovering and panting in the background, sharking their eyes in her direction.* Mayer's other handouts included a snuff box for its Hudson Whiskey brand, featuring the slogan "take a pinch." Inside the box was another harem girl in an "odalisque" setting, with the tagline "beats 'em all for high balls." This sets the tone for the wave of racy matchbooks, playing cards, and other giveaways that flooded bar counters.

The quality of the liquor often matched the tone of the advertising, but that didn't mean top-shelf brands weren't immune to general trends. Soon after James Pepper sold Old Crow to the New York financiers, Old Crow playing cards turned up in saloons, featuring two lingerie-clad hookers, smoking and giggling. An advertisement for I.W. Harper features a man on a couch playfully wrestling with a woman to get a bottle of whiskey she is holding just out of reach. The caption reads, "He won't be happy 'till he gets it." Another Harper ad shows a gown-wearing society woman above the poetic caption "Pull off my gown, and see the whiskey of greatest renown." The flip side of the ad featured the nearly nude woman holding a bottle of I.W. Harper.

Whiskey advertising also saw a flourishing of "Belle" brands: Belle of Nelson, Belle of Lincoln, Belle of Anderson. The word's French origins denote a combination of intelligence and beauty, and advertising for the Belle brands was much less risqué. Women wore typical Victorian garb: wide-brimmed hats, sashes, and long dresses with leg-o'-mutton sleeves. Occasionally, however, ankles would peek out from beneath the fabric, causing excitement. But even though women may have been drinking these brands, the advertising certainly wasn't directed toward them. It simply made drinking a little more respectable for men, toning down the racy advertisements of other brands while keeping an appealingly sexual vibe. Alcohol-related violence was one of the many driving forces behind the temperance movement, and a few savvy advertisers

---

*By placing nude women in settings that resembled ancient Greece or Middle Eastern harems, companies could better argue that their advertising was "art," thus avoiding the era's laws against pornography.

realized that slumming might be good for short-term profits, but it wasn't a good long-term strategy.

African Americans fared no better than women in Gilded Age whiskey advertisements. They were often featured with the cartoonishly huge lips and exaggerated features of minstrel show performers. One Old Crow ad features a black man with the body of a monkey tap-dancing on top of a bottle. Another ad for rye whiskey shows a black man in the middle of a dirt road, a stolen chicken tucked under one arm and a watermelon under the other. He stares fretfully at a bottle of whiskey lying on the ground, unsure of which of his stolen wares he should drop in order to pick it up. The caption reads, "I'se in a perdick-ermunt." Louisville's Paul Jones Distillery—founded by a Kentucky Confederate family that lost its fortune in the Civil War—advertised its whiskey with a painting titled *The Temptation of St. Anthony*. It's a picture of southern poverty, a small black boy sitting confused between his parents. His mother holds a giant watermelon and his father holds a bottle of Paul Jones. He doesn't know which one to choose.

As blacks increasingly migrated north, abandoning jobs as poor farm laborers and taking roles as waiters, porters, and bellhops, advertising shifted to reflect the change. In 1911, Cream of Kentucky Bourbon began depicting blacks in service roles rather than as poor farm labor. Nevertheless, they're still serving whites. In 1940, the brand commissioned Norman Rockwell, America's beloved illustrator, to do one ad casting a white man and a black servant awkwardly aping the *Amos 'n' Andy* show.

Other minorities were also typecast according to stereotypes. Chinese Americans were depicted with tiny slits for eyes and portrayed as the cheap labor used to build the railroads connecting the coasts and opening up the frontier.* Chicago's A. Bauer & Co. Distillery in the

*In 1883, the famed New York political cartoonist Thomas Nast, an opponent of anti–Chinese immigrant prejudice, lampooned the idea that if the Chinese drank American whiskey instead of importing Chinese spirits and wines, Americans would be more accepting of them. In the cartoon, a Chinese man embraces a giant bottle of whiskey.

1880s ran a popular advertisement set in the Wild West, featuring an Indian, a Chinese man, and a cowboy playing poker on a blanket. The Chinese man has won the pot with four aces just as the Indian lunges at him and the cowboy levels a six-shooter at his head. "Sam Toughnut's Saloon" sits in the background, advertising four of Bauer's rectified whiskies in the window. These are the brands that truly won the West.

Of course, by the time Bauer & Co. ran this ad, the frontier made famous by American lore was coming to a close, although it would continue to inspire whiskey advertising for ages to come. Mark Twain took notice of this fact when he spoofed a painting by Emanuel Leutze titled *Westward the Course of Empire Takes Its Way* that today hangs in the U.S. Capitol. It's a portrait of pioneers facing a sunny western horizon illuminated by the Golden Gate into San Francisco Bay. In *Life on the Mississippi,* Twain, famous for always having a fun go at American self-importance, appropriated the painting's title into "Westward the Jug of Empire takes its way." He wrote, "The earliest pioneer of civilization is never the steamboat, never the railroad, never the newspaper, never the Sabbath-school, never the missionary—but always whiskey!" Following the spirit's path were poor immigrants, then the traders, gamblers, desperadoes, and highwaymen. Trailing that group came the lawyers and undertakers.

Bourbon, so adaptable, would likewise adjust its advertising to the shifting horizons of America's growing empire. After the Spanish-American War erupted in 1898 and spread to fighting in the Philippines, one Cincinnati distillery began selling Dewey's Old Manila Whiskey, named after navy admiral George Dewey, who was victorious at the battle of Manila Bay. Greenbriar Whiskey advertised that Dewey's success at Manila wouldn't have been possible without "Old Greenbriar," and industry trade magazine *Bonfort's Wine and Spirit Circular* debated why bourbon should not become the national drink of Cuba when American military forces became involved on that island. A few years later, as America's presence increased around Panama, Edmund H.

Taylor Jr. suggested that the United States "Fortify the Canal Zone with Old Taylor."

But in order for men like Taylor or his brands to fortify anything, they would first need to protect themselves against the fraudulent imitators threatening the labels they had so carefully created and emblazoned with their names in the first place.

· CHAPTER NINE ·

PURITY AND POPULISM

When the Old Taylor Distillery was built in 1887, it was the most magnificent plant of its kind in Kentucky. It wasn't the biggest, but it was an enchanting corollary to the typical factory-like operations of the era. The facility sat near James Crow's old distillery on Glenns Creek, and was built of limestone to resemble the kind of medieval castle imagined in the pages of *Ivanhoe*. The springhouse was designed like a Roman bath, and Ionic columns held up pergolas that shaded visitors—who were welcomed, unlike at most distilleries—as they wandered sunken gardens and reflection pools. Visitors were all given free tenth pints of Old Taylor.

By the twenty-first century, however, the Old Taylor Distillery would sit in ruins. Engulfed by weeds, the distillery's outbuildings resembled a lost city in the Amazon. Glass and rubble crunched beneath the feet of visitors willing to crawl through breaks in the barbed wire to wander the property, its likeness to an old castle enhancing the sense of an American industrial age that has gone the way of Carthage.

Dozens of similar ruins lie scattered across Kentucky and the other whiskey states, the casualties of constant and consistent waves of industry consolidation.* The legacies of those shuttered distilleries are long forgotten, but Old Taylor is an exception. Almost every single bottle of bourbon you buy today carries the fingerprints of its founder, Colonel Edmund H. Taylor Jr. He combined into one cohesive whole all the different parts of the new bourbon industry: marketing, finance, quality control, and lobbying. It was a battle, and the greatest threat he faced was from rectifiers counterfeiting brands like his that were attempting to build their reputations on quality. Taylor joined with other reformers looking to reverse Gilded Age excesses by establishing many of the labeling rules and consumer protection regulations still in place today. Together, they would all help the better angels prevail in their eternal struggle.

. . .

Born in 1830 to parents who had made their living as slave traders, Edmund Taylor was orphaned when they died young. His uncles raised him, including his great-uncle Zachary Taylor (the future U.S. president), and another uncle (also named Edmund) who lived in Lexington, Kentucky. His uncle Edmund was a banker, and Taylor followed him into that career. It's a testament to bourbon's nature as a business that two of today's most exclusive brand lines—Colonel E.H. Taylor, Jr. and George T. Stagg—are named after men who worked primarily as bankers, focused on turning grain into money rather than just booze.

During the 1850s, Taylor traveled the Kentucky countryside opening bank branches for his uncle. There he became acquainted with James Crow and Oscar Pepper, whose Old Crow brand was just beginning to turn heads. It was the dawn of big brands, and growing distilleries struggled with how to finance construction upgrades and expansion projects. As a young man in his twenties looking to make his name, and

---

*In 2014, a group of investors who were no doubt inspired by bourbon's renewed popularity bought the eighty-two-acre site for just under $1.5 million, with plans to build a new distillery there.

with a powerful banker as a surrogate father, Taylor found himself in the right place at the right time.

After Crow died in 1856, Oscar Pepper decided to continue making bourbon just as the doctor had, and still under the Crow name. By 1860, Old Crow couldn't meet its demand, and Taylor stepped in to organize and finance Gaines, Berry, and Co., Distillers, which made and marketed Old Crow on a larger scale. When Oscar Pepper died in 1867, the firm gained the distillery, its whiskey stocks, and rights to the Old Crow brand name. This was also when Taylor adopted the fourteen-year-old James Pepper. Taylor had started in the whiskey business merely as a financier, but now he was in deeper.

Taylor's acquisition of the Pepper distillery created a pattern he would use for the rest of his career, and a template much of the industry would soon follow. In 1870 he sold his interest in Gaines but continued to manage it. Then he helped finance and start an assortment of other distilleries. Taylor's business portfolio soon became an elaborate network of distilleries he bought into and then sold out of. He'd start a company, define its strategy and tactics, and then contract roles like sales and distribution out to other firms. Partial interest in one place, full interest in another, Taylor's roster of business partners soon became a complex web.

Taylor quickly found himself trapped in a labyrinth of his own devising. His file cabinet bulged at the seams with leasing agreements, contracts, and other financial pursuits—construction projects, speculative ventures—that all moved according to their own rules. It wasn't long before one of the distilleries he had founded in Frankfort—known as Old Fire Copper (O.F.C.), located on the site of what is today the Buffalo Trace Distillery—came under the control of a New York firm, which quickly sold its holdings to St. Louis financier George T. Stagg, who had been Taylor's original partner in the venture.

Stagg probably thought he was doing Taylor a favor by purchasing the holdings. By buying O.F.C., he was bailing Taylor out of a bankruptcy mess linked to Taylor's financial adventures in the construction business. Nevertheless, the two were bound to clash over the fact that Stagg now controlled an emerging brand that was marketed with Taylor's name and signature. Even though the outfit was named E.H. Taylor, Jr., Company, Distillers, Taylor only owned two of the company's twenty-five hundred stock shares. Stagg basically owned Taylor's name, and since he was just as much of a wheeler-dealer as his former business partner, he eventually began selling shares of the venture to outside investors in New York. Those investors had their own ideas about how the company should be run, and soon Taylor wanted out. He also wanted to keep the valuable brand representing his legacy.

When Taylor broke away from Stagg, the nineteenth century's nebulous trademark laws allowed him to continue using his own name with the new operation: the Old Taylor Distillery. This was the distillery resembling a medieval castle, and when Taylor built it, he made sure to incorporate everything he had learned about the whiskey industry thus far, including knowledge from a tour of European distilleries he had taken a decade earlier. He used corrugated rollers instead of millstones to grind his grain, ensuring more consistent fermentation; he swapped out wooden mash tubs for copper vats because they were easier to clean; and he made his own barrels. He even briefly experimented with different barrel sizes, as small as forty gallons, although these he eventually abandoned for larger ones.

To age his whiskey, Taylor used a new kind of rackhouse with a tiered storage system that would eventually become an industry standard (it is the most widely used system today). Up to that point, barrels were usually stacked directly on top of each other in rows three or four barrels tall. But there were problems arranging barrels this way. The weight of the top barrels caused the lower barrels to leak and the tight arrangement prevented air circulation—mold grew more easily and could cause the whiskey to taste musty. Removing or checking barrels from the bottom layers was labor-intensive, requiring all the barrels to be rearranged.

With the tiered-rack system like the one employed by Taylor, barnlike warehouses consisting of five or six floors were built. Each floor contained three tiers of barrels, each barrel rolled into place along a wooden set of rails that supported their weight. Narrow hallways ran through the warehouses and floors made of loose planking or meshed steel allowed air to circulate freely.

Each warehouse like this is a separate biosphere full of various microclimates. These different climates determine how the whiskey will taste and are dictated by an assortment of variables that affect temperature and humidity. Is the warehouse made of stone or wood or metal siding? How much sunlight does it get? Is it in a valley that channels cool breezes?

The separate microclimates inside an aging warehouse mean that a barrel's exact location inside the structure will greatly affect a whiskey's flavor. Barrels in different parts of the warehouse age differently and take on different characteristics, even though they might have come from the same production batch. Top floors get hotter and experience more drastic temperature swings, causing whiskey to push deeper into the wood and evaporate faster. Whiskey that has aged for more than a decade on a top floor often tastes unbalanced and woody—in fact, more than a decade aging in a hot part of the warehouse can cause most of the barrel to evaporate entirely. Lower floors are cooler and age whiskey more slowly—whenever you find bourbon older than a decade, chances are that it comes from barrels in a cooler section of the warehouse, where the aging was subtler and evaporation rates weren't as aggressive.

During the aging process, distillers roam the warehouses, periodically tasting samples from the different barrels to check on their progress. Barrels are marked for bottling once they've achieved the desirable flavor profile. To achieve flavor consistency for a particular brand, distillers today mix many barrels together in batches so all their slightly different qualities balance each other. Once the whiskey is dumped together in giant vats, it is tasted to ensure that it matches past batches (distilleries keep scores of reference samples for comparison). A few distilleries, such as Maker's Mark, rotate barrels between floors so they all age evenly, primarily because the company makes one core brand and needs to keep everything within a tighter flavor range.* Four Roses uses low, single-story rackhouses, which don't have as many microclimates, to ensure more even aging between barrels because it also makes relatively fewer brands than most modern big companies.

Occasionally, distillers roaming their warehouses will encounter a "honey barrel," meaning a barrel that has found a sweet spot within a perfect intersection of the factors that make up the maturing process: time, esterification, oxidation, extraction. Distillers eventually learn what portions of the warehouse are most likely to produce honey barrels—window seats are a good bet, where sun and cool breezes speed up the expansion and contraction cycles. The cooler lower climes can also produce interesting results if you give them enough time. In the past, distillers typically set honey barrels aside for their own personal consumption or to give to close friends.

. . .

As Edmund Taylor settled into business at his new distillery, he spent years bickering with his former business partner Stagg about the use of his name. Trademark law was still in its infancy, and Taylor realized— just as George Garvin Brown and James Pepper were realizing around the same time—that ownership of a powerful brand name, and the loyalty it earns from faithful consumers, is priceless. Taylor and Stagg would shake hands on various rounds of concessions related to the use of the Taylor name, but rarely honored them. At one point, Taylor held a company called E.H. Taylor, Jr. & Sons, while Stagg continued calling his company E.H. Taylor, Jr. Company. Taylor sued and won in court, only to have the decision reversed on appeal—Stagg's distillery would keep using variations of the Taylor name until 1904.

As the reputation of Taylor's whiskey grew, others would also attempt to capitalize on his brand, unleashing an avalanche of counterfeits and rectified whiskies with similar names. When "Kentucky Taylor"—

---

* Aside from the regular Maker's Mark brand, there is also Maker's 46. This is regular Maker's Mark that spent six extra weeks in a barrel with seared pieces of French oak, which lend the bourbon a slightly spicier flavor. (Oak trees from France and Japan both tend to carry spicier flavors than American oak, which generally carry heavier notes of vanilla.)

the product of one Louisville rectifier—hit the market, Taylor attacked it in the courts, establishing important legal precedents and protecting his whiskey's reputation.

As the whiskey industry developed, and as businessmen like Taylor and James Pepper—who also fiercely protected his brand names—filed in and out of courtrooms, a few labeling rules came into play. Brands couldn't associate themselves with organizations with which they had absolutely no relationship. In one case, the Churchill Downs racetrack successfully prevented one distillery from naming its whiskey "Churchill Downs." Labels also couldn't convey what the courts called "false information," but this restriction's subjectivity made it largely toothless. Rectifiers skirted the rules, meaning consumers struggled to know with certainty a whiskey's true origins or how it was made.

Taylor, who had dabbled in local and state politics, responded by teaming up with Kentucky senator Joseph Blackburn to help pass the 1897 Bottled-in-Bond Act. The landmark law made the U.S. government the guarantor of a whiskey's quality and is still in place today (modern bottles that are still bottled-in-bond include some, though not all, versions of Old Grand-Dad, Very Old Barton, and Evan Williams). In order to get the government's seal of approval, the whiskey had to be made at a single distillery by one distiller. It had to be made in one season, aged at least four years, and be bottled at 100 proof. Labeling also had to clearly indicate the maker. If a whiskey met the standards, it was affixed with a green stamp bearing the image of John Carlisle, the Kentucky congressman who had lobbied for bonding increases after the Civil War and who by this time had moved into position as Grover Cleveland's treasury secretary. Counterfeiting the green stamp was a serious federal crime. When bottling became commonplace just a few years later, drinkers learned to look for the stamp.

But even with the Bottled-in-Bond victory, Taylor's battle to ensure bourbon's quality on the marketplace was far from over. Shortly after the act's passage, George Stagg, still happily trading assets and ownership shares of distilleries, entered a business partnership with Walter Duffy of Rochester, New York, who was known for making spirits used in medicine. His "Duffy's Famous Malt Whiskey" was pure snake oil. Duffy placed full-page advertisements in leading newspapers such as the *New York Times,* making claims that were outright lies. In one, a supposedly 148-year-old man claimed that Duffy's was the only thing keeping him alive (in fact, according to Duffy, every American over the age of 100 reached that age because he or she drank Duffy's). Duffy even bought endorsements from prominent medical professionals—such as renowned bacteriologist Dr. Willard Morse—to shill for his brand and claim its medical virtues.

Duffy's ads worked and the brand grew huge. As the company expanded, it invested in changes at Stagg's facilities as Stagg slowly removed himself from the operation. By the turn of the century, Duffy controlled the distillery, which still associated itself with Taylor's name. It made upgrades to produce "cheaper" whiskey and supply "a large demand for goods of a lower grade," Taylor complained. It was putting out lesser-grade contract whiskey and organizing other distilleries in the region into a trust resembling Peoria's larger Whiskey Trust.

Taylor immediately issued statements that he had nothing to do with Duffy's or with the trust. But fight as he might, he still only represented one small side of a whiskey industry divided into two camps. The other side, composed of rectifiers making inferior whiskey, continued to spread.

Taylor's problems were a symptom of Gilded Age corruption. Fraudulent imitators like Duffy were making fortunes in an unregulated system that failed to protect the efforts of those doing the best work. Writing in muckraking publications like *Collier's* and *McClure's,* journalists like Upton Sinclair and Ida Tarbell reported on how the exact same problems affected many industries besides just whiskey. Americans were growing increasingly angry and wary, a reaction that the economist Henry George had warned of back in 1879 in his book *Progress and Poverty,* which claimed that the Industrial Revolution's advancements in wealth and comfort had come at the expense of the working class. The Gilded Age, as George described it, was an elaborate banquet of opportunity and potential, waited on by poverty and corruption. He feared revolution.

In 1896, Congress was eventually moved to action and launched an investigation to determine exactly what kind of whiskey was being served at the grand American banquet Henry George had described. An investigation committee later declared that scarcely 2 million gallons of whiskey in America were being sold "in its original integrity," whereas 105 million gallons were mixed with rectified spirits and a myriad of other dangerous adulterants in a proportion, if the drinker was lucky, of about one to seven. A thin crust of society was drinking well, while everybody else was taking their chances with whiskey that was slowly killing them.

But in the year *Progress and Poverty* was published, the reform-minded Teddy Roosevelt was getting ready to graduate from college. His future deputy in the battle to establish food purity laws, Dr. Harvey Wiley, who would eventually team with Edmund Taylor, was also readying to climb his way up through the government bureaucracy. As Henry George had warned, revolution was around the corner, but it wasn't quite the revolution he had anticipated.

· · ·

One of the first things Theodore Roosevelt did as president was deliver a twenty-thousand-word speech to Congress about curbing the power of trusts and the need to protect consumers. His voice boomed through the chambers, falling on the ears of lobbyists and fixers crowding the adjacent hallways.

Roosevelt had suddenly inherited the presidency after the assassination of William McKinley, and most were surprised to see him in this powerful position. On the surface, Roosevelt wasn't a likely reformer. He came from the kind of wealthy and privileged family that the status quo generally favors—classically pro-business Republicans who went on safaris for vacation, and his grandfather had founded the Bank of New York. In fact, Roosevelt began his career as a staunch conservative, arguing against the government's role to regulate the private sector. He even once joked that members of the Populist Party should be lined up and shot.

But Roosevelt wasn't blind to reality. He wasn't much of a drinker, but his attitude toward adulterated whiskey and the federal government's role in public safety was guided by his experience with other tainted foods. While commanding the Rough Riders during the Spanish-American War in 1898, his soldiers had stockpiled thousands of pounds of canned meat from U.S. slaughterhouses. After seizing Cuba, Roosevelt's soldiers devoured the canned meat before realizing it was spoiled. Many fell sick and some even died, more from the meat than from battle, according to some sources.

The incident made an impression on Roosevelt. Now that he was president reform-minded members of his administration were no longer on the sidelines. Chief among the reformers was Dr. Harvey Wiley, the Agriculture Department's chief chemist. He was also a connoisseur of fine bourbon—he personally curated the bar at Washington, D.C.'s Cosmos Club, a prestigious private social organization—and had become a household name for his efforts during the previous decade to pass food purity laws. An eccentric man with an enormous wit and even bigger ego, he teamed with Edmund Taylor to ensure quality regulations for whiskey as he battled for passage of the Pure Food and Drug Act in 1906, which also helped establish rules around whiskey. During the early years of the twentieth century, the whiskey lobby, largely controlled by rectifiers, had delayed the bill's passage by prolonging debate over how whiskey should be defined and regulated.

But even though Roosevelt's political support was key to Wiley's success, the two men could hardly stand one another personally—Roosevelt once described Wiley as "nagging, vexatious, and foolish." Nevertheless, their poor relationship still didn't prevent Roosevelt from eventually allowing Wiley to briefly convert the White House Cabinet Room into a distillery so the two could share a drink.

. . .

Harvey Wiley's entry into the battle over whiskey labeling regulations began, oddly enough, after the controversial purchase of his first bicycle. Wiley had bought the bicycle at Purdue University, where he had accepted a job teaching chemistry in 1874 after a previous stint in Germany studying sugar chemistry. There he learned the many ways that sugar manufacturers adulterated their product using harmful chemicals as preservatives.

The bicycle was one of those ridiculous old-timey contraptions with an enormous front wheel and a tiny back wheel. The conservative old stalwarts on Purdue's board of trustees, never having seen a bicycle before, thought it both odd and improper for a faculty member to be seen on one of those things. Even though the trustees were generally pleased with Wiley's academic abilities, they were nonetheless skeptical that he was "too young and too jovial," nor did they like how he fraternized with his students in the school's athletic programs.

But it was the bicycle that really bothered them. One faculty member wrote in one of Wiley's reviews, "Imagine my feelings and those of the other members of the board on seeing one of our professors dressed up like a monkey and astride a cartwheel riding along our streets."

Fortunately for Wiley, he had caught the attention of U.S. agriculture commissioner George Loring, who in 1883 offered him the post of chief chemist at the U.S. Department of Agriculture. Soon thereafter, Wiley was embroiled in the raging debate about the use of chemical preservatives and adulterants like those used in many whiskey brands. In his 1899 annual report, Wiley claimed the mislabeling of food and drugs was a national epidemic threatening the health of millions of Americans.

With no truth-in-advertising laws in place, food labeling was a rampant problem. The "pure honey" sold in some stores was nothing more than flavored glucose with a dead bee placed in each jar for "authenticity." And even though states could impose their own quality control laws, the growth of interstate trade lacking corresponding federal laws made them useless. Many whiskey sellers lied outright about what was in the bottle. Producers in Ohio could churn out "Pure Kentucky Bourbon Whiskey, Aged 10 Years," although no word on that label was true—it could be one-day-old whiskey doctored with burnt sugar, carbolic acid, and prune juice for color. Even if a producer made a quality product, corrupt distributors undermined their efforts. During one congressional hearing on the matter, Joseph Greenhut, still the world's biggest distiller and the source of many rectifiers' blending spirits, even admitted that his powerful trust had no control over the matter. Distributors could label their products with "any fancy name they want," he told lawmakers.

The pure food and drug bill was essentially a labeling regulation, and Wiley strenuously argued before Congress that whiskey and other food producers should simply "tell the truth on the label." This stance earned Wiley powerful enemies among politicians working on behalf of specific interests in their states. Massachusetts's senators lobbied for the codfish industry, which used boric acid as a preservative; Maine fought for the herring industry, which boosted its profits by mislabeling herring as "Imported French sardines"; and New Jersey politicians protected canning factories in their state, which relied on benzoate of soda to preserve foods. Rectifiers, who controlled somewhere between 75 and 90 percent of the whiskey market, likewise began lobbying. They were in the same position as the rest of the food industry, and cheap whiskey passed off as an expensive straight whiskey, now having to be labeled accurately, would no longer be as lucrative. Whiskey's hired guns were Ohio senator Joseph Foraker and Kentucky representative Joseph Sherley, both sensitive to rectifying interests in Cincinnati and Louisville.

Wiley's enemies hired investigators to comb through his trash looking for anything that could discredit him. The reformer responded publicly by claiming he was the "target of a veritable fusillade of poisoned arrows from every track journal, newspaper and magazine which the adulterating interests could control." Then he put the crusade in simpler terms: "I have stood always for food that is food." Wiley was good at the clean sound bites. He announced that it was a "sin to be sick," and that adulterated foods were cheating people from achieving sound mind and body. He called his critics "the hosts of Satan" and said that his own efforts were "a struggle for human rights as much as the Revolution or the Civil War. A battle for the privilege of going free of robbery and with a guarantee of health. It has been and is a fight for the individual right against the vested interest, of the man against the dollar."

The debate over how best to label whiskey delayed passage of the pure food and drug bill by as much as two years. Other reformers thought the bill would pass more quickly if the sections on whiskey were removed, but Wiley insisted they should remain. The votes of temperance advocates were needed to pass the bill, he argued, a powerful contingent that would surely oppose the measure if it didn't address the whiskey question.

Much of the debate over whiskey hinged on the definition of "purity," a word that many brands centered their advertising around (McKenna was "Pure and Straight," Kentucky Dew was "The Standard of Purity"). Straight whiskey sellers, such as Edmund Taylor, contended that only straight bourbon or straight rye should be called whiskey. Rectified products, he argued, were so heavily adulterated that they should carry a label, such as "imitation whiskey." Rectifiers, understanding that nobody wants something called imitation whiskey, disagreed. They countered that straight whiskies should be called "fusel oil whiskeys," alluding to the kind of chemical compounds that, in minimal doses, give whiskey their flavor and complexity, but are harmful in larger amounts.

On this, the rectifiers had a point. Grain neutral spirits are technically more pure than aged whiskey because they are stripped of everything. Of course, the real argument here wasn't over rectified spirits in a simple, higher-proof form. It was over the harmful adulterants that some, though not all, added to their whiskey. It was also over producers lying about what they were selling.

The battle between straight and rectified whiskey quickly turned populist, with both sides attempting to utilize whiskey's humble everyman reputation. In one congressional hearing, an attorney for the rectifiers argued that straight whiskey wanted nothing more than to "put on airs" and seem fancy (he also claimed that fusel oils attacked the brain). Edmund Taylor, who was also at the hearing, shot back that rectifiers were trying to destroy the ancient ritual of making "honest" whiskey.

This last argument by Taylor was largely philosophical, but was nonetheless adopted by Wiley, despite his training as a chemist. He didn't support rectifiers because their product didn't live up to his own personal standards of connoisseurship. He argued that rectifiers didn't make real whiskey, simply because it didn't taste as good as the straight version. He admitted that while some "blenders are most honorable men," their whiskies were "like one of those beautiful painted forms that the milliner puts up and puts a gown on compared with a real girl," he told members of the Committee on Interstate and Foreign Commerce. He backed his argument by making "fourteen-year-old" bourbon right there in the chamber. It only took minutes as he added a dash of this and a dash of that to a base of rectified spirits that he then passed among the lawmakers. The congressmen who took sips scrunched their faces and gasped. It was horrid.

The Pure Food and Drug Act passed in 1906, more because of public fury over recent scandals involving meatpacking than because of the whiskey question. Thus the whiskey provisions were pushed through before the whiskey debate was fully settled. Rectifiers were required to start calling their product "imitation whiskey," "compound whiskey," or "blended whiskey." They quickly complained that these unpalatable new labeling regulations were a scheme by straight whiskey producers to steal their sales and pled with Agriculture Secretary Wilson to modify the rules. Wilson was willing, but a zealous Wiley quickly sabotaged the effort by appealing to the president. Roosevelt allowed Wiley to set up a small still in the Cabinet Room, and there he made insta-whiskey just as he had done for Congress. After tasting it, Roosevelt declared that the law should stand. Still outraged, rectifiers continued lobbying the White House to reverse the decision, but the president had already given his final say.

Blenders and rectifiers remained convinced that the bill was biased against them. Then, in 1909, they were given another chance to change the law. William Howard Taft was now president, and rectifiers petitioned him for another hearing. Taft offered a compromise. He declared that anything distilled from grain was whiskey, and that both blends and straights could therefore call themselves whiskey, so long as the type of whiskey was further clarified somewhere on the bottle. Nobody was required to use the term "imitation whiskey," and nobody was allowed to use the phrase "pure whiskey." The terms "straight whiskey" and "blended whiskey" were adopted as the two basic types, and are still in use today.*

Rectifiers weren't thrilled with the decision, but they accepted it. Wiley, on the other hand, was infuriated. His input on the matter had been snubbed by Taft and he took it as a kind of betrayal, its sting made worse by the suggestion that his powerful influence was eroding. For more than a decade he had enjoyed considerable prestige and national attention. Countless magazine profiles had called him a noble warrior of consumer rights and "father of the Pure Food and Drug Act." He sensed that it was all drifting away.

Then, adding insult to injury, Roosevelt denied him any credit for his accomplishments. The two men had never gotten along very well— Wiley had strong opinions on many matters, and had publicly disagreed with the president about parts of his Cuba policy. Roosevelt didn't once mention Wiley's name in his autobiography when he wrote about the landmark pure food and drug legislation. Wiley retaliated in his own autobiography, downplaying Roosevelt's role, but it's not hard to guess which autobiography sold more copies and how the history would eventually be written.

Wiley resigned from government service in 1912. Disenchanted, he reconsidered his views on alcohol. As war unfolded in Europe and discussion of America's involvement turned loud and thick, he advocated wartime rationing, arguing that grain should be used to feed soldiers.

---

*The term "blended whiskey" shouldn't be confused with the type of blending bourbon makers do when they mingle different straight whiskies from their warehouses to achieve a unique flavor profile. Those are still considered "straight whiskey" because that's all they contain (additional rules around this term, requiring that "straight whiskey" be aged for at least two years, would eventually be applied as well). In the United States, blended whiskies are often composed of straight whiskies mixed with grain neutral spirits. In Canada and Scotland, however, the blending spirits are usually distilled to a slightly lower proof and often receive some sort of aging. In both places, blending is much more respected and considered an art. To learn more about Canadian whisky, see Davin de Kergommeaux's excellent *Canadian Whisky: The Portable Expert.*

He fell in step with Prohibitionists calling to ban alcohol entirely, but not for the same moral reasons as the policy's other supporters. His reasons were populist. "I am not a prohibitionist from principle, but for policy," he explained. Speaking of the rectifiers, he said, "They have validated the adulteration of all whisky. . . . There is not much danger of drunkenness in pure whisky. In fact, it is too expensive except for the well-to-do. Under present conditions with adulterated and poisonous whisky freely sold it would be better to have prohibition."

But before Wiley could tumble completely into obscurity he pursued another track that would also make an impression on American life. After leaving his government post, he soon married Anna Kelton, a woman half his age, and had two sons. The move helped lift him out of his lifetime battle with depression, which he once described as an "awful ennui of the soul." He traveled the world, giving lectures and receiving awards, including the French Legion of Honor. Popular with consumers, he was made a contributing editor at *Good Housekeeping* magazine, and ran the magazine's famous product testing lab. If a product met Wiley's demanding standards he would bestow it with another of his legacies: the coveted *Good Housekeeping* seal of approval.

· CHAPTER TEN ·

THE HOLY BIBLE REPUDIATES
PROHIBITION AND DEAD PUPPIES

During the early 2000s Prohibition returned to America in a surprising form. Many of the hippest bars in the country modeled themselves after speakeasies from the 1920s, requiring reservations and secret passwords at the door—if you could even find the door. One place in Washington, D.C., marked its entrance with only a single blue light. Another spot in New York was entered through a phone booth along the side of a restaurant serving hot dogs. Gaining admission often required explaining oneself to a grim-faced hipster staring through a peephole.

The Prohibition era has slowly begun to muscle aside the frontier as a wellspring of whiskey marketing. In 2013, when Heaven Hill opened the Evan Williams Bourbon Experience, a multimillion-dollar tourism destination in Louisville to promote the distillery's flagship brand, the facility included a tasting room styled after a speakeasy (the trend had finally migrated from the coasts). Tours began with interactive displays of Evan Williams arriving at the frontier and opening a distillery, but ended with a visit to a tasting room pumped full of jazz music. Many whiskey brands created after 2000 have followed suit by focusing on Prohibition-era themes: Heaven Hill's Larceny Bourbon, Speakeasy Bourbon, Smuggler's Notch, and countless other brands named after bootleggers like Jack "Legs" Diamond, Al Capone, and bootlegging-legend-turned-NASCAR-celebrity Junior Johnson.

The Prohibition era lasted thirteen years beginning in 1920, and its appeal is easy to recognize. Crimes committed around bootlegging and speakeasies crackle with subversive glamour. Drinking became a symbolic gesture of fighting against the tyranny of a moralizing minority, and while the act technically might have been a crime, few really thought it *criminal*. Even President Warren Harding drank from a private stash of bourbon while in the White House, effectively sanctioning the rebellion and giving it a stamp of approval that would eventually help transform the era into marketing gold. Prohibition even helped birth NASCAR, a sport whose earliest stars learned to drive while evading the law. Their outlaw appeal created NASCAR's success even though the association's owners battled to scrub it into a clean form of family entertainment.

It was an odd series of events and full of contradictions. So how did it all even come about, and what happened to whiskey?

· · ·

Despite Prohibition's glamour, the era's liquor was notoriously bad. All those Prohibition-era cocktails so popular in today's reimagined speakeasies were created because the hooch needed disguising. The kind of consumer protection regulations and labeling requirements that Edmund Taylor Jr. and Harvey Wiley had just finished fighting for were abandoned as the entire industry was driven underground by a policy that a majority of Americans never supported in the first place.

America remained a whiskey-drinking nation, but thirteen years of Prohibition caused people to forget what it should taste like. Stolen stocks of aged bourbon, alongside smuggled stocks of scotch and Canadian spirits from abroad, were stretched thin and diluted with the same adulterants that had defined Gilded Age whiskey. One bottle of straight whiskey often became four or five after the addition of industrial alcohol, which tripled in production between 1920 and 1925. It then doubled again by 1930 to 150 million gallons—and not because it was being used for its intended purpose.

But thinned-out alcohol was the least of drinkers' problems. Much of the industrial alcohol making its way into Prohibition whiskey was made poisonous on purpose. In 1906, Congress had passed the Tax-Free Industrial and Denatured Alcohol Act at the request of companies arguing that industrial spirits shouldn't be taxed the same way as beverage alcohol. The U.S. government agreed, but required that alcohol used for industrial purposes be "denatured" with toxins so people wouldn't drink it. Washington approved seventy-six denaturants ranging from soap (tastes bad, but won't kill you) to formaldehyde (carcinogenic, will kill you eventually) and sulfuric acid (used in insecticides and antifreeze, will kill you immediately). Capable chemists could usually strip out the denaturants, but capable chemists weren't always available. Eventually, denatured alcohol began seeping through the cracks into people's cocktails, pushing alcohol-related deaths from a little over a thousand in 1920 to more than four thousand by 1925.

During Prohibition, American whiskey regressed back into its dark past. Once again, when people bought booze they had no idea what they were getting. The majority of the drinking population suffered, and only the thinnest of the upper crust was getting anything you might consider good.

And it wasn't even *that* good. Today, bottles of Prohibition-era whiskey can occasionally be found in the personal stashes of whiskey collectors. As they drink the rare whiskies or send samples to friends, these collectors funnel the liquid into increasingly smaller bottles to limit the amount of air trapped inside. Unlike wine or beer, whiskey in a bottle will last indefinitely, largely unchanged, as long as excessive air is kept out of the container. This prevents unwanted oxidation, which can slightly alter the whiskey's flavor over the years, although not nearly as much as it affects wine. If a bottle of whiskey is mostly full, it will keep, but if an inch of whiskey sits at the bottom of a standard-size bottle, covered by a cushion of air, it's time to either drink it or move it to a smaller bottle. The rough edges of a sample of Prohibition-era whiskey I once tried from a small vial were clearly covered up with prune juice added for color and sweetness, and carried an overwhelming flavor resembling celery salt. Nevertheless, the sample also showed the efforts of a careful blender trying to make the best of a bad situation. It's no wonder sales of ginger ale, which was widely used as a Jazz Age mixer, tripled between 1920 and 1928.

Considering the incredible gains whiskey had made during the nineteenth century, and all the seemingly lopsided battles that people like James Crow, Edmund Taylor, George Garvin Brown, and James Pepper had won in courtrooms and in the court of public opinion, tasting this disgusting whiskey begs one question: how did the powerful whiskey industry ever let something like Prohibition happen?

· · ·

Calls for an outright ban on alcohol had steadily increased during the decades following the Civil War, but whiskey makers only heard them once they reached a fever pitch, and by then it was too late. It wasn't until 1910 that George Garvin Brown, by then a leading industry figure, single-handedly made one of the few attempts on behalf of the industry to fight the encroaching ban. Prohibition advocates were claiming that distillers were pumping poison into America, and the creator of Old Forester responded by self-publishing a book titled *The Holy Bible Repudiates "Prohibition."* In 104 pages, Brown printed every verse from the Bible that mentioned wine or drinking, alongside his own interpretation of the passages. He pointed out that alcohol, consumed in moderation, was a blessing. In fact, he observed, the Bible had worse things to say about eating "hog-meat" than drinking booze. He asked why nobody wanted to ban pork as well.

Prohibition never had majority support in the United States, but it succeeded through brilliant organization and ruthless politics. Its arguments stirred Americans' worst fears about race, class, and religion, all while manipulating scientific studies. Whereas Brown self-published a slim book of measured arguments, the Prohibition movement flooded the nation with pamphlets covered with pictures of intoxicated demons and dead puppies, telling America that alcohol was the cause of both of them.

The whiskey industry's effort to battle Prohibition was disorganized. After passage of the Pure Food and Drug Act in 1906, lingering resentment remained between producers like Edmund Taylor and his rectifying counterparts, which effectively took an industry that should have been working as a cohesive whole and divided it into bickering factions. The balkanized distillers also suffered from rifts with beer brewers that prevented the two groups from working together. In the immediate decades following the Civil War, the two industries had periodically joined to fight the federal alcohol tax, but as the temperance movement hardened into calls for outright prohibition, they drifted apart as brewers began thinking of distillers as competition rather than allies. Beer's strategy was to preserve itself by throwing whiskey, its more potent cousin, under the bus. Brewers used their own separate lobbying machinery to argue that beer was a "temperance" beverage because it was so low in alcohol compared to whiskey. The brewer Adolphus Busch claimed that distillers produced "the worst and cheapest kind of concoctions," whereas brewers made "light, wholesome drinks." Busch ultimately died of liver cirrhosis, which didn't help his argument, not that Prohibitionists agreed with it anyway.

Many distillers ignored the Prohibition debate because few took the threat seriously. Before the personal income tax went into effect in 1913, alcohol taxes were a core component of government revenue and distillers knew that Washington wouldn't snip its own purse strings. Confident in that protection, they failed to take initiatives to clean up dirty corners of the industry's image lingering from days of the Whiskey Trust and of blatantly false advertising. Instead, they left very real problems to fester: there were few institutions addressing alcohol abuse and the rampant domestic violence that slithered out of it; saloon culture was notoriously linked with prostitution and gambling, which sparked more violence; and an industry that had grown large on the backs of rectifiers suffered from image problems in general. For all the distillers who had put their names in lights and trumpeted their brands, many others de-cided to hide from the industry's long-running shabby reputation. Many industry leaders would humbly list themselves as farmers in business di-rectories rather than proudly declare they were whiskey merchants.

In 1911, Kentucky distiller Peter Lee Atherton wrote a letter to his friend Congressman Henry Watterson suggesting ways the whiskey industry might lobby its way back into the nation's better graces. Per-haps whiskey makers should support "reasonable and enforceable laws to abate the evils of intemperance and condemn any interference by the liquor interest or any other interest in politics for selfish purposes," he wrote. Atherton also suggested that distillers support schools, tax re-form, and public infrastructure. It was an honest and well-meaning missive, but written more than a decade after the Prohibition move-ment had already whipped itself up into gale-force winds. Like Brown's book, the effort was a day late and a dollar short.

Bourbon distillers like Brown and Atherton were up against a jug-gernaut named Wayne Wheeler. A religious farm boy from Ohio, Wheeler traced his hatred of alcohol to a farming accident that occurred when he was stabbed in the leg by a pitchfork wielded by a drunken farmhand—a poetic beginning to his legacy. Wheeler was a tireless, around-the-clock crusader with a disarming, likable appearance. When he died in 1927 from exhaustion, at the age of fifty-seven, his elderly mother told reporters, "Wayne always was a good boy."

Compared to Prohibition zealots like Carrie Nation, who captured headlines by storming into saloons and smashing bottles with a hatchet, Wheeler was just so . . . *reasonable.* He made it easy to forget that what he stood for—a constitutional amendment banning alcohol and legis-lating Americans' moral behavior—was so radical. He was a household name, his influence so great that the *Baltimore Sun* wrote, "Nothing is more certain than that when the next history of this age is examined by dispassionate men, Wheeler will be considered one of its most extraor-dinary figures." But the *Sun*'s prediction never bore out and Wheeler's name would largely be forgotten. The template he created for single-issue lobbying, however, remains stronger than ever.

Wheeler found his way into the Prohibition crusade after graduating from Oberlin College in 1894, when he answered a job advertisement from the Ohio Anti-Saloon League looking for "a spirited self-sacrificing soul who yearns to help the other fellow." The ASL was run by a man named Howard Hyde Russell who years earlier had realized that Americans would never immediately support a full ban on alcohol—it would be too much, too soon. He instead directed public attention against the much easier target of crime-infested saloons, which would be the first stage of getting Americans to Prohibition with baby steps. It was grassroots organizing at its best—by taking on bite-size chunks and slowly building a string of limited successes, the ASL managed to attract uncertain supporters and increase its funding. Russell was building his base, and Wheeler was his first full-time employee. Once Wheeler was on board, the men worked eighteen-hour days canvassing Ohio and delivering antidrink sermons. In his few spare minutes, Wheeler got a law degree from Western Reserve University.

Wheeler and Russell's ASL was single-minded, focused only on the alcohol issue. This was a break from other temperance leaders, whose various organizations had become distracted. For instance, Frances Willard of the Woman's Christian Temperance Union had folded a stable of other reform measures—vegetarianism, postal policy—into her organization's platform. But by trying to go everywhere, the WCTU effectively went nowhere. When Wheeler became the ASL's legislative director, he avoided Willard's error and kept the ASL focused only on nonpartisan support for Prohibition. Working through church networks the ASL focused on swaying large blocs of voters to whatever candidates were dry, Democrat or Republican. In Ohio, the strategy ousted seventy sitting legislators from both parties, effectively giving Wheeler, who many now considered a political kingmaker, control of the state legislature. With his army of lawmakers in place, Wheeler then introduced a local-option bill allowing separate communities to vote on banning alcohol. Victory was assured.

In 1895, Russell traveled to Washington, D.C., and began establishing the groundwork for a national version of the ASL that mimicked the

Ohio strategy. He met with leaders of the nation's many different disorganized temperance groups and convinced them to come under the ASL's umbrella. After joining he told them the new plan and established state chapters to begin working on the new national strategy.

Alongside grassroots organizing, Prohibitionists were masters of propaganda. *The Headquarters for Murders* was the bloodcurdling title of one pamphlet, which claimed, "The saloon is the resort of the underworld [whose] inhabitants swarm like maggots." Another showed a leathery demon holding a drunkard over the burning pits of hell. This set the tone for an estimated one hundred million pamphlets that were distributed by the ASL's dutiful army in the early years of the twentieth century. Other pieces of propaganda targeted peoples' emotions with arguments that were dressed up to appear rational and scientific. One pamphlet claimed that alcohol could lead to spontaneous self-combustion. Another said that each year 10 percent of the population died because of drinking, and that 80 percent of America's criminals came out of saloons. Sources for these "facts" were rarely provided. One group, the Scientific Temperance Federation, forced dogs to drink alcohol for a publicity stunt. Then it published pictures of puppies born dead or deformed as a result in a pamphlet titled *Alcoholic Dogs Had More Feeble and Defective Puppies*. No distiller countered by publishing a book titled *The Holy Bible Repudiates the Murder of Cute, Innocent Puppies.*

In addition to using jerry-rigged statistics, Prohibitionists also stirred the race pot. Before the Civil War, temperance was strongest among northeastern Republicans who had also supported abolition. This kept the movement divided politically from southern supporters. After the Civil War, however, temperance gained steam in the South as a way to keep alcohol out of the hands of blacks. The movement joined with the KKK, which for its part published handouts portraying blacks as drunken fighters and rapists. "No prohibition law . . . would ever have been passed if it had not been for the negro," the *New York Tribune* wrote in 1909.

The crosshairs also found their way onto other minorities. Temperance was a way to control the Irish, Italian, German, and Jewish immigrants who had been arriving since the Civil War. Rural Republican strongholds like Wheeler's Ohio feared these immigrants landing in coastal cities, taking up all the jobs, and then voting for Democratic candidates who were backed by political machines. The new arrivals increasingly came from countries in Southern and Eastern Europe that many Americans believed were politically radical. One Boston pastor claimed that immigrant drinking was anchored in "the reactionary tendencies" of "the free-and-easy drinking customs of Europe." No mind was paid to statistics indicating that immigrant Jews and Italians had lower rates of alcoholism than the native-born American population, or that the United States was now actually drinking less per capita than it had been before the immigrant boom.

Alongside arguments for Prohibition from a social perspective, policy supporters also claimed it was better for the economy. Industrialists of the era claimed that alcohol ruined the productivity of workers, increased the threat of injury in America's increasingly industrial workspace, and lowered profits. The auto baron Henry Ford, a vocal anti-Semite, even singled out the success of the distiller Joseph Greenhut, the biggest distiller in the world, as evidence that the whiskey industry was part of a Jewish conspiracy to undermine American morality and business. Jewish involvement in the trade, Ford claimed, now meant that whiskey "ceased to be whiskey" and had become "rot-gut." Alongside Jews and whiskey, he also blamed America's fall into degeneracy on Hollywood.

But Ford's haranguing was another of Prohibition's many contradictions. The auto baron was a prime driver of America's transformation into the newer and faster version of itself that he apparently so despised. The workers he relied on to create his machines were banned from drinking both on and off the job to ensure their morality and, more important, their productivity. Ford paid handsomely but he demanded that workers in his company live "wholesomely," ensuring their compliance through a spy ring he named the "sociological department" to seek out drinkers and union agitators. Other industrial titans of the era—Rockefeller, Carnegie, McCormick, Du Pont—lined up behind

Ford to support Prohibition policies they also believed would boost productivity.

The forces of Prohibition were a political crazy quilt: liberal reformers from the Northeast, suffragists, the KKK, and industrialists like Ford. Politics makes strange bedfellows.

In 1905, the ASL's strategy started reaching a groundswell when it effortlessly ousted Ohio governor Myron Herrick, a Republican who had been elected just two years earlier with the largest plurality in the state's history. Ohio started going dry. "Never again," Wheeler crowed, "will any political party ignore the protests of the church and the moral forces of the state." Prohibitionists in other states jolted awake at what had just happened in Ohio, largely the result of two grassroots organizers working on salaries of less than $2,000 per year.

Two years later, the ASL succeeded in pushing through another round of state Prohibition laws, which sparked yet another groundswell of increased support for broader Prohibition. After falling a few votes short of passing national Prohibition through a constitutional amendment, the ASL doubled down in 1916 and successfully moved more dry legislators into office. The constitutional amendment was reintroduced the following year and easily passed both chambers of Congress.

As that legislative victory unfolded, the United States prepared to enter World War I. This gave Wheeler another tool he could use: anti-German sentiment. German books were burned in Wisconsin and the playing of Beethoven was banned in Boston. America's liquor trade, both in beer and whiskey, had been a foothold for many German immigrants, and Wheeler turned this against them. He declared that "the liquor traffic aids those forces in our country whose loyalty is called into question at this hour," while another ASL pamphlet called German Americans involved in the booze trade "the chief hope of the Kaiser in his plot to enslave and Prussianize this land." In 1917, dry advocates managed to push through the Food and Fuel Control Act, also known as the Lever Act, which banned the use of grain for distilling or brewing as a wartime emergency food conservation measure.

During the American Revolution, America's switch to whiskey had been considered a patriotic move. Now, almost 150 years later, the opposite was true.

The writing was on the wall. Prohibition would eventually pass, and thirsty Americans began making plans to evade the impending legislation. In 1918, Sears, Roebuck & Co. started advertising home distilling equipment in its mail-order catalogs.

After the amendment to ban alcohol was passed by Congress, it moved to the states. Thirty-three had already voted themselves dry under Wheeler's local-option strategy, and had seven years to convince a total of thirty-six to agree. The wets continued not to fight, perhaps from disbelief that states would actually tinker with the U.S. Constitution. Or as historian George Ade wrote, "The non-drinkers had been organizing for fifty years, and the drinkers had no organization whatever. They had been too busy drinking." In less than a year, thirty-six states signed (forty-six states eventually did so, with only Connecticut and Rhode Island declining).

Congress quickly passed the Volstead Act. On January 16, 1920, it went into effect, decreeing that any American involved in the production, sale, or transfer of alcoholic beverages would go to jail and have his or her property confiscated. It was the end of bourbon production in America, and it was captured perfectly by one story that circulated around Lexington, Kentucky, after the law's passage. Town lore claimed that one soldier returning home from World War I could only stare fretfully at the "Born with the Republic" slogan emblazoned across the shuttered James E. Pepper distillery as he passed into the city. Turning to his companions on the train he sighed, "Born with the Republic, died with democracy."

. . .

Henry Ford may have hated liquor, but it helped make his fortune. After the Volstead Act passed, bootleggers selling moonshine needed fast cars to outrun the police. Ford's cars were their favorites, and when his company upgraded from the Model T to the Model A in 1927, boot-leggers clamored for the zippier version, leaving Prohibition agents wondering whose side Ford was really on.

The engineering of Ford's cars was superior, making it easy for tin-kering mechanics to add upgrades. The cars' exteriors were deceptively plain, the engines inside anything but. Gear ratios were altered and extra batteries added so the entire power of the engine would go to the driveshaft and not be wasted on the generator. Extra carburetors were lined up on the engine head, delivering more gasoline when speeds zoomed over 100 miles per hour. Expanded cylinders fit larger pistons so the cars wouldn't pant so hard when the extra fire was fed into their bellies. Headlights were rigged to turn with the wheels, making it eas-ier to see at night as drivers whipped around curves. The upgrades were so effective that police had to use cars confiscated from bootleggers to even chase them. It was an arms race, and the constant demand for in-creased speed and durability led to one of the automotive industry's most fertile periods of innovation.

Some mechanics simply resorted to guise and guile, transforming hearses into whiskey haulers because they assumed the police would be less likely to stop a funeral procession. The best mechanics of the era, however, put all their efforts into speed. Red Vogt, who would go on to become a legendary NASCAR mechanic during the sport's early years, spent his days ripping up engines, tweaking stock parts, adding hot-rod accessories ordered from catalogs, and machining other pieces of gear he invented himself. He kept a secret workshop behind a false wall of his Atlanta garage where he worked on cars for the bootleggers Lloyd Seay and Roy Hall, who would also go on to become early racing stars. Bootlegging in souped-up cars thrived in the decades after Repeal, and some drivers had double careers—Seay didn't quit until he was shot dead by his cousin in 1941 after a dispute about their sugar supply.

The liquor splashing around inside the cars was responsible for giv-ing NASCAR's first generation its keen driving skills. Two hundred gallons of sloshing moonshine does mysterious and deadly things to the physics of a car that's hurtling down dirt roads and slicing through hairpin turns. Unstable and leaky small kegs were quickly abandoned for the wide-mouth Ball and Mason jars that soon became ubiquitous for moonshining. They didn't leak and could be packed more easily. One-gallon rectangular tin cans were also popular because they could be filled at an angle to eliminate what drivers called the "gurgle," meaning the slippery air bubble that allowed the liquid's weight to shift and alter the car's center of gravity. The gurgle could push a driver off the road while he was hauling tons of flammable liquid.

Driver Junior Johnson—who did jail time for bootlegging, and many years later was pardoned by President Ronald Reagan—claimed that driving with moonshine practically gave him a master's degree in racing before he ever even hit the track. "I had did all them spinning deals sideways and stuff like that. It just made my job so much easier," he later told one reporter.

Eventually, bootleggers wanted to show off their skills and make a little money by betting on their abilities against other drivers. Makeshift racetracks were carved out of deserted pastures and the South found a new hobby, led by a freckled and bucktoothed cavalry of men with names like Red, Buck, and Fireball. Slowly, the crowds grew and a few gifted drivers became celebrities. By the 1940s, a man named Bill France—whom older racing fans might know from his megaphone-amplified voice during races—realized the sport's commercial possibilities. He became NASCAR's first president and eventually bought out the league's other stockholders to become its owner—the entire league is still family-owned. France saw a workingman's sport with "distinct possibilities for Sunday shows. . . . We don't know how big it can be if it's handled properly," he once said.

The sport had huge potential, but France's biggest obstacle was NASCAR's moonshine-drenched past. It stood in the way of the sort of scrubbed-clean family image he coveted. For instance, a driver named Buck Baker once poured booze into a douche bag rigged with a drinking tube so he could drink *while racing*. Tim Flock once won the 1953 Grand National with a rhesus monkey dressed up in a racing suit riding next to him in the passenger seat (the monkey was retired after it ferociously attacked Flock's head during a pit stop at a later race). Curtis Turner was enough of a superstar that he could afford his own airplane, which he once landed on a residential street in Easley, South Carolina, so he could pick up a bottle of whiskey from a friend's house. When he took off again, he hedge-hopped a row of parked cars and took out a telephone pole while a police officer watched. (He died in a plane crash years later.) As France worked to clean up the sport's misfit image, drivers and mechanics were blackballed if they drew too much attention to the bootlegging heritage. France "transformed an unruly hobby into a monopoly, then rewrote the past," according to NASCAR historian Neal Thompson.

Today, NASCAR has over eighty million fans and is a multibillion-dollar industry that is followed by Americans of all stripes. The first racers were farm kids without any other options for how to spend their weekends—they souped up regular production (stock) cars that anybody could buy and raced them. Today, however, the cars have become so sophisticated that you need millions of dollars before even thinking about starting a team. In 2006, NASCAR president Mike Helton told reporters that the "redneck heritage that we had is no longer in existence." An outcry from offended fans caused him to backpedal, saying NASCAR "was proud of where we came from." The *Washington Post* later commented that the sport appeared to be "shedding its past as if it were an embarrassing family secret."

The sport's outlaw past—and Bill France's attempts to suppress it—helps drive its appeal, a rule that also applies to the moonshine that fueled its early days during Prohibition. It's hard to miss the parallels between the sport that whiskey built and whiskey itself. Both started as a collective endeavor, with humble roots they've attempted to transcend as they join the mainstream. The big come-up for both was rambunctious and rowdy, full of colorful myths that remain in the narrative when they're convenient, but are toned down in the struggle for respectability that corporatization demands. NASCAR is still a family-owned business that tightly controls access to historical records, just as getting access to old records at big liquor companies is no easy task. Both industries still maintain their appeal and are exciting as ever, but their foundations have unquestionably shifted with the times. They were built on steady mainstays, stock cars and mid-tier brands, but the sex appeal has drifted to the fancy stuff, cars that could double as spaceships and bottles emblazoned with words like "limited" and "exclusive."

Nevertheless, the bootlegging of moonshine was just one part of Prohibition, which today translates into a catchy kind of marketing. More important was its lasting effect on the structure of the industry itself, and the way a hypocritical policy would forever change how, and by whom, bourbon would be made.

An example of the whiskey industry's tradition of reimagining history for marketing purposes, this short-lived brand from the 1930s depicts the brutal alcohol trade between whites and Native Americans as a peaceful, mutually beneficial affair.
(Image courtesy of The Filson Historical Society.)

George Washington's distillery at Mount Vernon was the largest of its kind before it burned down in the early nineteenth century. In 2009, it was rebuilt with funds from an industry trade group, which helped burnish the whiskey industry's reputation by connecting it to America's most famous founding father. (Image courtesy of the Distilled Spirits Council of the United States.)

Cutting and harvesting ice from ponds as part of the "frozen-water trade." Beginning in the early nineteenth century, giant blocks were shipped from Massachusetts to as far away as India, one of the new markets created in part by convincing people that cocktails were best served cold.

(Image courtesy of the Library of Congress Prints and Photographs Division.)

This distillery in Anderson County, Kentucky, was built before the Civil War and was typical of its era (this photo was taken in the 1870s). Note the livestock in the foreground that fed on the spent mash and provided a sideline source of revenue, which was often more profitable than making whiskey. (Image courtesy of Jack Sullivan.)

A distillery in Lawrenceburg, Kentucky, photographed in 1900, demonstrates the growing scale of individual distilleries as consolidation whittled the industry down to a smaller number of larger operators.
(Image courtesy of Jack Sullivan.)

Johnson drinking James E. Pepper, Sunday, July 3, 1910, before the Championship of the World Battle

As brand names became widespread after the Civil War, sporting events grew into common marketing arenas. In 1910, James E. Pepper Whisky sponsored boxing legend Jack Johnson in his bout against Jim "The Great White Hope" Jeffries in Reno, Nevada, during the "Fight of the Century." (Image courtesy of Georgetown Trading Co.)

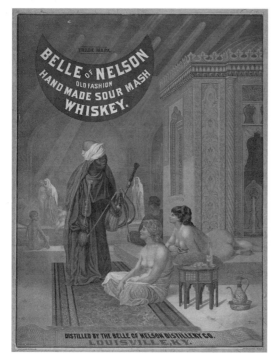

In addition to sports, whiskey marketers would soon learn that sex was also a good way to sell liquor. Brands circumvented laws against pornography by dressing up advertisements as classical art, placing nude images in "exotic" settings such as ancient Greece or the Middle East.
(Image courtesy of the Library of Congress Prints and Photographs Division.)

Minorities usually fared poorly in pre-Prohibition whiskey advertising.

(Images courtesy of Jack Sullivan.)

Joseph Greenhut was the biggest distiller in the nation before Prohibition and entertained U.S. presidents at his many homes (his mansion in Peoria, Illinois, is shown below). Greenhut's name faded from history, however, as the corrupt and unaccountable industry he presided over was transformed by government regulations. Greenhut was also the target of anti-Semitic remarks made by auto baron Henry Ford, who claimed that Jewish distillers represented a conspiracy to undermine American morality and business. These remarks exemplify how Prohibitionists leveraged xenophobic outrage against American immigrants during their crusade.

(Images courtesy of the Peoria Public Library.)

Colonel Edmund H. Taylor Jr. would become the "father of the modern whiskey industry" by fighting for stronger industry regulations, trademark protections, and production standards.
(Image courtesy of Buffalo Trace Distillery.)

The Old Taylor distillery was the finest of its kind during the late nineteenth century, but by 2015 it would sit in ruins, the result of industry consolidation and bourbon's drop in popularity during the late twentieth century. The brands once made there were sold to competing companies.
(Image courtesy of the author.)

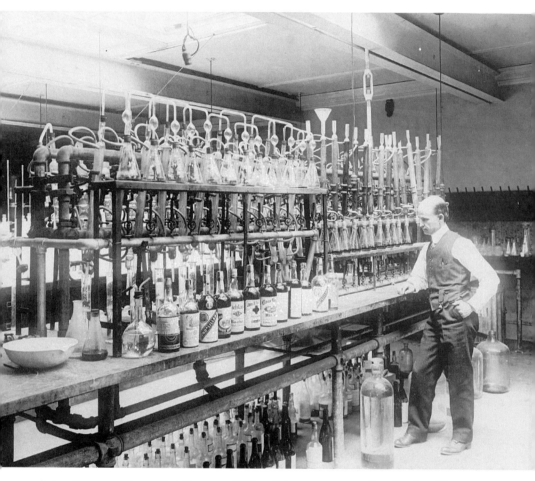

A chemist tests adulterated whiskey circa 1906 and the passage of the Pure Food and Drug Act.
(Image courtesy of the Library of Congress, Prints and Photographs Division.)

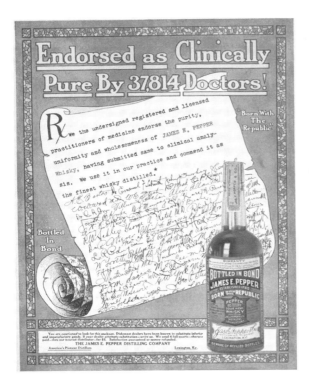

Even respected brands, such as James E. Pepper Whisky, would regularly advertise through questionable practices like exaggerating whiskey's medical benefits.

(Image courtesy of Georgetown Trading Co.)

Whiskey is poured into a sewer at the dawn of Prohibition, a prophetic symbol of the poor quality of spirits Americans would later be forced to endure as organized crime took over the whiskey trade. (Image courtesy of the Library of Congress, Prints and Photographs Division.)

Exterior and interior shots from a typical rackhouse. Barrels of whiskey age differently depending on where they are placed in these barnlike structures—the warmer top floors produce a different flavor profile than cooler floors on lower levels.

Before consolidation channeled marketing efforts toward a small number of widely known national brands, companies catered to regional markets. Both of these examples targeted southern drinkers. Also note the prominent age statement on the Jeff Davis label, named for the former president of the Confederacy and made by the famed Stitzel-Weller Distillery. Whiskey isn't better simply because it's older, but youth is rarely a selling point. Therefore, companies that disclosed such technical details in the name of consumer education immediately set themselves apart from the rest of the fray.

(Top image courtesy of The Filson Historical Society; bottom image courtesy of Jack Sullivan.)

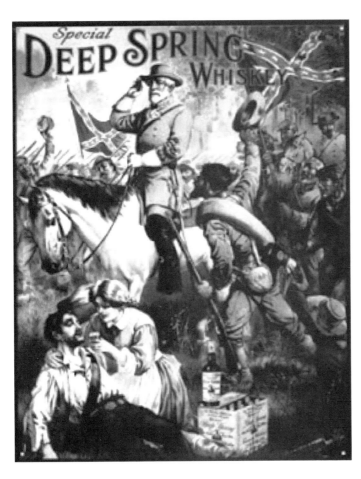

A scion of Establishment respectability, W. Forbes Morgan helped the whiskey industry rehabilitate its image after Prohibition by serving as the head of its chief lobbying organization in the 1930s. *Time* magazine called this behind-the-scenes operator the industry's "Front Man," as he worked to divert the nation's attention away from the spirits industry's sordid past. (Image courtesy of the author.)

The Beam family's legacy stretches back to Kentucky's frontier days, although its enormous success is largely attributable to modern Beams (left to right: Carl Beam, David Beam, Baker Beam, Booker Noe, and T. Jeremiah Beam in the 1960s). As the "first family of bourbon," generations of Beams have worked in the industry, many of them for competing brands. (Image courtesy of Jim Beam.)

"Now they were whiskey men."
The five Shapira brothers (pictured above, along with Charles DeSpain, a distillery executive) founded Heaven Hill shortly after Prohibition ended. During its early years, the company would use the image of William Heavenhill (left), a farmer who had once lived near the location of the Shapiras' new distillery, to help create a sense of heritage and authenticity around the company. By 2014, Heaven Hill would be the largest family-owned distillery in the United States, responsible for labels such as Evan Williams and Elijah Craig, as well as scores of others.
(Images courtesy of Heaven Hill Distilleries, Inc.)

Up until the mid-twentieth century, distilleries often celebrated whiskey's nature as a highly processed, industrial product on labels (top) or even on business cards (bottom). This connection has faded as modern food politics, alongside romantic nostalgia surrounding America's agrarian past, have transformed whiskey's agricultural qualities into better marketing tools.

(Top image courtesy of The Filson Historical Society; bottom image courtesy of Jack Sullivan.)

An executive from Seagram's, one of the four companies that would come to dominate nearly three-quarters of the American whiskey trade in the twentieth century, confidently addresses members of Congress in 1939 during a hearing to investigate the industry's monopolistic business practices.

(Image courtesy of the Library of Congress, Prints and Photographs Division.)

Julian "Pappy" Van Winkle was the marketing guru behind the legendary Stitzel-Weller Distillery, helping boost the popularity of "wheated" bourbon during the latter half of the twentieth century. Years after his death and the shuttering of Stitzel-Weller, Van Winkle's grandson would market a brand named after him, sourcing its production from Buffalo Trace.

(Image courtesy of Buffalo Trace Distillery.)

Hybrid pot-column stills being manufactured at Vendome Copper & Brass Works in Louisville, Kentucky. Vendome is responsible for the still technology used by many of America's distilleries, both large and small.
(Image courtesy of the author.)

Distilleries like Coppersea in Hyde Park, New York, are both reinventing and resurrecting American whiskey by bringing back forgotten techniques, such as "green malting," and by using pot stills (pictured here) that are direct fired.
(Image courtesy of the author.)

· CHAPTER ELEVEN ·

A COLLECTION OF CONTRADICTIONS

The bootlegger George Remus loved to refer to himself in the third person. He would say things like, "Remus is going to the store," or "Remus does not agree with you." By only using his last name, Remus gave his quirk a sort of locker-room feel, which the creators of HBO's *Boardwalk Empire* would later use to their advantage when portraying him on their show. Eighty-five years before *Boardwalk Empire*, F. Scott Fitzgerald had also noticed Remus's dramatic potential, allegedly using him as a model for Jay Gatsby after meeting the bootlegger in a Louisville bar.

Remus at his Prohibition peak grossed over $25 million per year by figuring out how to tap into the ocean of bonded bourbon sitting in padlocked warehouses. A lawyer by trade, he utilized loopholes to make broad chunks of his criminal empire legal. A few other bootleggers copied his template, and after Repeal would convert those enterprises into parts of some of the biggest liquor companies in the world today.

Remus was a teetotaler who ran a whiskey empire, left a lucrative law career to break a law that he considered the epitome of hypocrisy, and murdered the one person in the world he loved most. But that last bit of violence aside, he kept his affairs strictly about business. After suffering a rare defeat from another attorney suing him over a construction contract, he walked across the courtroom to his adversary, extended his hand, and offered him a job. With his annoying third-person habit, he said, "Anyone who can beat me and my coterie of lawyers deserves to be Remus's lawyer."

. . .

When Prohibition began, Remus was a fidgety criminal defense lawyer in Chicago earning $50,000 a year—a lot, but not nearly as much as what his bootlegging clients made. He considered most of them nothing more than thug kids, but he couldn't ignore how casually they snapped thousand-dollar bills from fat rolls of pocket cash to pay $10,000 fines, right there in the courtroom. If these foot soldiers had that kind of money, Remus could only imagine what their bosses— men like Jim Colosimo and Johnny Torrio on the South Side—were making.

As soon as Prohibition was passed, Remus, as he would later say, saw the new law as "a chance to make a clean up." All around him, beer casks were smashed open and drained into Chicago's gutters. High- quality bourbon and rye, however, were saved, twenty-nine million gallons of it inside bonded warehouses. Legally, the spirits were still private property, so the government couldn't confiscate it, but the whis- key's owners couldn't sell it either. All of America's whiskey sat in pad- locked warehouses, scattered across the rural, unguarded countryside. Pilfering became an immediate problem, but that's not where Remus fo- cused his attention—simple snatch-and-grab jobs weren't where the big- gest fortunes sat. Besides, the government quickly moved to establish "consolidation warehouses" in which the contents of 292 whiskey ware- houses were gathered in ten different locations, all patrolled by guards.

Instead, Remus sat in his office and read every word of the Volstead Act. His attention was caught by Title II, Section 6, a clause that allowed for the sale of "medicinal whiskey." Sales of whiskey as medicine—a holdover notion from the nineteenth century—were al- lowed so long as sellers had a government-issued permit and took the whiskey from bonded warehouses. Anyone with a doctor's prescription could get it. If your doctor was high-end, you'd get your bourbon in the distillers' own bottle, just like it had been before Prohibition, only with a caveat on the label stating, "Unexcelled for Medicinal Purposes." That's how Old Grand-Dad was sold—the exact same as before, with four extra words. If your doctor wasn't quite as reputable, you'd get it in a pint-sized vial, most definitely diluted. Physicians were allowed to prescribe one pint of 100-proof spirits per patient every ten days. Dentists and veterinarians were also licensed.

Remus, a licensed pharmacist who as a youth had worked in his uncle's drugstore while going to law school at nights, quickly realized that this loophole would make him rich. He considered the real crime here to be the law's hypocrisy—the U.S. government had banned alcohol, knowing that it was a deeply flawed policy, and then rigged the whiskey industry in a way that sanctioned breaking the rules. In Remus's opinion, as he would later say, the loophole was "the greatest comedy, the greatest perversion of justice" imaginable.

Six companies were given licenses to continue selling 100-proof bonded spirits for medical reasons: Brown-Forman, Frankfort Distilleries, the A. Ph. Stitzel Distillery, Schenley Distillers Corporation, the American Medicinal Spirits Company, and James Thompson and Brother. In 1928, when most of the six were running out of whiskey, the government passed an exception allowing them to distill a total of three million gallons more.

Many of the distilleries that closed during Prohibition never reopened. They sold their stocks of aging whiskey and rights to their brands to one of these "Big Six." Each of the six companies consolidated valuable brand names as a way to preserve them, usually buying them cheap because their owners needed the money. This was how Brown-Forman acquired Early Times, how A. Ph. Stitzel got Old Fitzgerald, and how the American Medicinal Spirits Company managed to acquire fifty-eight new brands (AMS was actually the carcass of what remained of Joseph Greenhut's Whiskey Trust, and would become National Distillers after Repeal). Alexander Hamilton, who had so fervently championed the industry's consolidation, never would have imagined that this was how it would happen.

These deals made during Prohibition drew much of the blueprint for how the industry would look after Repeal. A little foreshadowing here: in the first decade of Repeal, get ready to see the names of some of the Big Six change in order to account for various mergers, agreements, and buyouts. The names of these companies would transform, and today continue to do so, into the names of the giant liquor companies that modern drinkers know and love. Schenley in particular would emerge as one of the biggest liquor companies in the world, and its owner, Lewis Rosenstiel, would become one of the most influential figures in the whiskey industry during the latter half of the century, making decisions and lobbying for reforms that still greatly affect the spirit today. A Cincinnati native, Rosenstiel had dropped out of high school during the first decade of the century to work in his uncle's distillery—the Susquemac Distillery Company in Milton, Kentucky—but had left to sell bonds after Prohibition started. In 1922, while vacationing in the French Riviera, he met Winston Churchill, who speculated that the United States would eventually overturn Prohibition, and that the businessmen who had prepared for Repeal would become rich. Rosenstiel took his advice, and upon returning to the United States he would follow a strategy similar to that of Remus, buying up shuttered distilleries and their whiskey stocks while taking advantage of the medicinal whiskey loophole.

. . .

Aside from being a godsend for organized criminals, Prohibition was likewise a boon for American drugstore chains that now, thanks to the medicinal whiskey loophole, found themselves a conduit for booze. The Chicago-based Walgreens chain grew from 20 stores in 1920 to 525 by the end of the decade. The company's gobsmacking growth spurt is often credited to milkshakes, which the chain started selling in 1922, and which no doubt included more than just milk and ice cream. In *The Great Gatsby*, Daisy Buchanan describes the mysterious bootlegging title character as having "owned some drugstores, a lot of drugstores." The identical paths of Remus and Gatsby seem lifted from the same manual on how to achieve the American dream—that is, after the pages of that manual fell into a shredder.

Fifty years earlier, a man like Remus would have moved west to seek his fortune in something like gold or railroading. But after studying the Volstead loopholes, he moved east to Cincinnati, after calculating that 80 percent of the bonded whiskey in the United States was sitting in padlocked warehouses within a three-hundred-mile radius of the city. It was a good portion of the best straight bourbon and rye in the country. Each warehouse was watched by a government gauger—similar to the ones who were paid off during the Whiskey Ring scandal—who made sure that whiskey volumes, paperwork, and taxes all matched up when whiskey was withdrawn. Remus gathered $100,000 in savings and planned his move. He then asked his secretary, Imogene Holmes, a woman he was deeply in love with and who had become his closest confidante and friend, to marry him.

Remus bought his first distillery for $10,000, making him the legal owner of all the bonded whiskey sitting on the distillery grounds. Then he combined the remaining $90,000 with his persuasive charm and entered the good graces of a local bank that would underwrite the part of his ambition that exceeded his savings. He soon owned ten distilleries scattered across the Midwest, including Pogue Distilling in Kentucky, Jack Daniel's (which had temporarily relocated to St. Louis after Tennessee voted itself dry), the Squibb Company in Lawrenceburg, Indiana, and the Fleischman Company of Cincinnati. Alongside the distilleries, he also purchased a mansion in the fashionable neighborhood of Price Hill that he and Imogene planned to renovate.

Rome wasn't built in a day, but Remus—who shared his name with one of that city's mythical founders—seemed to build up his Cincinnati empire in about that much time. He employed hundreds of drivers, guards, and office personnel and was one of Cincinnati's biggest employers. While he was accumulating distilleries, he also bought a drugstore in Covington, Kentucky, and renamed it the Kentucky Drug Company. Since he was a former pharmacist, the perfectly legal acquisition barely raised eyebrows, as did the purchase of other drugstores and their allotted number of medical whiskey permits. Remus then started removing whiskey, in thousand-case lots, for sale on the medicinal market, to the millions of Americans who had suddenly started asking for medicinal whiskey prescriptions once alcohol was banned.

A portion of Remus's operation was actually legal, bolstered by his government-sanctioned permits. Of course, if he wanted to get the higher black market price, he'd just have his own men hijack the shipment, then play dumb during police questioning. When he didn't have enough legal permits he turned to government officials he had bribed (on just one day in October 1920, forty such officials were invited to Remus's office and each given $1,000). When the permits eventually ran out, he simply broke the law—at the Jack Daniel Distillery, he ordered his men to tap into the barrels, siphoning the contents through an underground warren of hoses and pipes into waiting tanker trucks. He replaced the whiskey with water.

In the early years of Prohibition, Remus was bootlegging's most impressive baron—Al Capone was still clawing his way up through the ranks of Johnny Torrio's outfit. As the scope of Remus's operations spread, so did bribes to government officials. He had started making regular trips to New York since his shell companies there were important sources of liquor permits. Settled into his suite at the Hotel Commodore during one trip to the city, he reached out to an old lawyer friend, Elijah Zoline, for a series of introductions. His operation was national, and that meant an insurance policy protecting him at that level. America's biggest mover of bourbon planned to buy the protection of Harry Daugherty, attorney general of the United States.

Remus's meeting with Zoline was to establish contact with Jesse Smith, who knew Zoline and was a poker buddy and drinking partner of President Warren Harding. Smith had known Daugherty since childhood and ascended through Ohio politics with both him and Harding. Smith was one of the administration's primary gatekeepers, and almost impossible to get an appointment with.

Smith was also involved with Prohibition matters and could get the permits that Remus needed. He was a double dealer, along with

Harding's chief Prohibition officer, a man named Roy Haynes, who occasionally sidestepped his official duties to send bourbon, under the protection of armed federal officers, to what was known as the "Little Green House on K Street," where Harding would join Daugherty, Smith, and others for poker games. Harding was a heavy drinker, and the Washington rumor mill would eventually disclose that Remus was likely the source for much of the bourbon making its way into the White House.

Remus's meeting with Smith cut straight to the point. He asked for more withdrawal permits and Smith agreed. But one thing Smith made clear was that the arrangement was only for permits, not for any kind of legal protection. Remus, one step ahead of him, pulled out $50,000 in cash. Smith extended his hand again and told Remus that he was safe. He warned that there would be investigations, arrests, and even prosecutions—appearances would need to be upheld—but Remus would never end up in jail. Bourbon, like the rest of the nation, was finding ways around the rules.

Remus's payoff of the attorney general put him in the safe zone for the time being. It was audacious and gutsy, but par for the course at the level he was now playing at. The man didn't do things that were diminutive or subtle. For New Year's Eve 1921, Remus and Imogene threw a party lavish enough to confirm his Gatsbyesque status. The couple had just finished renovating their mansion, thirty-one rooms sprawled out in gray stone. The indoor swimming pool—a marble-columned Roman bath surrounded by a lush crescent of palm trees and exotic plants— alone cost $100,000. A hundred couples celebrated in the mansion's warm glow as a full orchestra played in the background. A team of professional synchronized swimmers performed water ballet, to be joined later by a drunken Imogene waltzing to the end of the diving board and splashing in. Remus beamed and applauded alongside the other guests. He then turned to the crowd and told them that he had always wanted a pool like this, jumping in beside his wife and soaking his tuxedo.

Of course, Remus the teetotaler couldn't keep up with that festive pace all night. When the ball dropped and the party was at its fever pitch, he slipped quietly up to his library to read. At dawn he made his way back downstairs to find all his guests still celebrating, waiting on rumors of extravagant parting gifts. Remus told his servants to gather everyone's coats so they could go outside and find their party favors. The crowd shuffled toward the door and, squinting out into the morning light, found one hundred brand-new cars lined up on the front lawn.

For a while, Remus's arrangement worked just like Smith said it would. Remus worked out in the open, casually whipping out all the proper paperwork during police raids and pullovers. And, just as Smith had warned, Remus was prosecuted. His largesse had made him a prime target for Mabel Willebrandt, the seemingly incorruptible assistant U.S. attorney general, who wanted to use him to set an example. Nevertheless, Remus wasn't particularly worried, but he was cautious enough to have given Imogene the power of attorney over all his assets. Smith regularly let Remus know that he was in the clear and not to fret.

But despite Smith's reassurances, Willebrandt's case was gathering steam. She drew testimonies from his witnesses with knowledge of operations that by this point had become too big to hide. On April 15, 1922, Remus was indicted by a federal grand jury. Smith told him not to worry, that the case needed to be prosecuted vigorously for the sake of appearances, but that he'd make sure Remus didn't go to jail. A commutation would occur or the sentence would be repealed. Besides, he could always get Remus a pardon.

On May 16, Remus was convicted and sentenced to two years in Atlanta. He continued to smile, figuring he was in safe hands with Smith and Imogene. But then on May 30, Smith was found dead in his pajamas, his head in the trash can he had used to prevent blood splatter when he shot himself. He had been ill for a while and had decided that it was finally his time to go.

With his prime source of protection dead, George Remus was going to prison. Everything was now in the hands of Imogene, to whom he had given power of attorney. She would run everything—a bootleg-ging syndicate worth about $40 million—while Remus was in jail.

Nevertheless, Remus considered it little more than a hiccup. He had secured a spot at a country-club prison and was planning to use his stay to lose some weight. Imogene would be able to visit regularly.

Things began smoothly. Imogene was a capable operator, managing to dodge charges when she inevitably came under investigation herself. Eventually, Remus decided to seek early parole after learning the name of the man who had orchestrated his conviction: Franklin Dodge, a rising star in the Justice Department. Dodge was apparently "approachable," according to the prison grapevine, and Remus asked Imogene to reach out to him.

Imogene did just that, but Remus nonetheless sensed something wasn't right. His wife didn't seem to be pursuing his parole very aggressively, although he did hear rumors that she was spending a lot of time with Dodge. When Remus's release was two days away, he learned that Imogene had filed for divorce. And when he stepped out of prison, curious to ask her about events, federal authorities rearrested him on charges related to old cases he thought had been buried. He would soon serve another year, during which Dodge quit his government job and began using Remus's permits to sell booze alongside Imogene. She had originally approached Dodge, just as Remus had asked, but the two somehow fell in love, sleeping with each other for the first time in the warden's office. Remus boiled, and was starting to hear rumors that Imogene and Dodge were planning to kill him.

. . .

After Remus was released on parole, his first step to rebuild his empire was to retaliate against Imogene by testifying about her role in the case involving the bleeding out of the barrels at the Jack Daniel Distillery. His second goal was to find Imogene alone—the two occasionally met for the divorce proceedings, but those were like military summits, each side armed with guards. Eventually, Remus discovered the hotel where Imogene was staying with the couple's daughter. He told his driver to take him there. Pulling up to the hotel, he saw Imogene and his daughter driving away in a taxi, and told his own driver to step on it.

Remus's car easily overtook the taxi. He jumped out and ran toward her, chasing her up a hill before finally catching up. Imogene turned around, pleading. Remus responded by jamming his pistol so far into Imogene's gut that onlookers barely heard the sound when he pulled the trigger.

Remus immediately turned himself in after shooting his wife. When the police told him that Imogene had died at the hospital, he replied, "She who dances down the primrose path, must die on the primrose path. This is the first peace of mind I've had in two years."

Remus the criminal defense attorney was going to trial for murder. Even though he had won freedom for former clients with insanity pleas, he didn't want to use the defense for himself. He was too proud, arguing that his murder of Imogene was the sane thing to do and that he "owed it to society." But the cooler head of former Cincinnati district attorney Charles Elston, whom Remus hired for his defense, ultimately prevailed. Elston argued that it was insane not to plead insanity in a case like this.

Despite his impressive defense team, Remus argued most of his own case. The jury sat and "listened to stout, baldheaded, raucous George Remus, attorney, defend stout, baldheaded raucous George Remus, accused of murder," *Time* magazine reported. Even though Remus had killed his wife in cold blood in front of the couple's daughter, the prosecution still had a hard time getting the jury to sympathize with her. Remus's defense strategy was seamless. The famed lawyer Clarence Darrow, whom Remus knew from his days lawyering in Chicago, even testified on behalf of his character. Elston, himself slick and to the point, told the jury that Remus's behavior could only be considered "an insanity brought about by a series and set of circumstances and acts which turned an otherwise normal man into an insane man."

The jury bought it, and Remus went free. "American justice! I thank you!" Remus shouted from his chair. The *Cincinnati Post* was less sanguine, running the headline, "A Chicago Bootlegger Gets a Chicago Verdict."

Temporary insanity. It kind of summed up the whole decade, but Remus was able to walk away from it all. When he tried to walk back into his old business, however, he found it was too late. The holes had closed and others had moved in. Men like Lewis Rosenstiel had moved in to exploit the medicinal whiskey clause and gangsters like Al Capone had risen in the ranks.

Remus's single act of violence against Imogene paled in comparison to the increasingly brutal gang wars erupting throughout American cities. Incidents like the 1929 Saint Valentine's Day Massacre in Chicago, when gangsters disguised as policemen executed seven other mobsters, continued to remind people that Prohibition was a failed policy and would always be defied. Calls for repeal grew louder.

Repeal's most powerful lobbying force—its Wayne Wheeler, so to speak—was a woman named Pauline Sabin. Heir to the Morton Salt fortune and married to the president of J.P. Morgan, Sabin was the first female member of the Republican National Committee and had originally been a powerful advocate for Prohibition. But like the reasonable majority of most Americans, she soon realized that the policy was impossible to enforce. Whereas Remus justified his criminal enterprise on the grounds that Prohibition was a hypocrisy, Sabin claimed that efforts to continue the failed policy, knowing that it was futile, were also "an attempt to enthrone hypocrisy as the dominant force in this country."

Sabin organized other women who, like her, had supported Prohibition but were now against it. Most came from high society as well. They toured the nation and gave repeal a fashionable face backed by smart arguments. After the stock market crash of 1929 and the beginning of the Great Depression, she began arguing that repeal would provide crucial tax revenue—Prohibition cost $40 million a year to enforce and diverted $1 billion per year in taxes to criminals. Convinced, Congress eventually met in a lame-duck session and passed the Twenty-First Amendment. A symbol of a nation that realized the error of its ways and changed course appropriately, Sabin was an essential force behind bourbon's return. In 1933, liquor would again be legal, in no small part because of her efforts.

As for George Remus, the man spent the rest of his days in relative modesty, shuffling between Covington, Kentucky, where he had bought his first drugstore, and Miami, where he occasionally popped up at the dog races. He made front-page news once again in 1952 when he quietly died. The *Cincinnati Enquirer* announced, "Fabulous George Remus Dies; Made Millions as Bootleg King." The headline was a reminder of how American history is just a continuous cycle of fortunes made and lost, lessons learned and forgotten.

· CHAPTER TWELVE ·

THE RESURRECTION

Thousands of Virgin Mary statues populate the rolling countryside of Kentucky's Nelson County, located in the very center of bourbon country. In fact, these Catholic sentries guard the homes and small businesses of many of the counties clustered near Louisville: Jefferson, Bullitt, Franklin, Woodford, Anderson. Today, this little chunk of north-central Kentucky produces close to 95 percent of the world's bourbon, and the Virgin Mary statues scattered across the rural landscape are nestled into makeshift altars fashioned from old bathtubs cut in half and stood on their ends. The locals lovingly refer to them as "Marys on the half-shell," and they're the unsung heroes of bourbon.

The distillers in this area historically have come from a variety of religious backgrounds, but the Catholic influence has always been strong. During the late eighteenth century, much of the land here was purchased, sight unseen, by people in Maryland—originally a colony for persecuted Catholics—who needed a place to send their young sons, the ones buried under piles of older brothers, who wouldn't be inheriting the family businesses. One of those sons was David Bard, who founded Salem, Kentucky, in the 1770s. The locals soon started calling his settlement "Bard's Town," and today it is the Nelson County seat and known as Bardstown. The Bardstown Diocese was formed in 1808, and was one of four in the United States, alongside Boston, Philadelphia, and New York. It was the center of all Catholic matters west of the Allegheny Mountains.

Just outside of Bardstown is the Abbey of Gethsemani, the Trappist monastery where the jazz-loving monk Thomas Merton, author of *The Seven Storey Mountain*, lived. After World War II, Merton traveled the world studying interfaith spirituality and promoting social justice, and that connection has drawn a number of Buddhist monks to the region today. Trappists usually earn a living by making homemade foods such as beer, cheese, or fruitcake—the ones at Gethsemani make bourbon fudge. The abbey is practically within shouting distance of distilleries for Jim Beam, Heaven Hill, Wild Turkey, Brown-Forman, Four Roses, and Maker's Mark and is about an hour's drive west of Buffalo Trace and Woodford Reserve.

After Repeal, the relatively open attitude of American Catholics toward alcohol helped whiskey distilling reemerge in north-central Kentucky. During Prohibition the Vatican had even weighed in and criticized the U.S. policy, which infuriated the Protestant forces working hardest to maintain it. In other parts of the country, Congress was redistricted to more accurately reflect America's increasingly urban (and wet) population.

But even though Repeal was a blow to Prohibitionists, they still held considerable power. During 1936, in the thirty-one states that still permitted local-option laws like those utilized by Wheeler during his grassroots campaign, dry advocates promoted three thousand referenda and won half of them, scuttling attempts to return whiskey to large parts of the South and in other distilling centers like Tennessee. They wielded heavy power in Kentucky as well, but not as much in the areas where the Virgin Mary statues, living in their old bathtubs, stood guard. Eighty-six of Kentucky's 120 counties—many of which orbit today's Bourbon Belt—were still dry as late as the 1960s, and 48 remained dry as of 2014.

Kentucky has always had a special relationship with bourbon, but it wasn't until after Repeal that bourbon and Kentucky became truly synonymous. The state had always enjoyed a strong reputation for making good whiskey, matched only by distillers from a handful of other states like Pennsylvania and Maryland, but those distillers quickly dwindled after Prohibition.* Many eastern distilleries, as well as those around Cincinnati and Chicago, sat closer to cities. Their proximity to such places would also work to rural Kentucky's advantage—the land occupied by those former competitors was too valuable to sit unused for fourteen years and was quickly converted to other purposes. The closing of eastern distilleries was also a blow to the production of rye whiskey, which would continue to fall in proportion to bourbon.† Before Prohibition, bourbon accounted for about 70 percent of American whiskey sales, a number that would grow more lopsided as the squeeze of industry consolidation smiled upon Kentucky. It had never been the country's biggest whiskey producer by volume, but it soon would be, fully enshrining the state's reputation.

The whiskey industry after Repeal would be very different than before. Almost every brand on liquor store shelves today came after Repeal, regardless of whatever ancient date is plastered on the bottle. Even old stalwarts like Old Forester were retooled—new yeast strains, new distillery locations, little recipe tweaks here and there. As a product, bourbon's DNA remained the same, but no brand with roots extending past Prohibition would taste exactly the same as it did before 1920—everything went under the knife for cosmetic surgery.

When F. Scott Fitzgerald wrote that "there are no second acts in American lives," perhaps after observing the fate of George Remus, he was wrong. Americans, it turned out, love a second act as much as they love a second round. After Repeal, the bourbon industry got its new beginning. All along, the Virgin Mary statues in northern Kentucky weren't mourning the loss of bourbon, they were simply waiting for its resurrection.

---

* Although better known for making rye, many of these distilleries made bourbon as well.
† Rye's welcome revival this century has been accompanied by a modern myth that it was America's dominant whiskey up until Prohibition.

. . .

After Repeal, the nations of the world pounced on the United States. Here was a nation of big drinkers and big spenders ready to buy alcohol again, but with very little supply of its own. Even in the midst of an economic depression, it was the biggest consumer of spirits in the world, most of it whiskey. Beer and gin could be made quickly enough, but aged whiskey stocks, held over from the medicinal clause, could only supply about a quarter of demand. The United States would have to import, and the rest of the world was waiting for the feeding frenzy.

Spain was one of the first to move. The Spanish Wine Institute in Madrid paid for a set of American phone books and mailed out pamphlets a month before Repeal was officially announced, wagering that it could spark America's interest in Spanish wine. It was a noble attempt, but Americans weren't about to quench their thirst with Garnacha. Spain was muscled aside as major whiskey producers like Scotland and Canada stalked closer.

Franklin Delano Roosevelt used the U.S. whiskey market as trade leverage. During his presidential campaign, Repeal was billed as a way to boost the struggling economy and whiskey was a blue chip in international trade negotiations. FDR's new Executive Commercial Policy Committee hinted to trading partners such as Great Britain that scotch whisky imports would depend on its willingness to take pork and butter exports from the United States. Trade barriers were also lowered in order to discourage the still rampant bootlegging. U.S. distilleries were pumping out three times more whiskey than domestic demand, to get it aging in storage, but shortages would be normal for the rest of the decade. Extremely young whiskies made their way onto store shelves by the mid-1930s, but the best stuff was still years away.

Speculators swarmed the market. Within twenty-four hours of Illinois's ratification of the Twenty-First Amendment, Hiram Walker, the Canadian company responsible for Canadian Club, announced that it would build a huge distillery in Peoria, a move that boosted the company's stock by 2,700 percent. It wasn't long before Seagram, also from

Canada and the biggest distiller in the world, followed. As for the U.S. companies, National Distillers held in its saddlebags 50 percent of the U.S. aging whiskey stocks left over from the medicinal whiskey clauses, and saw its stock jump close to 700 percent, from $17 to $117. Seton Porter, president of National, was on the cover of *Time* magazine. Schenley, which held 25 percent of U.S. whiskey stocks, acquired sweetheart import rights to foreign brands like Dewar's scotch.

In America's long contest between Jeffersonian and Hamiltonian ideals, Repeal was a decisive victory for Hamiltonians. Of the nearly two hundred distilleries operating in Kentucky before Prohibition, only about half resumed business in 1933, and many of those quickly folded for lack of the kind of large capital an atmosphere of intense consolidation would now require. Rounds of corporate reshuffling to accommodate the entrance of the two Canadian companies converted the Big Six into the Big Four: National, Schenley, Seagram, and Hiram Walker. George T. Stagg joined Schenley and the other two outfits that had been part of the Big Six—Brown-Forman and the A. Ph. Stitzel Distillery—moved slightly into the background. They were still big players, but with far less muscle than the industry's Goliaths.

Also present was a smattering of much smaller independent distilleries. Most were either starting fresh, knowing that Repeal would be lucrative, or rebuilding companies from before Prohibition. The cards were being redealt and the more moderately successful independents, distillers like Jim Beam—a respected but not widely known name—now had a chance to recreate themselves. The page was still white, and smart moves at key moments—better financing, shrewder partnering—would determine how it would be written. If these smaller operators played their cards right, they might someday become big corporations themselves.

· · ·

In 1933, Jim Beam was in his seventies, and his tired old bones must have loved walking away from the rock quarry where he had worked to make ends meet while waiting for Repeal. He had also dabbled in

Florida citrus groves, but without any great success. Other members of the Beam family had moved to Canada and Mexico to make liquor during Prohibition; once it ended, they would also come back.

Beam returned to a business that many others had abandoned. Other independents alongside Beam included Leslie Samuels (whose son would create Maker's Mark twenty years later), the Tom Moore Distillery, and A. Smith Bowman. For old-timers like Beam, distilling was all he had known. He had the pride of knowing his craft, and at his age it was his only real option to make a living, as the rock quarry and the failed citrus grove had proved. But in order to make a go of things, these distillers would need money. Aside from a few farms, some rock quarries, lots of a thing called "authentic heritage," and an army of Virgin Mary statues, the Bourbon Belt doesn't have much.

Beam was in the same boat as many of his smaller Kentucky counterparts. Many came from respected old families with years of distilling experience—in Beam's case, his family's whiskey-making roots legitimately extended back to the frontier, when a German Mennonite farmer named Jacob Boehm migrated there during the 1780s. Most of these old distilling families had started their businesses organically, as side projects to farming that were slowly built up over time. But after Repeal, the bar was significantly higher and required more capital. Aside from their know-how, the only thing that Beam and Kentucky's other old distilling families had to sell was the valuable sense of heritage that could be created around their names. In a business greatly disrupted by Prohibition, having the steady normalcy of an old name was an enormous asset. But was there a market for such old names? If so, survival meant finding a benefactor.

The investors mostly came from the crescent of northern industrial cities above Kentucky: Chicago, Cincinnati, New York. They had money but didn't know anything about making whiskey. For many old distilling families, the opposite was true, and thus began a flurry of business partnerships. In many ways, these new marriages were like Henry Ford's worst nightmare: scores of Jewish names—Abelson,

Bronfman, Getz, Lehman, Rosenstiel, Shapira, Wertheimer—swooping in and trading cash for the names of distillers whose families had been there since frontier times. But despite the worries of anti-Semites like Ford, these investors were helping preserve, not destroy, a part of America's legacy.

The courtships were chaperoned by lawyers buckling under stacks of paperwork. Beam's suitors were three men from Chicago: Phillip Blum, Oliver Jacobson, and Harry Homel. The three Chicago men pooled together $15,000 and struck an arrangement with Beam. They would own the company outright, and Jim and his son, T. Jeremiah, would run it. On August 14, 1934, the James B. Beam Distilling Company was founded.

The arrangement was bliss. The Beams returned to work and had control over the whiskey portion of the business. Their investors stayed content in the background, waiting to see if their investment panned out. In 1941, Homel and Jacobson sold their shares to Blum for around $1 million, giving him control of a brand name that would eventually be worth far more.

Heritage was important, but Repeal also offered a perfect chance to shed parts of history that didn't fit in with the future. The Beam family's best-selling brand before Prohibition was called Old Tub. It had been moderately successful and respected, but wasn't a particular standout. The company briefly tried to revive it after Repeal, but soon learned that it had lost the rights. Perhaps that was for the best, as the unappetizingly named Old Tub was put to rest and the company's new signature brand was named after Jim himself.

Beam's financiers learned that heritage could be purchased outright, while others discovered that it could also be acquired by different means. New distillers could adopt a kind of "loaner heritage," then trade it in once their real heritage grew out of its diapers. The formula went something like this: start with a story of a Kentucky pioneer, then gradually replace it with the real story of your company once it fully matured. This was the strategy of Heaven Hill, which alongside

Beam would eventually become one of the most important Repeal-era start-ups. Like Beam, it started small, with just one or two brands, but over the decades it would acquire or create many more.

Heaven Hill was founded by the five Shapira brothers—Ed, David, Gary, George, and Moses, along with some other outside investors. The Shapiras had owned a small chain of department stores in Louisville and decided that Repeal made whiskey a smart investment. Although they "didn't know a barrel from a box," as Heaven Hill president Max Shapira would say seventy-five years later, they did know where to find people who did. The Shapiras struck an arrangement with Joseph Beam and a handful of other Beams (a few branches away on the family tree from Jim) to get the distillery on its feet and make the whiskey.

Basics in place, Heaven Hill cast about for its heritage. The Shapiras knew that you can't have a "brand new" whiskey company. Bourbon drinkers always crave tradition—they want their whiskey brands to at least *seem* like they've been around for a long time. Heaven Hill needed some sort of history, even if it was manufactured anew. This the brothers found with William Heavenhill, a long-dead farmer-distiller who a century earlier had worked the land where the new distillery had just been built. Heavenhill's backstory fit the bill: he was born in 1783 in the middle of a surprise Indian attack. His mother had escaped into the woods and hid behind a waterfall, where she gave birth to him. Heavenhill also had the right look: his beard was a brambly thicket, untamed and wild as if a flock of birds lived within its tangles. The distillery called itself Heavenhill after the man, but shortly after it opened the name was separated into two words. Company lore claims the reason was because the typist filling out the company's first distilling permit misspelled it. Heaven Hill couldn't afford to reapply with the correct name. In a move of frontier practicality that would have made William Heavenhill proud, the distillery decided to just roll with it.

Heaven Hill had proved once again—just as James Pepper had done a half century earlier—that in the whiskey business, the appearance of authenticity and heritage is often more important than the real thing. In the process of creating such a fantastic backstory, the distillery had also upped the ante, raising a bar that later generations of companies would be forced to outdo. Bulleit was created in the 1990s, but would present itself as something dating to the 1860s. Templeton Rye was created in Iowa in the early twenty-first century, but would tell customers it was the same whiskey that Al Capone drank (the whiskey was in fact sourced from MGPI). The Michter's brand on store shelves today started in the 1990s, giving itself a patina of age by sourcing old stocks of whiskey from outside suppliers and printing the year 1753 on its labels. The truth about Michter's, however, is that its brand name didn't exist until the 1950s, when liquor executive Lou Forman invented it by combining the names of his sons, Michael and Peter. The Michter's plant that Forman owned—unrelated to the modern brand—was located on land that was owned in 1753 by a Pennsylvania farmer-distiller named Johann Shenk. Like most farmers of his era, Shenk owned a little pot still to convert his excess grain into spirits, and historians speculate that he might have sold some of his spirits to George Washington's army. So, by purchasing rights to the lapsed trademark of a brand that was completely unrelated to Shenk but was briefly located on the site of his old farm, Michter's today suggests that it once sold whiskey to George Washington during the American Revolution (the modern Michter's isn't even headquartered in the same state). Regardless, stories like these have helped many brands build their considerable success.

Even though many brands get their start by sourcing whiskey from outsiders, Heaven Hill in the 1930s started by making its own product. Like any new distillery, the company was forced initially to rely on sales of extremely young whiskey. It created a temporary brand called Bourbon Falls, aged for a scant two years, that enabled the company to keep the lights on. Bourbon Falls was eventually phased out as the distillery's namesake brand, a four-year-old bourbon, came on the market by the early 1940s. Heaven Hill also sold bulk whiskey and created custom brands for liquor stores and bars.

In 1943, Heaven Hill was on more solid footing and its initial investors outside of the brothers decided to sell their interests. The family acquired their shares and kept on expanding. During the following decades, Heaven Hill adopted a strategy of purchasing brands that other companies no longer wanted and of building new brands named after old icons. Heaven Hill introduced Evan Williams in 1957 and eventually started or purchased the brands Elijah Craig, Henry McKenna, J.T.S. Brown, and Mattingly & Moore. Today it's also responsible for Fighting Cock, Old Fitzgerald, Larceny, Rittenhouse Rye, Pikesville Rye, Mellow Corn, and owns dozens of rum, vodka, gin, tequila, and other whiskey brands. It also makes whiskey for many other non-distiller producers who bottle it under their own labels and sell it as their own. In 2000, the distillery honored Isaac Wolfe Bernheim, the whiskey icon who didn't think his Jewish name would market well, by naming its wheat whiskey after him. And by 2014, Heaven Hill would remain family-owned—the biggest distillery in the country to claim that honor—and the second biggest owner of aged whiskey stocks in the United States. Members of the Beam family were still its master distillers.

Over time, Heaven Hill moved the story of William Heavenhill to the margins. The story of the Shapira brothers is what the distillery emphasizes today, featuring a photo of them that has finally accumulated the weathered look that whiskey companies covet. In the image, the brothers all stand around a barrel, their suit jackets casually tossed aside so the men don't seem too formal, and their neatly combed hairstyles presenting a stark contrast to William Heavenhill's brambly beard. A caption below the image reads, "Now the Shapira brothers were officially whiskey men."

· · ·

As whiskey companies resurrected—or simply just invented—themselves, the industry began cultivating new parts of its image. Much of this involved downplaying parts of the past—attempts to form monopolies, the association whiskey had with domestic abuse and other social problems—that had gotten the industry into trouble with Prohibitionists in the first place.

Early efforts to make over bourbon's image began with an increased focus on luxury. Walter Greenlee, an executive at Schenley, told his industry counterparts that they needed "increased accent upon the *quality appeal* in liquor merchandising." He told them to be careful about window displays and to avoid "cheap and flashy containers." Millard Bennett, from the Hunter Gwynbrook Distillery, ordered his sales force to sell its brands "as a luxury item wherever we can convince the distributor that whiskey is not bought or consumed like soup."

In 1935, one association of distillers from Kentucky published a mea culpa in *Spirits* magazine, an industry trade publication, apologizing for its various past attempts to establish monopolies to combat Joseph Greenhut's Whiskey Trust. The cartels had all been well-intentioned efforts to bring order to a mercurial industry, they told customers, but their implementation by the industry's forebears "did not work exactly as they had figured out on paper," the distillers explained in their attempt to make amends to the public.

With the apologies out of the way, the distillers turned to convincing the public they were in fact a bunch of choirboys. "The Kentucky distiller is not, nor ever was, merely a manufacturer of whiskey," another industry trade group told the nation in a public letter. "Nor was there ever a more honorable set of businessmen. And, in the main, there was never a more honorable group in any industry than that found among the rank and file in the Kentucky distilling business." Another paid advertisement read, "Genuine, old-fashioned, hand-made, sour-mash Kentucky Bourbon" could only be made "by a trained, native Kentucky distiller, as only a trained native Kentucky distiller knows how to make Bourbon Whiskey."

They were laying it on thick, coaxing America back into bed after the long estrangement. In order to get the new message out, the five largest Kentucky distilleries invested more in advertising during the three years after Repeal than the entire state had invested before

Prohibition, according to one industry estimate. Just as Kentucky had done during the days of Daniel Boone, it was demonstrating its unparalleled ability to use rhetoric to enhance its mystique. The whiskey makers were becoming masters of modern marketing.

. . .

Amid all the rebuilding and reinventing, the whiskey industry was well aware of the kind of havoc that changes to old recipes might wreak. One of a bourbon brand's key assets is the sense of heritage and history that it conveys to consumers, and no smart distiller or marketer disrupts that. In 1935, a trade association of Kentucky distilling interests addressed customer fears about disrupted heritage by publishing another open letter that would put minds at ease. The "old-timers may have operated, for the most part, by the rule of thumb," they admitted in a rare acknowledgment that the old ways, while easily romanticized, were sometimes a little slapdash and inconsistent. But drinkers, the distilleries assured, shouldn't fret. "The only change which might be mentioned in the methods of manufacture is, if anything, for the best," the group calmly reassured customers. After that, the changes were hardly ever mentioned again.

The A. Ph. Stitzel Distillery, which had barely survived under the medicinal whiskey clause, took particular note of the changed whiskey landscape and decided to evolve. It would pay lip service to tradition, but it would also steer bourbon in creatively novel directions that remain popular today. After Repeal, the company merged with W.L. Weller and Sons, an NDP it had partnered with during Prohibition. Among the company's new leadership was a marketing salesman named Julian "Pappy" Van Winkle, who had started in the whiskey business in 1893 working for the Weller side. Van Winkle wasn't from a family line of whiskey people, but fell into the profession as a marketer because "I wanted a job," he later explained after the new company he helped establish, which was called Stitzel-Weller, became a tastemaking legend.

Stitzel-Weller approached the challenge of adapting with aplomb and creativity, setting out to bypass shortages by producing a bourbon that tasted better at a younger age—something that held up well in the five- to seven-year range, when most bourbon is just starting to really earn your attention. Using a recipe devised by Stitzel, the distillery replaced rye from the classic bourbon recipe in favor of winter wheat, which he assessed might take a little less time to age, and thus built a foundation for a style of bourbon that has since grown much more popular.

Wheat had certainly been used to make whiskey before, but the grain was far from popular. During the early nineteenth century, distillers praised wheat's flavor, but advised against using it because the alcohol yields weren't as high as corn or rye and because it was relatively expensive. But despite those economic disadvantages, wheat carries an appealing and delicate flavor; sweet and redolent of tropical fruits and coconut, as opposed to the heavier spice notes of rye. Wheat is as sophisticated and complex as rye, but its flavor is just a bit lighter on the palate. In the same way that the marriage between rye and corn creates a whole greater than the sum of its parts, wheat is also often at its best when combined with the other grain.

In the mid-1940s Stitzel-Weller came under the control of the marketing impresario Van Winkle, who focused the company's efforts almost exclusively on making the wheated bourbons it had developed. The standout was Old Fitzgerald, which came in four-, six-, and eight-year-old varieties and was bottled at 100 proof. The company also made Cabin Still (four years old and 90 proof), W.L. Weller Special Reserve (seven years old and 90 proof), Weller Antique (seven years old and between 107 and 114 proof), and Rebel Yell.*

Stitzel-Weller's bourbon stood out for the care and consideration given to its production. The corn wasn't ground quite as fine as many distilleries typically grind it, a step that helps create a richer flavor but is expensive for distillers because it doesn't yield as much alcohol per bushel of grain. The oak staves used for the distillery's barrels were also a little thicker than average, which produced a heavier oak flavor that

---

*Today the Weller brands are made by Buffalo Trace, while Rebel Yell and Old Fitzgerald are made by Heaven Hill.

helped balance out the wheat's sweet lightness. Barrel entry proofs were also relatively low—another expensive measure that doesn't allow the alcohol to be stretched as far but preserves flavor and dissolves compounds out of the wood a little more gently. Stitzel-Weller also used pot stills and proclaimed in advertisements that its bourbons were made "the old-fashioned way." Nevertheless, in many ways the company's whiskey was refreshingly new.

Stitzel-Weller had been forced to adapt, but it still maintained a commitment to quality production standards. Beam and Heaven Hill would also insist on making their single brands as full-bodied, straight whiskies, although they would generally continue to use rye as the flavor grain. National and Schenley also prioritized the production of straight, full-bodied whiskey, but not across the board for all the brands they owned. Old Crow, Old Grand-Dad, Old Taylor, James E. Pepper, and Ancient Age were all geared back up as straight whiskies, but many less popular old straight whiskey brands were now offered as blended products, made by stretching a small amount of straight whiskey with grain neutral spirits. As for the scores of other smaller brands the industry giants had acquired during Prohibition, many were retired to reduce competition for the headliner brands they would now push harder on a national level. In 1934, 85 percent of the American whiskey inventory was less than one year old, and the move to lightening the whiskies was considered a temporary holdover. What the companies didn't realize was that this decision would ripple throughout the market for decades, as many consumers acquired a taste for the lighter products.

Everyone found ways to adapt, but the demands of instant gratification forced some distilleries to use aging shortcuts. The Publicker Commercial Alcohol distillery in Philadelphia was able to produce ninety thousand gallons of spirits per day and claimed in advertisements that it could "make seventeen-year-old whiskey in twenty-four hours." Publicker's president, Simon "Si" Neuman, and its chief chemist, Dr. Carl Haner, claimed their process of "artificial aging" could be done through a process of shaking the barrels and applying them with direct heat in order to speed up the aging process. The company hinted at other methods it used to quickly extract wood flavors—probably measures like wood chips and pressure cooking—but refused to provide the public with any more details.

"But the Great White Father down in Washington won't let Publicker dupe the people like that," *Fortune* magazine responded to Publicker's antics in 1933. Because of the regulations that had gradually rolled into place since the era of Edmund Taylor, Publicker would be forced to label its whiskey for exactly what it was. The distillery's response was a $2 million advertising campaign "to reeducate the people," the company claimed in a way that made it sound vaguely like some sort of Soviet apparatchik attempting to brainwash its customers. Publicker slammed the proven methods, telling customers, "Don't fill your stomach from a misty old keg."

Fortune was skeptical that the public would buy into the shortcuts. "Maybe Mr. Neuman's whiskey will revolutionize the industry. Or maybe Si Neuman is crazy," the magazine speculated.

It turned out that Neuman *was* crazy, and his endeavor ultimately failed, despite the enormous whiskey shortage and Publicker's advertising campaign to change the rules of connoisseurship. Regardless, the lesson bears repeating, because history always repeats itself and similar shortcuts and misleading reeducation campaigns would rear their heads again seventy-five years later, when America would find itself with another influx of new distilleries and shortages of whiskey.

. . .

As whiskey companies rebuilt, the federal government decided to step in and help. It would establish rules and regulations that would replace an industry it couldn't control before with one that it now could. In the wake of Repeal, legislators scrambled to implement the changes, many of which would favor bigger, more consolidated producers. Thomas Jefferson, from his grave at Monticello, surely bristled.

The new changes were a mixed bag, and continue to this day to affect drinkers. On the positive side, the new regulations helped protect consumers against the kind of corrupt practices that had turned many

Americans against liquor before Prohibition. In 1933, sale directly from the barrel became illegal and spirits needed to be sold in standard bottle sizes, ensuring consistency and limiting adulteration or watering down by middlemen. By 1936, the federal government also determined the standards of identity, setting even more precise guidelines for the manufacture and aging of spirits and ensuring certain quality baselines. As of 1938, anything called "straight whiskey" officially had to be aged in brand-new charred oak barrels for at least two years, which gave consumers a little more clarity about how their whiskey was produced.

One of the other big changes, still in place today though controversial, was the regulation of distribution channels through what is called the three-tier system. Under this arrangement, power was given to the individual states to regulate alcohol sales, and the industry was organized into three tiers: producers, distributors, and retailers. No single entity could own all three tiers, which was a way to limit the kind of monopolizing common before Prohibition. While the system can help improve diversity by limiting monopolies, today it can also make certain small brands difficult to find if none of your local distributors carry them. This is why a small brand produced in California can be hard to find in New York, and vice versa. You can't simply ask your local retailer to order a bottle of a small brand you're curious to try—the retailer needs to go through distributors, which often have complicated relationships with various competing brands (the separate tiers aren't allowed to bypass one another, except for very limited circumstances, like brewpubs). During Repeal, this trifold system created three distinct layers of taxation that were a revenue windfall for the Depression-era government, but it has perhaps outlived its purpose and today increases prices by involving an arguably unnecessary middleman.

At first the federal government gave the whiskey industry a chance to determine its own rules. Unfortunately, the draft plan worked up by the companies themselves was a dismal failure and promptly discarded. No copies of that plan remain today, but it apparently didn't satisfy Washington's idea of how an industry with a reputation that was still festering—and with Prohibitionists still brandishing pitchforks and torches at the gates—should act. The whiskey industry would need to be on its best behavior as it carefully rehabilitated its image (*Time* in 1937 compared it to "baseball after the 'Black Sox' scandal," referring to how gangsters in 1919 had rigged the World Series).

FDR responded by assigning members of his Agriculture Department to help the whiskey industry write its new rules. As part of his New Deal legislation, he also included the spirits industry under his National Industrial Recovery Act, which temporarily suspended antitrust laws. Rules, prices, and production quotas could be fixed, as long as industries spread their workloads to as many people as possible in order to get the nation working again and to generate tax revenue. The antitrust laws were reinstated by the middle of the 1930s, and a few years later the government would ironically investigate the industry for monopolistic business practices—Alexander Hamilton and Thomas Jefferson, wherever they resided in the afterlife, still probably weren't on speaking terms.

Working with the government, the whiskey industry also adopted a voluntary "Code of Responsible Practices" as part of its makeover. It agreed not to advertise with pictures of women or children or advertise on the radio, so as not to invade the "family circle." Likewise, it wouldn't advertise in Sunday papers or appropriate images of "men in the uniform of our armed services."

Whiskey's new relationship with the federal government also meant more lobbying, more traveling to Washington and sitting around smoking cigars and drinking whiskey with influential lawmakers. The new lobbying organ was called the Distilled Spirits Institute, otherwise known as the DSI, and its initial leadership consisted primarily of Owsley Brown, president of Brown-Forman; Samuel Bronfman, head of Seagram; Seton Porter, head of National Distillers; and Lewis Rosenstiel, head of Schenley.

None of these men, however, offered the kind of charm or other qualities needed to serve as the organization's official head. Owsley Brown's company was much smaller than his counterparts and would have struggled to wield influence. Seton Porter seemed like a perfect fit—he was a Yale-educated WASP and a "gentleman whose best recognized attribute was his Racquet Club orientation," according to his profile in *Fortune* magazine. But a large portion of his company, National Distillers, consisted of companies that had once resided under the Whiskey Trust, a connection the industry would have wanted to downplay. Then there was Samuel Bronfman, who headed the biggest liquor company in the world but was Canadian, making it problematic for him to serve as the official face of an organ dedicated to lobbying U.S. lawmakers. Besides, Bronfman lacked the needed charm. The *New York Times* once described him as "mean, tough, ruthless and unbelievably bad-tempered. He swore so often and so indiscriminately that his employees were sometimes not sure whether he was angry at them or merely making conversation. Like many other autocratic types, he was famous for things like cracking the glass top of his desk with his bare hands and throwing ashtrays at his subordinates."

But even more problematic than Bronfman's personality was his company's checkered past supplying bootleggers during Prohibition. His background was always suspect, although it wouldn't be until the 1950–51 U.S. Senate investigation into organized crime known as the Kefauver Committee that the gangster boss Frank Costello would testify that Bronfman was one of his main suppliers during Prohibition (Costello, along with Carlo Gambino, was the inspiration behind Vito Corleone, Marlon Brando's character from *The Godfather*). These were connections that Bronfman would spend his whole life trying to hide, and in a 1979 *New York Times* profile of him the great Nora Ephron wrote that "Bronfman never told the truth. From the time of Repeal until his death in 1971, he devoted himself to erasing his past. He gave millions to charity, spent hundreds of thousands printing sanitized versions of his company's history. His desire for respectability became so great that he claimed to have been born in Canada instead of Bessarabia." Ephron then pointed out that Bronfman was a human embodiment of a very complicated industry. "The distribution empire Bronfman built with mobsters and former bootleggers and then with their Harvard-educated sons is fascinating," she wrote. Regarding his own past and links to organized crime, Bronfman typically offered only wry smiles and knowing winks, once commenting, "It would be a fascinating story, if I could only tell the truth of what happened."

That left Schenley's Lewis Rosenstiel as the last big liquor company head to potentally lead the DSI. The problem here, however, was that Rosenstiel's career was just as suspicious as Bronfman's. He had built his company by purchasing shuttered distilleries just as George Remus had done, and in 1929 he had been indicted, although never convicted, on bootlegging charges. (It wouldn't be until the 1970s, when the state of New York investigated how deeply organized crime had infiltrated legitimate business, that witnesses would discuss the connections Rosenstiel had to gangsters like Meyer Lansky and Al Capone. Indeed, Lansky himself once complained, "Why is 'Lansky' a gangster, and not the Bronfman and Rosenstiel families?") His past notwithstanding, Rosenstiel's personality was also so prickly that years later the *New York Times* had no qualms about describing him, in the first lines of his obituary, as "a domineering man with a quick temper." He was also widely rumored to be bisexual, which certainly would have flown in the face of the era's social prejudices and the whiskey industry's attempts to cultivate a more family-friendly image. One of his many ex-wives even claimed she once saw him having sex with two boys as FBI director J. Edgar Hoover—an acquaintance of Rosenstiel's and widely rumored to be a homosexual and cross-dresser—wore a dress and watched from the bedside. The ex-wife later admitted that she had made up the claim to smear Rosenstiel's character, and would do prison time for perjury, but the incident nonetheless demonstrated the highly negative feelings the man stirred in others.

So with that, it was determined that none of the big whiskey company heads was suited to serve as the public face of the industry's main lobbying arm. What DSI needed was a "Tsar of high power, smoothness and influence," *Time* speculated. With this in mind, all of the company heads met to discuss who would lead the organization. Their choice would become part of the industry's new image, but the part nobody ever really sees: W. Forbes Morgan, DSI's new executive director—or as

Time called him in its business section, the "Front Man." A pillar of re-spectability, Morgan was the nephew of J. P. Morgan, uncle by marriage to Eleanor Roosevelt, and had personally raised $2.7 million for FDR's first campaign as treasurer of the Democratic National Committee. His Oxford accent—a result of his transcontinental upbringing and school-ing at Eton—was part of the soundtrack of FDR's inner circle, and the photograph accompanying his announcement showed him wearing a sumptuous silk necktie nailed to his chest with a diamond pin the size of a doorknob. He was plugged into just about every power socket imag-inable, and his confirmation happened at the Waldorf Astoria Hotel, right where it should have been.

In more ways than one, bourbon was moving into the modern age.

· CHAPTER THIRTEEN ·

COCKTAILS FOR HITLER

Just as bourbon found itself recovering from Prohibition, struggling to regain its footing during Repeal, the outbreak of World War II once again shattered the industry. Shortages loomed: rationing measures for grain shut down distillation between 1942 and 1946 and distillers were forced to stretch aged stocks with grain neutral spirits.* Soldiers on the front were grateful to drink anything they could get their hands on—troops drank their Aqua Velva aftershave, according to James Jones in his novel *The Thin Red Line,* while sailors filtered the denaturants out of torpedo fuel and drank that.

But even though bourbon production ceased during the fighting, most distilleries found themselves busier than ever. The War Production Board took control of the industry after Pearl Harbor and converted distilleries from the production of beverage alcohol to industrial alcohol. Lewis Rosenstiel at Schenley commissioned the construction of a modified column still to make high-proof, industrial alcohol quickly, then handed the plans for it over to other distilleries at no cost. Schenley also marshaled its large stable of chemists for the war effort, directing them to work on penicillin production, which relies on the growing of mold in a way similar as is required to grow yeast.

---

* There were three one-month distilling "holidays," which usually coincided with corn surpluses, when distillers were allowed to make beverage alcohol.

The spirits industry called its wartime production of alcohol "cocktails for Hitler." One gallon of industrial alcohol was required to manufacture every 155-millimeter howitzer shell, while the construction of a single jeep required twenty-three gallons. In total, roughly 126 million gallons were used just for antifreeze, and the synthetic rubber for tires, hoses, and the rayon for parachutes required over a billion more gallons. Overall, the spirits industry supplied 44 percent of the 1.7 billion gallons of 190-proof industrial alcohol used during the war. Taxes on whiskey that had been aging since before the war increased from $3 per gallon in 1941 to $9 per gallon by war's end, raising over $6 billion for the fighting.

The United States continued to look abroad for whiskey imports, but its best suppliers were also crippled by the war. The British government confiscated trucks owned by scotch distilleries for military use, and any scotch that did make it out for export was threatened by German U-boats. U.S. newspapers reported on aged whiskey stocks the same way it would report on strategic petroleum reserves after the Arab oil embargo of the 1970s: as a matter of national security. Drinkers stormed liquor stores and hoarded bottles as the government and distilleries pleaded with them to keep calm and share the wealth. A surprisingly populist ad for Hiram Walker's Imperial brand blended whiskey featured a shark chasing minnows and read, "There can't be feasts for the big or there'll be oblivion for the little." Hoarding whiskey meant that "someone else may be underfed," the ad continued. As long as everybody maintained a cool head, there would be enough whiskey to go around, the liquor industry assured drinkers.

The whiskey industry deserves credit for its wartime contributions, but actions during war are rarely black and white. Industry leaders had proved themselves patriots, but not entirely selfless ones. In 1944, Congress charged the whiskey industry with attempting to boost its profits by circumventing measures set by the wartime rationing board. The accusation came after reporters noticed that distilleries possessed nearly double the stocks of aged whiskey that they claimed publicly. A subcommittee of the Senate Judiciary Committee asserted that the DSI misled the public when it ran ads in hundreds of newspapers—titled

"The Truth About the Whiskey Shortage" and signed by fifty-seven liquor company executives—that cited the lower numbers for aged whiskey, which were subject to price controls. The blended whiskies offered to the public instead were more expensive than they should have been because the neutral spirits used in them weren't subject to the same wartime price ceilings. (The biggest brand of the war was a Schenley label called Three Feathers, which was only 5 percent straight whiskey and 95 percent neutral spirits that, because of grain rationing, were typically made from potatoes or cane sugar.) Whiskey makers were hoarding the good stuff to sell after the war, when rationing measures would be lifted and it could fetch a higher price. Coordinated efforts to misrepresent supply in order to manipulate prices were a violation of the Sherman Antitrust Act. Since the Big Four now owned 70 percent of the nation's whiskey, they were spearheading the industry's slide toward "monopolist tendencies," the lawmakers concluded.

The incident was an echo of whiskey's checkered past as well as a lesson for its future. Americans will always love bourbon unconditionally, but the companies responsible for making it will forever be tempted to step out of line. Today, the industry is regulated by the Alcohol and Tobacco Tax and Trade Bureau (TTB), which still occasionally finds distilleries in violation of federal regulations. For instance, after 2010, when markets hummed with whiskey's resurgent popularity, various non-distiller producers increasingly began implying to customers that they were making whiskey themselves instead of sourcing it from somebody else. A handful of brands were hiding their whiskey's origins for marketing purposes, a violation of Section 5.36(d) of the Code of Federal Regulations. Around the same time, with companies finding that bourbon's popularity had stretched whiskey supplies thin, other companies started to present age statements in questionable ways. In some cases, companies choosing to drop age statements from their labels continued to include the numbers on the label and only removed the words "years old" from under them, suggesting an age that the company technically didn't have to honor (this was the case with Very Old Barton, Old Charter, and numerous others). It wasn't officially illegal, so the federal government couldn't do anything about it, leaving vigilant whiskey writers to warn consumers about the practice.

But even though whiskey companies will occasionally veer from the straight and narrow, whiskey-loving Americans will always forgive them. During World War II, customers seemed less concerned about whiskey's misdeeds than they were with simply finding a bottle of the stuff. Shortages being what they were, Americans reluctantly turned to substitutes. An enchanting potion Americans initially referred to as "cactus wine" began creeping over the southern border. Drinkers eventually learned that it was called tequila, and greeted it with suspicion that bordered on hostility, as if this strange new spirit distilled from the agave plant was planning to steal bourbon's job. "The only liquor I have ever tasted that I regard worse than tequila is slivovitz," cocktail book author David Embury wrote in 1946. Embury told readers that tequila's odor could be offset with a "dilute acid," concocted by mixing salt and citrus juice. The "Mexican Itch" was born, a move consisting of licking salt from the back of one's hand, sucking on a lime wedge, and downing a shot of tequila. Slamming the empty shot glass down on the bar and picking a fight with the bouncer was optional.

It would be decades before tequila got a warmer embrace in the States. In the meantime, cheap and plentiful rum, courtesy of Caribbean distillers that hadn't been shut down during the fighting, saw sales triple between 1941 and 1945. The Bacardi brand was a particular favorite, owing to its having been smuggled into the United States during Prohibition. That made it a sparkling jewel that big liquor companies wanted for their portfolios—they had started buying up nonwhiskey brands to diversify their product lines and insulate themselves from whiskey shortages. Lewis Rosenstiel at Schenley won the scramble for Bacardi's coveted import and distribution rights and began promoting it heavily. For a time, rum regained some of the popularity it had lost during the American Revolution. Liquor companies reminded people that grain was needed for the war effort, thereby making rum the patriotic alternative.

Of course, Americans weren't always thrilled with the alternatives, and hoarded whiskey whenever they could find it. The big liquor companies continued trying to spread demand to the variety of new products in their portfolios, but whiskey demand continued to overwhelm, and bootlegging remained a problem. In 1943, one liquor store in Washington, D.C., announced that it had eight thousand bottles of bourbon and rye just in time for Christmas, slashing prices on gin and rum to free up shelf space. A giant mob waited ten freezing hours outside for a chance to carry away a bottle. "The public is behaving very badly about the liquor situation," a Chicago-based representative of Hiram Walker moaned to reporters in 1944. "When they go to a store and can't get butter, they realize there's a war on. But when they can't get whiskey, they raise hell."

. . .

Even though the war ended in 1945, Americans still had to wait one year more for the return of regular whiskey production as Prohibitionists waged their last attack. Drys argued that grain was needed for the livestock that would feed a war-torn and starving world. This was the kind of argument they would have won before World War I, but the Prohibition movement was now facing a much more formidable adversary. The whiskey lobby responded that spent mash was actually better as animal feed than unfermented grains. The whiskey industry, therefore, was doing world hunger a favor by making as much whiskey as possible. The knockout punch thrown, distilling resumed with no restrictions on production. The war had brought the nation out of the Depression, and as soon as the whiskey was ready, all the discretionary income of the booming postwar economy would be waiting for it.

Whiskey companies had come together during the war, but now, with the fighting over, they turned their attention back to competing with each other. Victory would go to the outfits that successfully predicted what the market most craved. Would drinkers choose full-bodied straight whiskies, or the blends that had been intended as a holdover but that some drinkers now preferred? Schenley, Stitzel-Weller, Beam, and Heaven Hill bet on straight bourbon, forecasting that America would return to robust, rich flavors. Seagram, however, went the opposite direction, speculating that blends would dominate. Other companies hedged, balancing portfolios between the two styles. When the market showed its hand, everybody won the pot. Straight whiskey came back, but the blends still kept a sizable portion of sales. Straight whiskey went from 12 percent of the market in 1946 up to 40 percent by 1955 (it would be half by 1963, although sales fluttered up and down during the 1950s). Blended whiskey fell from 88 percent in 1946 to 60 percent by 1955.

All this time, American whiskey's eternal battle of big versus small, each side represented by its respective patron saint of Alexander Hamilton or Thomas Jefferson, continued unabated. This fight would be a zero-sum game, and continued to tilt in Hamilton's favor. Between 1933 and 1958, the number of distilleries fell from 130 to 76 as control of the industry pooled into the hands of a smaller number of larger corporations, dominated by the Big Four, which now controlled more than three-quarters of the market. Labor and other supply shortages would also force many distilleries out of business or into consolidation rounds.

Eventually, the number of conglomerates would also begin acquiring each other—from 1938 to 1958 the number of holding companies fell from 110 to 35. The conglomerates were like a pod of whales that had grown big on schools of fish—when the fish ran out, the whales started eating each other. They grew so big that throughout the 1950s, each of the Big Four was consistently listed among America's top ten advertisers, alongside companies like General Motors. *Fortune* magazine reported that whiskey was essentially becoming a giant "banking and inventory business."

Whiskey's consolidation rounds were a perfect symbol of the rest of the postwar business world, where integration and diversified portfolios meant the reduction of financial risk. The Big Four were no exception. "The giants are turning increasingly to other fields of endeavor," *Barron's* reported. National was still making Old Taylor, Old Grand-Dad, Old Crow, and fifty-five other liquor brands, but it also decided to invest $82 million in the chemical industry, changing its name to the National

Distillers and Chemical Corporation. Seagram got into oil exploration and Schenley created a toiletry and pharmaceuticals division. Not all of these endeavors were as lucrative as making whiskey, but the U.S. Justice Department had begun to frown at the rate at which the Big Four were purchasing their smaller competitors, forcing them into other pursuits.

As more brands came under control of the conglomerates, these giants began trading the labels among each other as if they were baseball cards. If a company had too many whiskey brands and not enough gin brands, it would trade with a company that found itself in the opposite scenario. Just as they had done during Repeal, the companies continued to buy up small brands simply to discontinue them so the market could be focused on fewer star players. *Barron's* in 1954 noted the trend "in the whiskey industry toward a concentration of consumer preference in a relatively small number of recognized brands—the same trend at work in the automobile, beer, and cigarette industries. The largest distillers now account for an estimated 75 percent of the U.S. market, with the five best selling labels doing over 40 percent of the business." Tracking who owns what is to this day a full-time job, since the portfolios shift every year, everyone rebalancing depending on how their brands prosper and where they think the overall market is headed.

The Four Roses brand is a perfect example of how consolidation affected many once-famous labels. The brand was widely respected and had roots legitimately stretching back to the 1880s—it had drifted under the Frankfort Distilleries umbrella during Prohibition, but family shareholders wanted to sell it during World War II. In 1943, Seagram swooped in and saved the brand from extinction by purchasing it for $42 million. Then Sam Bronfman gutted it after the war by turning it into a blend, because that's where he had wagered the market was headed (it continued to be sold as a straight product for export markets). Immediately, the once-respected brand gained a reputation as cheap rotgut.

But things for Four Roses would eventually come full circle. In 1945, Four Roses had been a part of America's most famous image of victory over Japan in World War II. A giant neon advertisement for the brand is present in the background of Alfred Eisenstadt's *Life* magazine photo of a sailor and a woman kissing in Times Square during the celebration of the war's end. Over the next decades, Japan was rebuilt and brought into the fold of worldwide economic integration. Today Four Roses is owned by Japan's Kirin Brewery Company, another consortium that lovingly retooled the brand's recipe to make it a straight whiskey and return it to respectability. In a twist of irony, Kirin today happens to sit under Mitsubishi, the global conglomerate that made the A6M Zero fighter planes used by kamikaze pilots in the war that the *Life* magazine couple had just endured when caught by Eisenstadt in the middle of their kiss.

. . .

Amid the brutal consolidation rounds, a few smaller holdouts continued to stand independent. Some even found themselves moving up the ranks, most notably Stitzel-Weller, Beam, Heaven Hill, Glenmore, and a handful of others. In a way, they resembled a small group of frontier travelers who have grouped the wagons together to fight an encircling horde of bandits attempting to buy them out.

Or maybe they were just waiting for the bandits to make a good offer. The Blum family still owned Beam, which by the late 1950s had grown into a "moderate-sized" company, according to the *Wall Street Journal,* and was touted as an appealing purchase for a bigger player. At the time, Beam was an anomaly; whereas the conglomerates had diversified their portfolios, Beam was doing 90 percent of its sales volume in its single Jim Beam brand. Beam had worked its way up the ladder with an impressive strategy: it had started by concentrating on sales in California, then gradually moved the brand east, which allowed it to get strong distribution without spending a lot on advertising. "To the industry's astonishment, Jim Beam has now jumped into third place in national sales volumes among straight whiskies," *Barron's National Business and Financial Weekly* reported in 1958. The Blums held out on the smart little brand until 1966 when they sold Beam to American Brands, a New Jersey outfit that also owned Mott's Apple Products, Jergens Lotion, and a biscuit company.

There was much complaining about consolidation, and the U.S. Justice Department once again became suspicious of monopolization. From a purely symbolic standpoint, it didn't look great. Bourbon, as an icon of frontier independence—of Jefferson's yeoman farmer—was becoming anything but. Ownership of almost every brand in the country could ultimately be traced to just a handful of individuals who spent their time in boardrooms outfitted with really nice wet bars. Then, contrary to the nation's collective notion of Jeffersonian ideals, there were cases of some smallholders who were thrilled about being squeezed out of the industry. *Time* noted that many companies were witting accomplices that got paid handsomely in the buyouts. The payout that went to Four Roses was considered extremely generous for the time and the family shareholders gladly took it. They had just inherited the company and wanted to avoid paying taxes on it, according to company historian Al Young in *Four Roses: Return of a Whiskey Legend*. The buyout allowed the brand to survive and for rich family members with little interest in the whiskey business to go off and do something else. Forty-two million dollars offered for a company in a cutthroat industry during a time when the nation was embroiled in a world war? That deal had looked pretty good.

But not everyone saw it that way—some naturally wanted to remain in control of the businesses they had built. In 1952, the House Judiciary Committee held a hearing on whiskey monopolies. The heads of many smaller companies showed up to testify, making it sound as if they were men fighting with their backs to the sea, their only choices being to succumb or die. Pappy Van Winkle told lawmakers that bigger producers were guilty of "skullduggery" and "squeeze moves" against smaller operators like himself. He pointed out that the Big Four now owned eight of the fourteen independent cooperages that had existed before the war, allowing them to prevent smaller companies from getting barrels. Van Winkle also claimed that some big distillers had rented warehouse space from him, then pulled their stock but kept the insurance plans they had taken out so that he couldn't use his own storage facilities.

A standout among the smaller operators, Van Winkle by this point resembled the farmer who builds his house on land that a developer later wants to put a highway through. He was the man reflexively turning down offers from other companies, spitting on the ground as the dollar figures crept higher. The most notable offer came in the 1960s from Heublein Spirits Group, the company that owned Smirnoff vodka and itself would eventually become part of RJR Nabisco. When Van Winkle died in 1965, he did so as the head of a company that had remained relatively independent, always the master of a house he had built with his own hands. If whiskey consolidation was a war—and many articles from the era refer to it that way—Pappy had won his battles.

But once Pappy was gone, Stitzel-Weller was fair game for a take-over. People familiar with the running of the distillery claim that Pappy's son, Julian Jr., who was now in charge, struggled to match his father's business acumen. According to Julian's daughter, Sally Van Winkle Campbell, Stitzel-Weller's other investors sidestepped her father to force a sell to the millionaire industrialist Norton Simon in 1972, for $20 million. After that, the distillery fluttered between a few more owners until it was finally shuttered in the early 1990s and its unique and flavorful bourbons were lost.

Rights to Stitzel-Weller's brands were divvied up among the conquerors, and today reside primarily with Buffalo Trace and Heaven Hill. These companies would continue making them according to similar recipes, and they're still quite good, perhaps even better than ever, but they're not exactly the same as they once were. The little things that make separate distilleries unique were inevitably lost as companies continued to pool together and the industry streamlined. Bourbon was growing a little more homogeneous, and special standouts were being lost as consolidation took its toll.

· CHAPTER FOURTEEN ·

AMERICANS ABROAD

If you're a fan of older bourbon—anything older than eight years—you can thank the Korean War and one man's misinterpretation of international affairs. During the buildup to war, Lewis Rosenstiel wagered that hostilities would again go global and that the U.S. government would be forced to ration grain and shut down distilling, just as it had done during World War II. This time, however, Rosenstiel planned to distill a large surplus of whiskey to carry him through the drought. Schenley went full blast, helping push America's whiskey stocks past 637 million gallons, enough to supply the country's projected demand for almost eight years. Rosenstiel's foresight was typical of his business savvy, but the decision almost ended in disaster.

The problem began when the Korean War turned out to be a much smaller conflict than Rosenstiel had anticipated. There were no shortages and no rationing, and Schenley found itself holding a huge whiskey surplus. Now a single company owned almost 70 percent of the nation's older whiskey stocks, according to its competitors. When the taxes on all that whiskey came due in eight years, according to the bonding period established by Congress back in the nineteenth century, Rosenstiel would be forced to sell to a market without enough demand to meet his supply. Prices would plummet, Schenley would sell at a loss, other producers would have to slash prices to compete, and parts of the industry could be torn asunder—it reflected the same boom-and-bust cycles that had plagued the industry eighty years earlier. *Time* claimed that Rosenstiel's "mistaken theory that a shortage was in store" was a "hammerhead," while the *New York Times* ran the banner headline, WHISKY INDUSTRY IS FACING A CRISIS.

Rosenstiel responded by leaning on his counterparts within the DSI to help him buy some time. To avoid the impending tax crunch, he wanted to lobby Congress to increase the bonding period past eight years, allowing the whiskey to age longer and remain untaxed as he figured out what to do with it. The plan seemed simple enough, but the DSI's other members balked, turning against their powerful colleague. Hiram Walker and Seagram particularly opposed the aging increases, telling reporters that it would "put the Government in the position of underwriting Schenley's inventory expansion" and place other companies at a pricing disadvantage. They supported tax relief, but wanted a provision preventing Rosenstiel from labeling his whiskies as over eight years old until the rest of them had a chance to build up their own inventories of similar whiskey. Rosenstiel had made a mistake, they argued, and was now lobbying for rule changes that would reward his error.

Rosenstiel was just trying to convert his weakness into a strength. The strategy would give him a huge advantage, and his competitors were simply trying to block what they knew would be his next play: Schenley would use its older bourbon to take advantage of a growing luxury market created by a booming postwar economy. Sidney Frank, Rosenstiel's son-in-law and Schenley's vice president and sales manager, told reporters that the company was refocusing toward "the class market." (Decades later, Frank became a billionaire by upmarketing Grey Goose vodka the same way, taking a relatively simple product and convincing customers to pay more for it.)

The timing for Rosenstiel's luxurification strategy was perfect, and gave him one more significant advantage. By 1956, the luxury trend in spirits had caught fire, but bourbon makers had no real way to capitalize on it since the product they offered wasn't typically associated with high luxury. The very nature of bourbon itself stood in the way: a simple and uncomplicated product requiring little more than some fermented grains, a wooden barrel, and a little bit of patience—it was just whiskey, not a Fabergé egg. To make their product seem more exclusive, bourbon makers increasingly sold their whiskey in cut crystal decanters and marked up the price. The whiskey, same as before, also found itself adorned with unregulated and ill-defined terms like "extra-aged," which meant nothing because it was entirely relative and lacked specificity. (In later years the "extra-aged" term would be joined by other vague descriptors like "handmade," "artisanal," "small-batch," and the ubiquitous "craft," other terms without strict definitions that are used to justify charging a higher price.) In 1956, the *New York Times* condemned the trend with the headline, "Can't Improve Whiskey, So Distillers Turn to Its Container." As the *Times* elaborated, "This holiday season will see more fancy glassware than ever before, and some in the industry (whisky, not glass) are saying privately that they're a little concerned about the extreme to which the trend has gone."

If Rosenstiel's lobbying strategy to extend the bonding period worked, his older bourbon would allow him to confidently distance himself from ambiguous marketing terms and advertise tangible qualities with specific age statements. Plus, he'd have a five-year head start on most of his competition. The only problem was that Rosenstiel's Big Four counterparts were undermining his strategy, and he was about to fight back. He had not built an empire now worth $438 million because he was someone others could squeeze. He was the one who usually did the squeezing—in fact, Rosenstiel, who had a penchant for bugging his home and office spaces, was allegedly part of the reason why FBI director J. Edgar Hoover had been reluctant to pursue the Mafia. Hoover periodically attended parties at the liquor magnate's house, where prostitutes and organized crime figures also made occasional appearances, and the blackmail potential of Rosenstiel's tapes ostensibly kept Hoover at bay. The other Big Four heads were up against a powerful adversary, which Rosenstiel proved with his next move: he left DSI and started a separate lobbying group, calling it the Bourbon

Institute. (In 1973, the Bourbon Institute would merge with DSI and another trade group called the Licensed Beverage Industries to form DISCUS.)

In 1958, Rosenstiel and the Bourbon Institute successfully lobbied for passage of the Forand Bill, which increased the bonding period from eight to twenty years. The move happened against "the fury of the three other big distilling companies," according to the *Economist*, but was such an enormous success for Rosenstiel that a few decades later it would get two entire paragraphs in the man's lengthy *New York Times* obituary.

Not only was the Forand Bill good for Rosenstiel, it was good for bourbon. Many master distillers today claim that their favorite bourbons typically fall within the range of six to twelve years, depending on variances in aging conditions. The Forand Bill gave them more time to mature whiskey without having to pay taxes on spirits that would eventually evaporate. The twenty-year aging period allowed by the bill was extremely generous—after twenty years, bourbon aging in most parts of the warehouse has evaporated out of the barrel, leaving very little left to sell. What is left is often undrinkable, made bitter and astringent by too many wood tannins, with the few rare exceptions of bourbon aged in cool, relatively mild parts of the warehouse, where evaporation and absorption into the wood are less extreme.

Once the Forand Bill was passed, Rosenstiel did just what the rest of his industry counterparts had feared. In 1961, Schenley announced a $21 million advertising campaign promoting the age factor in its whiskies. Rosenstiel made it all look intentional, telling reporters that his aging program "represented years of planning and an investment of $1 billion in inventories of aged and aging whiskies." The new ads focused on age: "Age Makes the Difference," "Are you getting all the age you should get for your money?," and "We Stand Alone," which was Rosenstiel's less than subtle dig at his Big Four counterparts, reminding them that they were a few years behind him.

These advertising campaigns were left to outside experts, whom Rosenstiel had learned early in his career were the best people for the job. When his company was still young, he had once trained five thousand parrots to say, "Drink Old Quaker" and then gave the birds to bartenders. (The campaign fizzled in all the disastrous ways one imagines it would.) For Rosenstiel's campaign to market older bourbon, he instead relied on a list of advertising agencies that reads like the credits of *Mad Men:* W.B. Doner (clients: General Electric, Coca-Cola, DuPont), McCann-Erickson (Chevrolet, the Spanish government of Francisco Franco), and Doyle Dane Bernbach (Volkswagen, Mobil Oil, the presidential campaign of Lyndon B. Johnson).

There was a lot of spin, all stemming from what had originally been a misreading of the market, but the effect on bourbon couldn't have been better. Schenley boosted bottling proof and began increasing the ages of its bourbon brands so they were square in the middle of the perfection zone. James E. Pepper went from six to ten years, George T. Stagg went from four to seven years, J.W. Dant went from four to seven years, Melrose Rare went from seven years to ten or more, and Schenley Reserve went from five-, six-, and seven-year-old expressions to eight years. Old Charter became a twelve-year-old whiskey ("the whiskey that didn't watch the clock"), as did I.W. Harper. These surpluses turned the period during the 1950s and early 1960s into a golden age for consumers, when supply for well-aged bourbon met demand and prices were relatively low.*

Rosenstiel's strategy to sell older bourbon in the United States by emphasizing luxury coincided perfectly with his next plan: sell more of it abroad. There was sizable demand overseas, if not entirely comparable to the large domestic appetite. Nevertheless, Lewis Rosenstiel still had surplus whiskey he needed to sell. When he announced his new $35 million campaign to begin taking bourbon global, he decided to hold the press conference not in a Kentucky cornfield but from his office in the Empire State Building.

---

* The period stretching from the 1990s until about 2011 was another consumer golden age, when perfectly aged bourbons were plentiful and inexpensive. The intensity of bourbon's resurgent popularity after 2011 caught many distilleries by surprise and caused limited shortages that drove up prices, arguably ending this golden age.

. . .

In 1958, the British writer Graham Greene published *Our Man in Havana*, one of the Cold War's best spy thrillers, which detailed how the world's biggest superpowers were traipsing the globe in a comedy of errors, turning smaller nations into pawns in their game of chess. The United States and Britain were allies, but the book perfectly captured the contest that was about to erupt between bourbon and scotch as the two whiskey styles began competing for world market share.

Greene's protagonist, James Wormold, is a hapless vacuum cleaner salesman in Cuba who has convinced the world's intelligence agencies he's a master spy. Havana's police chief, Captain Segura, becomes suspicious of Wormold and challenges him to a game of checkers for his freedom. Instead of standard game pieces the men use mini-bottles of whiskey—bourbon for Wormold and scotch for Segura. The brands are classics: Old Taylor, Old Forester, Four Roses, and Kentucky Tavern for the bourbons, and for the scotches, Cairngorm, Dimple Haig, Red Label, and Grant's Standfast. Each man drinks every mini-bottle he captures. The better a man plays, the drunker he gets. It's a paradox in which success diminishes the chance of winning, and the victor is ultimately the man with the higher tolerance.

Scotch held an overwhelming advantage against bourbon. It was (and still is) the hands-down leader in global whiskey sales. At the peak of the British Empire, scotch had accompanied the Crown to every corner of the globe, and for most people it comprised the very definition of whiskey. But now, with the Cold War grinding forward, it was America's turn to blanket the globe with military bases. American soldiers drank American whiskey, but base exchanges were choosy about what brands they carried, and soldiers were sensitive to price. In one maneuver that allowed it to vastly increase its market share and advertise its name in the years to come, Beam decided to install bottling plants in Germany, which helped it lower costs and supply the soldiers standing guard next to the Iron Curtain (it was still made in the United

States, but bottled abroad). Beam also became popular in Australia, where it's still the best-selling whiskey brand. In some parts of the world you can still trace which bourbon brands established their bulkheads during the Cold War: Four Roses is an old standby in Spain and Wild Turkey is huge in Italy (and is actually owned by Gruppo Campari, an Italian conglomerate). By 1966, I.W. Harper was in 110 countries—today it is *only* available overseas, but is particularly big in Japan.

Bourbon's biggest obstacle to gaining an international foothold was that nobody knew what it was or how it was different from scotch. It was more foreign to foreigners than vodka was to Americans, *Time* quipped while reporting Rosenstiel's announcement of his global roll-out. Bourbon generally peaks faster than scotch and often doesn't have to be aged as long, but international customers were only familiar with scotch. Younger bourbons might very well be superior to their older scotch counterparts, but it wouldn't matter, people would still think they were inferior because they were younger.

The reason scotch is often able to hold up to longer aging than bourbon is because Scotland's climate is milder and most whisky there is aged in used barrels (meaning less oomph from the wood, akin to reusing a tea bag and steeping it for a longer period of time). The relatively higher humidity and lower temperatures in Scotland also mean less evaporation, so scotch producers lose less liquid by aging longer. In one experiment, American and Scotch producers exchanged barrels of whiskey and found that the bourbon aged in Scotland took much longer to mature and that the scotch aged in Kentucky developed much faster than it would have otherwise, simply because of the climate differences. Most people never get to try truly overaged whiskey, however, because most companies pull barrels from the hotter parts of the warehouse before the whiskey goes over the line. If there isn't a market for it, they sometimes store it in metal containers, to stop it from aging while waiting for the markets to improve, although this move is usually prohibitively expensive and rare.

Regardless of the realities between scotches and bourbons of different ages, Rosenstiel's older bourbons were better able to compete with scotch, and the overseas markets would give him a place to dump any overaged bourbons, passing them off to customers who believed they were good simply because they were old. This strategy was a godsend during huge surpluses that would again occur a couple of decades later, when a few bourbon companies were able to dump overaged bourbon on a Japanese market that based its understanding of whiskey entirely around the rules of scotch.

As for luxury appeal in overseas markets, scotch also held the advantage. When bourbon and scotch were getting their starts during the late 1700s and early 1800s, both Kentucky and Scotland were considered remote and rather isolated backwaters, manned by fierce independents who drew uncomfortable stares from polite society. Scotch's image, however, would evolve into something more urbane during the middle of the nineteenth century. Before then, wine and brandy were the tipples of European high society, just as they had been in America. But starting around 1860, the *Phylloxera* aphid decimated the European vineyards that wine and brandy both rely on, a tragedy that required years of rebuilding and replanting. Shortages of wine and brandy thus forced Europeans to look for alternatives.

Scotch was the obvious choice, moving into society's spotlight just as Scotland began riding a wave of voguish popularity. A few decades earlier, Sir Walter Scott had romantically depicted the misty crags of Scotland's landscape in his novels. Then he arranged for King George IV to visit the Scottish countryside and wear a tartan while doing so, glorifying public perceptions of Scottish tradition and heritage while making the region a popular tourist destination. In 1852, Prince Albert and Queen Victoria purchased Balmoral Castle in the Scottish Highlands, lending even more respectability. By 1870, the whisky made by Scottish distillers such as John Walker and Tommy Dewar had grown increasingly prominent, bolstered by advertising that relied heavily on tartans and bagpipes. By the 1890s, whisky and soda was the preferred tipple of English gentlemen, turning Dewar and Walker into millionaires. Tommy Dewar entered the House of Lords and was the third British man to own an automobile (the first was tea baron Thomas Lipton, the second the Prince of Wales). Scotland had become a classy place, and so had its whisky.

Bourbon country had never enjoyed a similar makeover, which might have allowed American distillers to take advantage of consumers' class perceptions. Even though Kentucky's charms are many, and it has had some contemporary success attracting the kind of tourism enjoyed by Napa Valley's wine industry, it still occasionally suffers the prejudices of people who consider it one of those "flyover" states where the cornfields simply blend into the horizon. Of course, with American customers, anyway, this disadvantage is spun in bourbon's favor when the spirit's humble roots become part of its appeal—even if it's a premium brand, bourbon retains its status as a blue-collar choice of the workingman. Drinking it sends a signal that you're not pretentious.

But that message doesn't always translate to foreign countries. As export markets became bourbon's new frontier in the 1950s and '60s, advertising would need adjusting. Clever marketing would be used to reimagine bourbon's image in places where scotch—the literal drink of kings—had written the rules of the game. Beam turned out to be so good at shapeshifting that in 1965 it received special accolades from none other than the *Wall Street Journal* for catering to "snob appeal." Its "ads overseas feature tuxedo clad men in posh surroundings" and helped "bourbon [develop] the same kind of status overseas that scotch has in this country." To this day the brand enjoys enhanced status in Germany and Australia, places where import duties boost its price—which customers almost always interpret as a sign of higher quality—and where the company has modified its advertising appropriately. The same goes for other humble American whiskey brands utilizing similar overseas marketing strategies—Four Roses Yellow Label sits on the top shelves of Spanish and Eastern European bars, as does Jack Daniel's, which flies off shelves at the Dubai Airport duty-free shop. It's yet another reminder that we taste and judge as much with our minds—susceptible as they are to outside signals of quality and value—as with our senses.

. . .

In May 1964, the U.S. Congress passed a resolution declaring that bourbon was "a distinctive product of the United States." The announcement came with little fanfare, making only a slight blip in the press. It was an inauspicious beginning to a resolution that, through sentimental nostalgia, has since become famous.

But the resolution was in fact another one of Lewis Rosenstiel's brainchildren, and an important part of his strategy to successfully market bourbon overseas. In 1958, Schenley sent a case of bourbon to every American embassy in the world and then began devising a way to "seek through international law and treaty to confine the name 'bourbon' to bourbon whisky produced in the United States," according to the *New York Times*.

The resolution was meant to give bourbon the same kind of trade and labeling protection afforded scotch and cognac in export markets. Much of the "bourbon" sold overseas was counterfeit. "Spurious bourbons," according to the *Times,* were particularly bad coming out of Canada and Panama. "A rose by any other name may smell as sweet, but members of the Bourbon Institute are taking a sour view of use of the name 'bourbon' for any whiskey not made in the United States." Senator Thruston B. Morton and Representative John C. Watts, both of Kentucky, introduced the bipartisan bill before it landed with the colorful chairman of the House Ways and Means Committee, Arkansas representative Wilbur Mills.

Throughout Mills's illustrious career, bourbon had occasionally surfaced. He is sometimes, although erroneously, credited with spearheading the legislation mandating that whiskey must be aged in charred new oak barrels for at least two years in order to be labeled "straight" bourbon or rye. The truth is that Mills entered office in 1939, shortly after cooper and timber unions had successfully lobbied for that mandate. The use of new barrels was already widespread, and was considered a best practice in the industry, but the New Deal legislation made it official and helped safeguard jobs. The unions had a powerful presence in Mills's home state of Arkansas, where almost three million acres of national forest sit at an elevation ensuring that trees grow at a rate giving them a density that's ideal for bourbon—the wood is soft enough that the spirit can penetrate deeply, but dense enough to prevent excessive evaporation and leakage. Missouri and West Virginia, other states with an abundance of timber companies and cooperage mills, also pushed for the legislation.

When the 1964 resolution originally landed in the House with Mills's committee, nobody was quite sure what to do with it. Mills moved it to the Interstate and Foreign Commerce Committee, a "catch-all" committee handling legislation ranging from weather-related issues to oceanography. The committee assigned the bill to a staffer who was an expert on the merchant marines, not liquor. The reason? The committee simply thought it would be funny, given that his name was August Bourbon.

August Bourbon did his namesake proud, and "after sober consideration," the *Washington Post* cleverly reported, the resolution quickly made its way through Congress and was passed. The name was protected and bourbon had "got its visa" to move overseas, as another wag put it. Bourbon would be given the same protection that scotch, cognac, and champagne enjoyed.

· · ·

It seems cynical and contrarian to reflect on this period, a time defined by consolidation, big business, lobbying, and cutthroat marketing. The reality of bourbon was the exact opposite of how it usually appeared in advertisements, an era that was arguably influenced more by men like Lewis Rosenstiel than by any of the master distillers who at the time were roaming their rickhouses searching for honey barrels (and who would eventually get their names and pictures on bottles).

Rosenstiel, however, soon became a victim of the kind of industry he helped create. In 1968, he was ousted from Schenley by Meshulam

Riklis, a man described as a "merger magician" in the press. Riklis, who controlled a conglomerate of various unrelated companies, made a tender offer to Schenley stockholders and quickly seized 88 percent of the company. Shortly after he fired Rosenstiel, Riklis purchased the former executive's six-story Manhattan town house, literally buying the man's home out from underneath him in every way imaginable. Rosenstiel retired to Miami Beach and spent the remainder of his life—he died in 1976—donating more than $100 million to various charitable and philanthropic institutions. A few Schenley executives objected that Riklis simply wanted to raid Schenley's massive treasury, to which Riklis replied, "They are just afraid they will be fired." In 1987, Riklis sold the remnants of Schenley to Guinness, which was eventually absorbed into Diageo, the outfit that by 2015 would be the largest spirits producer in the world.

Bourbon lost many things during these decades of upheaval, but consumers also got more choices, better-aged bourbon, and a spirit that was now enshrined as a national treasure. Rosenstiel had no master plan, but he was a force of will, scrambling to convert a near disaster into success. The industry had changed in ways that don't often pull at the heartstrings, but this wasn't because bourbon was abandoning America. In fact, as the 1960s began to heat up, America was actually on the verge of abandoning bourbon.

· CHAPTER FIFTEEN ·

FOREIGN INVASION

I n August 1959, Soviet leader Nikita Khrushchev sat in the cabin of U.S. vice president Richard Nixon's Boeing 707 and prepared to taste his first bourbon. As the plane rested on the tarmac of Moscow's Vnukovo Airport, jazz drifted from the cabin's high-fidelity sound system and Khrushchev was given the whiskey as a peace offering following a vicious argument he'd had with Nixon a week earlier. Khrushchev sniffed the glass and would soon give his opinion.

The argument between Khrushchev and Nixon had erupted during a cultural exchange intended to promote peace between the United States and the Soviet Union at the height of the Cold War. The two superpowers built exhibitions in each other's countries, and Nixon had flown out to give Khrushchev a tour of the American display, which resembled a modern-day IKEA: a walkway snaking through models of perfect American living rooms and kitchens, each fully loaded with high-tech gadgetry. As Nixon showed Khrushchev a color television, the Soviet premier launched into a tirade about U.S. policies, and the two men began arguing. The debate continued as the two men drifted into a model of an American kitchen, where the leaders stood like a married couple on the verge of divorce fighting during breakfast, stabbing their fingers at each other and shouting. Khrushchev kept interrupting, and Nixon yelled that the Soviet premier should "not be afraid of ideas. After all, you don't know everything," according to the press corps accompanying the diplomatic mission.

A week later, as Nixon was about to depart for America and the men's tempers had cooled, Khrushchev visited Nixon on his airplane for a tour. Khrushchev started picking through the plane's wet bar, sniffing at an American-made vodka and asking who had made it. Not even bothering to wait for an answer, he picked up a second bottle. "What's this?" he asked, and was told it was bourbon whiskey. Later, after Khrushchev sat down, he was offered a drink.

"You propose vodka or whiskey?" he asked before answering his own question: "We are on your territory. We will take whiskey."

Khrushchev was served a highball: bourbon poured over ice and mixed with seltzer. He took a sip and proposed a toast to the United States and his guests. "This is very good whiskey," he told the group through his interpreter, "but you Americans spoil it. You put in more ice than whiskey."

Khrushchev had no idea how prescient his words would be in the decade that would follow. Bourbon sales in the United States were relatively strong up until the middle of the 1960s, then began to plummet as consumer tastes changed. Full-bodied straight bourbons were hit particularly hard, and panicked distillers began scrambling to lighten their recipes and to lobby Congress for changes in the official production standards. Just a few years earlier, bourbon had thrived, but now it was folding like a bad musical as sales hurtled toward a historic low point. Of the many causes, the main one came straight from Khrushchev's homeland: vodka.

. . .

It took vodka about fourteen years to establish a beachhead from which it could launch an attack on bourbon. In 1933, the same year as Repeal, the United States officially recognized the Soviet Union, which technically cleared the way for vodka imports. But hardly any came, save for the odd case that arrived alongside Polish or Latvian vodkas, ending up behind grocery counters in ethnic neighborhoods like New York's

Brighton Beach or Chicago's Stock Yard district. Then, in 1934, a Russian immigrant named Rudolph Kunnet (shortened from Kunetchansky) contacted the sons of Russian distiller Pierre Smirnoff and bought the rights to his name. Kunnet's distillery in Bethel, Connecticut, was producing about twenty cases a day when it was purchased for $14,000 by Heublein (the same Heublein that would later try to buy Stitzel-Weller).

After that, very little happened. Vodka was a sleeper cell, hiding on American soil until receiving its orders. Most Americans had been unaware of its existence as a drink until the Tehran and Yalta conferences held during World War II between Franklin Roosevelt, Winston Churchill, and Joseph Stalin. FDR insisted on making dirty martinis for everyone, using a personal recipe that required a copious amount of olive brine. The non-Americans were confused and wary of what many historians have described as the worst martinis ever, and the Russians chose to toast with vodka instead, hoisting glasses of it into the air as if they were tiny trophies. Americans looked and wondered.

Distilled from grain at an eye-popping proof of around 190, much vodka is basically grain neutral spirits, intentionally stripped of all oils, compounds, and impurities, leaving it bracingly antiseptic and by definition "a neutral spirit without distinctive character," according to the U.S. Code of Federal Regulations. It's the opposite of bourbon, whose character is created when the same compounds that are stripped from vodka interact with a wood barrel. Vodka's qualities, or rather its lack of qualities, were quickly appreciated by alcoholics who noticed that the spirit didn't dirty their breath. Smirnoff later capitalized on this feature by launching its "Smirnoff Leaves You Breathless" campaign.

Vodka's main assault on bourbon began in 1946. Sales of the white spirit remained weak, and a Heublein executive named John Martin was wondering how to boost them when he ran into a bartender friend who was trying, unsuccessfully, to push imported ginger beer at his bar in Los Angeles. His creation: the Moscow Mule, a cocktail composed of ginger beer, vodka, and half a lime, served in a copper mug. Like all cocktail origin myths, there are alternative explanations for the drink's creation, but this one seems most likely. "The Moscow Mule was a Trojan horse," the adman in charge of the Smirnoff campaign around the drink later quipped. "It introduced vodka to the American people."

The Moscow Mule was vodka's insertion team, infiltrating the American countryside and rallying hearts and minds. It had a beachhead in Los Angeles, but where next? What place in America might be susceptible to its message? It turned out to be right where the House Un-American Affairs Committee thought that every other communist threat from Mother Russia seemed to find safe harbor: Hollywood.

According to cocktail lore, vodka's October Revolution occurred a year later, in 1947, at actress Joan Crawford's house. The screen legend and tastemaker threw a party where she commanded that only vodka and champagne would be served. Her guests, a collection of stars responsible for setting the nation's trends, got a taste of the spirit and began serving it at their own parties.

Vodka spread faster than a dance craze. Sales went from 40,000 cases in 1950 to 4.4 million in 1955. Bourbon still far outsold the clear spirit, but some straight bourbon producers began to take notice, particularly because the uptick in vodka sales was accompanied by increased sales of lighter blended whiskey. National Distillers assessed that the increased popularity of less punchy liquor was a harbinger. Between 1954 and 1958, the company offered 86-proof versions of Old Taylor, Old Grand-Dad, and Old Crow alongside the standard 100-proof offering, a move that also allowed it to cut excise taxes and lower retail prices. The brands were some of the oldest and most storied names in bourbon, and the proof drops were a little akin to suddenly transferring three of your finest Navy SEALs to desk jobs. Brands at other companies—I.W. Harper at Schenley, Brown-Forman with Old Forester, and many others—took the same precaution. By 1963, some of the lower-proof versions were outselling the heavier versions, and distillers were "seeing the light," *Time* quipped.

Vodka marched on. By 1967, as the Cold War escalated in Vietnam, vodka sales surpassed gin, the popular white spirit that capitalists used in power lunch martinis and that FDR had served at Yalta. With gin defeated, vodka now had bourbon in its sights, although the brown spirit was still a formidable presence. Jim Beam in particular had strong sales, partly a result of its shrewd overseas marketing and ability to get itself firmly ensconced on military bases. As the Vietnam War gathered momentum, newspaper reporters regularly added color to stories by depicting the field offices of colonels, making sure to describe what liquor they saw. The descriptions followed a format: tents, folding tables, ammo cases, and the ubiquitous bottle of Jim Beam. Rarely did they mention other brands.

As Vietnam erupted, Jim Beam fought fire with fire. In 1967, the James Bond movie *You Only Live Twice*—the one where Sean Connery plays Bond as he battles SPECTRE—was released, and Jim Beam hired Connery as a spokesman. Off camera, Connery was a Scotsman who presumably would have preferred scotch, but he also understood the larger implications the West faced as it fought communism and bourbon battled vodka, and put aside any conflicting principles to appear in the ads. It was a brilliant maneuver on Beam's part, recruiting the Cold War's most potent weapon.

But there was just one catch—Bond isn't normally a bourbon drinker, *he's a vodka drinker*. Bond's famous martinis replaced the traditional gin with vodka and were aggressively shaken rather than stirred. Bond's violent bending of the rules established his maverick personality—as a government man, he was the ultimate insider, but he wasn't constrained by the ultimate Establishment cocktail. By drinking vodka, Bond was building immunity against his Soviet adversaries, but with a glass of Beam in his hand he was something different. It was a masterstroke of psychological warfare to confuse his enemy. Because really, who truly understands James Bond?

Despite the Bond recruitment, vodka was able to overcome. By this point it had won the hearts and minds of America's impressionable youth. The baby boomers were reaching drinking age but also turning against the old ways of their parents. Bourbon became a symbol of the patriarchy and the Establishment. Vodka, on the other hand, hailed from a country that was America's mysterious enemy—drinking it was an act of subversive defiance. With its absence of any distinctive character, vodka was also a blank canvas the young generation could use to reimagine itself. The drink could be mixed with whatever flavor (orange juice, Kool-Aid) suited the moment. As Vietnam fell apart, boomers protested the war that was being led by all those old colonels with bottles of Jim Beam on their desks. The drinks of the older generation, *Esquire* wrote at the time, stood "for everything from phony bourgeois values and social snobbery to jaded alcoholism and latent masochism."

The generational standoff was awkward—the grayhairs sat across the table from the longhairs, blinking hard. Bourbon—so old-fashioned, so addicted to the past—struggled to find appropriate words, and sometimes embarrassed itself. In the 1960s, Beam created an advertising strategy geared toward women, but instead of breaking down whiskey's traditionally masculine image, it made the rift worse. Beam didn't promote *to* women; instead, it told women they should buy more bourbon for their husbands. "Pretty Nice Wife, Wouldn't You Say?" one ad read. In 1963, Seagram vice president Edgar Miles Bronfman, son of Samuel Bronfman, had a similar misstep. He claimed that the switch to lightness was because of women, "who prefer drinks without a lingering taste, and of young people, who find the 'lights' easier to learn on," according to *Time*. It was awkward, it was tone-deaf, and it came out during the same decade that Bob Dylan released a record titled *The Times They Are a-Changin'*.

By 1969, bourbon connoisseurs only could have felt a sense of impending doom. For his part, Lewis Rosenstiel, recently ousted from Schenley, even donated $1 million to the J. Edgar Hoover Foundation "to combat Communism or any other ideology or doctrine which shall be opposed to the principles set forth in the Constitution." Rosenstiel, a fervent anticommunist, was commonly described as a "father figure" to Roy Cohn, the organization's founder and the onetime controversial chief counsel to Senator Joseph McCarthy. The Hoover Foundation was chartered "to safeguard the heritage and freedom of the United States of America and to promote good citizenship through and appreciation of its form of government and to perpetuate the ideals and purposes to which the honorable J. Edgar Hoover has dedicated his life." After Rosenstiel's donation, the foundation's presidency was taken over by former Schenley executive vice president Louis Nichols, who had been the number two man under Hoover at the FBI until 1957, when he had left to work for the liquor giant.

Bourbon and vodka fought their most pitched, epic battles in the 1970s, as vodka slowly gained on bourbon's lead. By now, bourbon makers were running scared, abandoning thoughtful strategy. They started lobbing Hail Mary passes. In 1971, the big liquor companies lobbied Congress to change labeling and production regulations, saying that such revisions were needed for their survival. The U.S. government, which still got more federal tax revenue from liquor sales than any other source aside from the income tax, quickly complied. The resulting fallout emerged in the form of a product called "light whiskey." Whereas straight bourbon has to leave the still at less than 160 proof, preserving richer flavors, light whiskey could come from distillate leaving the still at between 160 and 190 proof. It could also be aged in used barrels, instead of the new barrels that the law dictated for other whiskies. It had to be aged for four years, but the result was still something that "resembles whisky-flavored vodka," *Time* reported.

The resulting headlines and advertisements stemming from the light whiskey campaign were far better than the whiskey was: "Let There Be Light," "Lighten Up," and "Major U.S. Distillers Are Now Following the Light." Four Roses ran a campaign with the theme "Prepare to Be Underwhelmed," for something called Four Roses Premium, a light whiskey that actually cost fifteen cents more per bottle than the brand line's heavier offerings.

Unsurprisingly, the light whiskey campaign was a failure, and by 1975 most companies had quietly stopped promoting it. Whiskey sales were still losing ground to vodka, however, pushing whiskey makers to dilute their old stalwart brands even more. Between 1973 and 1975, more than a hundred brands, including Seagram's 7 Crown, Four Roses, Hiram Walker's Imperial American, and Jim Beam, had reduced the proof from 86 to 80. Alongside the drops in proof, the return on investment for whiskey in general dropped to around 7 percent, well below the 12 percent that many investors consider a breakeven point.

In 1976, the same year as the U.S. bicentennial and two hundred years after whiskey had supplanted rum to become the nation's preferred spirit, vodka sales surpassed those of whiskey. Three years later, Hiram Walker closed its thousand-employee distillery in Peoria. It was another factory shuttered, just like countless others. "The day we got the news, there were men crying at their desks," one woman who had worked at the plant told the *Baltimore Sun*.

Bourbon suffered the sting of defeat and was in a dark place. But there was one brand representing a light at the end of the tunnel and a comeback. It would ultimately be bourbon's secret weapon.

· CHAPTER SIXTEEN ·

IT TASTES EXPENSIVE

Bill Samuels Jr., "Chairman Emeritus" of the Maker's Mark Distillery in Loretto, Kentucky, grew up among Kentucky legends. He is the godson of Jim Beam, who died in 1947 when Bill was seven years old, and as a teenager he briefly had a job chauffeuring around Colonel Harland Sanders, founder of Kentucky Fried Chicken. As a driver, Bill quickly learned that the colonel had a foul temper after watching him rip a deep fryer from the wall and scream at staff for messing up the secret recipe. Back in the car, the young Bill asked Sanders if the tantrum had really been necessary. "Yes," the colonel calmly told him. "Because now I know that I'll never have to do it again."

"He was a product guy, not a brand guy," Bill told me during one afternoon I spent with him in Louisville. "It was about the coleslaw and the gravy and the chicken."

The story is meant to illustrate the importance of creating a good product before building a brand around it. Bill uses the tale to illustrate the strategy his own family used to build Maker's Mark, one of the most distinctive bourbons on the market. It's sweeter than average, due to the wheat used in the mash bill instead of rye, with heavy accents of vanilla and caramel.

Bill eases into the Maker's story by telling me about another Kentucky legend he knew growing up. In 1951, when Bill was just eleven,

Pappy Van Winkle gave him his first drink of bourbon. It happened as he was tagging along beside his father, Bill Sr., who was meeting with Pappy in his office at Stitzel-Weller just before the elder Samuels started the Maker's Mark brand. As the three prepared to go have lunch, Pappy smiled and promoted the younger Bill to the next rung of manhood by shoving a glass of sloshing brown liquid into his little hands. Then he told him, "We don't go to lunch until after two fingers."

"I didn't know how to drink it," Bill said in a Kentucky drawl that is most noticeable when he swears, which is frequently. Now in his early seventies, everything he says is direct, confident, and punchy. He responded to Pappy by downing the drink in one gulp.

Maker's Mark is one of the few brands that during the 1980s helped launch a turn toward "craft" labels that lifted bourbon out of the doldrums of the 1970s. At the time, the brand was a study in opposites. Other companies were retiring labels amid a crumbling industry, but Maker's was starting one. When others slashed prices, Maker's increased them, then proudly advertised that it was more expensive. Many considered the strategy a kind of brand suicide. Indeed, Maker's failed to significantly profit for more than two decades. Industry insiders assumed the company was just a way for rich hobbyists to kill time.

Then, through luck and happenstance at the dawn of the 1980s, the label found itself setting the tone for the entire industry's revival. By 2015 Maker's would grow into one of the nation's biggest bourbon brands by catering to niche markets fixated on luxury and craft. With that, Maker's Mark wrote the playbook that this century's emerging craft whiskey distilleries have used to design their own strategies. Bill receives multiple calls each week from upstart distillers seeking advice, and is arguably the nascent movement's elder statesman. Of course, by this point Maker's is so big that many have questioned the distillery's "craft" status—making Bill Jr.'s story about KFC even more prophetic—although the bourbon that drove the brand's rise remains relatively unchanged. Confronted by a foodie movement that sometimes values "smallness" simply for the sake of itself, Maker's would in many ways become a victim of its own success, offering lessons for those attempting to follow in its footsteps.

. . .

The Samuels family was one of the many small distilling clans populating Kentucky's Bourbon Belt in the late nineteenth century, and its roots stretch back to the state's early settlers. After Repeal, the T.W. Samuels Distillery was one of the many outfits that ultimately failed to stay open during the consolidation era. The reason, according to Bill, was that it tried to recreate what it had done in the nineteenth century, failing to adapt to the new industry. In other words, it didn't take the path of outfits like Stitzel-Weller, experimenting with new ideas and recipes. Bill's father had wanted to take a new approach, but he was shot down by his own father, Leslie Samuels, who was in charge of the operation. Looking back on advertisements the family ran in 1935, Bill tells me, "God, they were so stupid."

The failure of the T.W. Samuels Distillery bothered Bill Sr. Bill Jr. as a young boy remembers him "whining about" it around the house. His pride was bruised, and the lingering memory became a source of tension in the family, particularly after Bill Sr. retired and was home more. His retirement had come early, after he was forced to sell out of other distillery investments, including one buyout that included rights to the family name. The sale, however, left him money he could use to build another bourbon brand. "He didn't have to work," Bill Jr. says. "He never went to the banks for money . . . it was a personal thing."

The elder Samuels received a considerable amount of help from close friends in the industry. He decided to make a wheated bourbon and Pappy, who was already making bourbon in this style, shared recipes and technical tips (for example, wheat shouldn't be cooked under pressure the way that rye is). Pappy also supplied him with Stitzel-Weller's white dog so that he knew how it should taste after it left the still. Bill Sr. also received yeast samples from friends at Brown-Forman, Jim

Beam, and Heaven Hill. It was the expertise of bourbon's old guard that helped Bill Sr. create something new and "kept him from going down blind alleys," according to his son. The location for Bill Sr.'s business was on the site of an old gristmill and "really was the first 'craft' distillery after Prohibition," Bill told me.

The new distillery started in 1953 and released its first batch of Maker's Mark in 1958. When it hit shelves, Maker's resembled the vanity project Bill Sr. had envisioned. The bottle was unique: square, stout, and dipped in red wax, which made it resemble fancier cognac bottles and distanced the brand from bourbon's downmarket image. It was also relatively expensive, arriving at a time when most bourbon brands were slashing prices. Maker's boldly targeted upmarket audiences, its first ad a two-page spread in the *New Yorker.* You can see a little bit of Bill Sr. in all of this: a defiant maverick who wanted his product to be seen as a principle as much as a product. He was putting it on par with cognac and scotch, which American consumers generally considered more exclusive and sophisticated.

But principle aside, there was very little profit, which came as no surprise for a product that had zero name recognition and was pricey. Its initial output was tiny, sold mainly in the immediate vicinity of the distillery and just profitable enough to keep the company from going under.

During this time, while Maker's Mark was getting started, Bill Jr. received an engineering degree and went to work as a rocket scientist for Aerojet General on the Polaris missile system. When one of his motors failed during a test launch, he was fired. After that, he attended law school at Vanderbilt. He moved back to Kentucky after graduation to work in the family business.

The push-pull dynamic of a headstrong father-son duo was soon to emerge. Bill describes his father as a "products guy" who had managed to engineer a bourbon that was respected by a small community of connoisseurs. But one senses that Bill's notion of success was more expansive—even in his mid-seventies he is restless and energetic, whirling his hands in the air and talking fast, as if his mouth can't keep up with all his ideas. He didn't think the whiskey was living up to its full business potential and that his father wasn't doing enough to push it on people. "His idea of marketing was sit on a rock and wait for Muhammad to come to that mountain," as Bill describes it to me.

The elder Samuels put Bill in charge of finding more customers, and his role eventually grew to include advertising. Bill stayed focused on the class market, and in 1965 Maker's Mark's ran the ad it is still most famous for: "It tastes expensive . . . and is." The ad was a jujitsu move, turning the brand's biggest weakness into its strength. Bourbon doesn't have to be expensive to be good, but Maker's realized that this concept is lost on a consumer culture programmed to reflexively equate quality with price. They shrewdly didn't push prices too high, though. Today it still generally retails for around thirty dollars and is very much an affordable luxury.

During the 1970s the brand slowly grew, from about six barrels per day up to nineteen barrels over the course of the decade. It was still small, but its growth coincided with a budding food movement around American culinary originals. In 1971, Alice Waters opened Chez Panisse in Berkeley, California, and around that same time *New York Times* food writer Craig Claiborne began championing "lost classics" from regions such as the Deep South. The message was one of getting "back to basics" and seemed aimed at the Space Age food crazes of the previous decade: Tang, TV dinners, astronaut ice cream. Slowly people began making the switch from iceberg lettuce to arugula, setting trends that would ultimately come to define bourgeois dining in the United States.

Tapping into this movement, Bill Jr.'s real masterstroke was his ability to get Maker's onto airline beverage carts. People would try it for the first time while traveling, then ask for it at their local liquor stores, creating national demand. In 1980, the airline strategy caught the attention of *Wall Street Journal* reporter David Garino, who published an article headlined "Maker's Mark Goes Against the Grain to Make Its Mark" on the newspaper's front page. The article explained how the rural distillery was an anomaly that was finding success through a strategy that most people would consider missteps.

The story was a game changer. It sparked an avalanche of orders the distillery could barely fill, marking the beginning of double-digit growth over the next two decades.

Bill is regularly given credit for shrewdly evaluating public taste and steering Maker's to its present success, but he simply credits it to lucky timing. What he does take credit for is that other bourbon makers followed suit by starting to sell upmarketed products. "Looking at our accident," he explains, "the market caught on." In 1984, the Ancient Age Distillery* (known as Buffalo Trace since 1999) released Blanton's, a single-barrel brand and a standout. The success of Maker's was certainly an inspiration, as was the rising popularity of single-malt scotches, which were what encouraged the use of the word "single" in the new offering (the term "single barrel" technically isn't regulated, and some supposedly single-barrel brands are actually mingled from multiple barrels, for consistency's sake, but most of the reliable brands note on the bottle the precise barrel the liquor came from). In 1992, Jim Beam responded to the new market by creating its excellent "small batch" collection: Knob Creek, Basil Hayden's, Booker's, and Baker's. ("Small batch" refers to a brand whose flavor profile is created with a collection of barrels that is smaller than normal. Like "single barrel," the term technically isn't regulated and can be used on any bottle.)

Slowly, increased sales of "premium" bourbons to niche markets started to boost the profits of bourbon makers. However, sales of classic mid-tier brands—Old Forester, Wild Turkey, Evan Williams—remained relatively flat. There was a bourbon revival of sorts, but it wasn't a tide that lifted all boats. The old stalwarts might have been excellent, but they were also reminders of bourbon's blue-collar past during an era obsessed with luxury and exclusivity—the U.S. economy eased out of recession in 1983, and the trend for super-premium bourbon exploded around the same time that the movie *Wall Street* hit theaters. A big part of this new demand originated not from the United States but from Japan, where the economy was also surging and where whiskies, both scotch and bourbon, were

---

*Ancient Age operated on the plot of land once used by Frankfort Distillers, one of the outfits with a medicinal whiskey clause during Prohibition.

popular. Single-barrel brands sold for over $100 across the Pacific, which was a price no bourbon—not even a super-premium offering—could yet command at home.

In his 1980 *Wall Street Journal* article, David Garino had also noted that potential buyers of Maker's Mark were "drooling on the sidelines." Bill Sr., however, insisted the brand should remain independent. Nevertheless, one year later the drinks giant Hiram Walker bought the company. It was a wholly owned subsidiary, operating mostly as it always had, but was now technically part of one of the industry's biggest corporations. After that, it drifted from corporate umbrella to corporate umbrella, as brands under consolidated umbrellas tend to do. British drinks giant Allied Domecq acquired Hiram Walker in 1987, and eventually sold Maker's Mark to Fortune Brands, a giant holding company that by this point was also the owner of Jim Beam. In 2011, Fortune Brands split and all the liquor that had once resided under it became part of what was known as Beam Inc. In 2014, Beam Inc. was purchased by the Japanese whiskey giant Suntory and became known as Beam Suntory. This is where Maker's Mark now resides.

· · ·

In 2010, Maker's Mark sold one million cases for the first time. That, coupled with its residency within a multibillion-dollar corporation, has caused it to lose some of the craft appeal that originally drove its success. In 2014, the brand was actually pulled from a couple of trendy and well-known whiskey bars in Louisville and New York, Maker's Mark master distiller Greg Davis told me. This means nothing in sales for the company now, but it is important for image, which can drive future sales. Speaking as the craftsman of a brand that has remained largely unchanged over the years, Davis confided that the pullouts definitely "hurt the soul a little bit." Bill's thoughts on the matter were similar: "We work hard to keep Maker's a product rather than a brand, and it's very hard. . . . We're not as cool as we used to be, but we're *so* authentic," he said.

Around 2010, some of the earlier craft darlings of the modern whiskey renaissance, distilleries like Stranahan's in Colorado and Tuthilltown in New York, which makes the Hudson line of whiskies, began flirting with outside investors. This led to the inevitable question of whether or not these companies should still be considered "craft," even though the potential buyouts wouldn't immediately change their size or day-to-day operations. In terms of image, a buyout requires careful navigation. Bill Sr. in 1980 told the *Wall Street Journal* that his company should remain independent, then sold out to Hiram Walker one year later, the kind of move that undermines a brand's credibility with connoisseurs but can also launch its success into the stratosphere by allowing access to better distribution channels and a bigger marketing budget. Attracting the investment needed for growth while cultivating an image of creative independence promises to be a looming issue for any new distillery navigating the touchy politics of today's foodscape. When I ask Bill how this will affect distilleries of the nascent craft whiskey renaissance, he responds with a blunt reality of American business. "Oh, they're all being built to sell out," he says with a shrug.

The task of determining a company's true craft bona fides is also inhibited by the fact that the term "craft" has no definition. The expression is unregulated and can be used by marketers however they see fit. Since most consumers instinctively think of products bearing a "craft" label as handmade, locally produced goods where supposedly better quality justifies a higher price, this means companies freely use the term as a marketing tool. Smallness (intimate, personal, Jeffersonian) will forever hold an appeal that bigness (distant, impersonal, Hamiltonian) does not. While announcing a new line of whiskey at an investor meeting in 2013, Larry Schwartz, president of Diageo North America, which is part of the world's biggest spirits producer, said, "We're going to be the number one craft distiller in North American whiskey in the U.S."

Schwartz's statement confirmed that the term "craft" is little more than an ambiguous buzzword. Diageo makes fine whiskies, but its status as the world's biggest maker of whiskey almost certainly contradicts most people's interpretation of "craft." The American Distilling Institute, the trade organization that represents America's smallest distillers, has attempted to put boundaries around the term by defining it as producing less than one hundred thousand proof gallons per year. This definition, however, is equally meaningless, because it pegs the term to size and not quality. Many small companies make horrible whiskey and many big companies make excellent whiskey, leaving consumers in the lurch if they want to use "craft" as a measure of quality. (Instead of defining "craft," a transparency rating would be more helpful. Higher scores would go to outfits that divulge technical information, such as production methods. This way, customers could form their own evaluations using hard data rather than marketing jargon.)

And while small, tailored operations hold unique advantages for many endeavors, we forget that some industries benefit from bigness. Take the car company Cadillac, which in the 1930s billed its cars as hand-built luxury goods—these "craft" cars were expensive and notorious for needing constant repairs. It took General Motors engineer Nicholas Dreystadt to drop cost and improve quality by implementing production standards and economies of scale utilized by other auto manufacturers. In this case, the benefits of mass production and scale were clear, but the argument for them rarely transfers to food—homemade jams, pickles, and cheese are almost always better. Made in small quantities, with a close eye and control over quality and ingredients, small wins almost every time.

But whiskey stands apart from other foods in that it sometimes contradicts the rule that size matters. The size of a still, big or small, pot or column, has far less impact on a whiskey's quality than the skill and know-how of the distiller operating it. In terms of aging, holding enormous volumes of spirits is another distinct advantage. Since every barrel matures a little differently, having a vast palette of barrels to mingle together to achieve brand consistency is another undeniable asset, and one that small distilleries struggle with. Many distilleries, big and small, source grains from common suppliers, but the bigger companies often receive volume discounts. Even if a small distiller used inferior ingredients (most don't), they would still be forced to sell their product at a higher price because of their smaller economies of scale and higher relative overhead.

In all these cases, larger scales lower costs and achieve consistency without necessarily sacrificing quality. As long as a company is devoted to achieving a certain standard, and stays focused on the process, the size of an operation is irrelevant. This is why distilleries like Wild Turkey and Buffalo Trace are able to make bourbon that is vastly superior to that made by many of their smaller competitors, and still priced for less. Ironically, the part of the process most responsible for how a whiskey tastes—around 60 percent of flavor, in the estimate of most distillers—involves the least amount of work: pouring a spirit into a barrel and simply waiting for it to be ready.

Perhaps the reason why whiskey confounds the expectations we hold for most foods is because it is both agricultural and industrial. Today we tend to think of these things as competing forces, but whiskey combines the two: it starts as a grain in a field, then is heavily processed by machines. In all parts of the world where whiskey has flourished, it did so in the wake of an Industrial Revolution that transformed economies from agricultural to industrial while political leaders like Thomas Jefferson and Alexander Hamilton debated about what all the changes meant. For a time, Americans considered industry compatible with agriculture, revolutionizing farming in helpful ways that freed the masses from the toil of fieldwork. Many whiskey brands up until the mid-twentieth century boasted that their distilleries were industrial factories. In the 1940s, Hiram Walker even commissioned the artist Thomas Hart Benton for a series of advertisements reminiscent of images from the TV series *Industry on Parade*.

But industry in America eventually overshadowed agriculture. In 1870, close to 70 percent of Americans were employed in farming, the number falling to 2 percent by the twenty-first century. The toil of field work was replaced by assembly lines, and then by the drudgery of desk work. As American rural life moved into the margins, whiskey advertising, forever drawing on nostalgia, put aside the Thomas Hart Benton advertisements of industrial efficiency and revived romantic visions of an agrarian past. Today, words like "heirloom" and "heritage" have taken on the marketing power that words like "purity" once held, when its use on whiskey labeling was debated during the passage of food and drug reforms. The sexiest of today's newest distillers, calling themselves "grain to glass" producers, proudly brag that they grow their own grains, usually in a field behind the distillery (imagine a yeoman farmer making the same boast as his neighbors stand around wondering why that's a big deal).

Agriculture is important to understanding one part of bourbon's nature, but if we truly want to understand whiskey we must also think of it as an industrial product. The British writer Andrew Jefford put it best when talking about his beloved scotch: "It may be disagreeable to most whisky lovers, then, but it is hard to reach any conclusion other than that a modern bottle of whisky is, like a can of cola, a post-agricultural triumph whose ideals are more industrial than agricultural," he writes. "Whisky aroma and flavor are overwhelmingly a consequence of the processing of those raw ingredients (malting, brewing, distillation, wood aging) rather than the ingredients themselves." Whiskey, Jefford concluded, was more a product of "manufacturing techniques and brand-building endeavor than of earth, stone, and sky."

But even when whiskey confounds expectations—big versus small, agricultural versus industrial—perceptions drive reality. Consumers inevitably value the sense of intimacy found in smallness or the simplicity found in agrarian life, even if those things are just illusions. Does it really matter if a distiller grows his or her own grains or is using antiquated equipment? The only way to judge is through a blindfolded tasting.

The bourbon in a bottle of Maker's Mark might have changed very little as the company grew, but opinions of the brand are nonetheless influenced by outside factors—it's yet another reminder that we taste with our minds as much as our senses. People are loyal to brands, but often wary of the corporations that own them. Some longtime drinkers of Maker's suspect that the pressure to meet increased demand and to grow as a company have caused the company to lower the bourbon's age a bit since the 1980s, which is something that's hard to know for sure because Maker's doesn't carry an age statement.* In 2013, those pressures became public when Maker's Mark cut its proof from 90 to 84 in an effort to boost its supplies. The decision came under Bill Jr.'s son Rob, who took control of Maker's in 2011. In a press release, the company told customers that they wouldn't be able to tell a difference.

Maker's customers were livid, flooding the company with angry responses. For a brand that built its reputation as a connoisseur's drink, playing to the sensibilities of people who pride themselves on being able to detect such differences, Maker's decision was surprisingly tone-deaf. Within a week, Maker's Mark reversed the decision and issued an apology. "We totally got it wrong. . . . You spoke. We listened." Rob Samuels later told reporters that the company's customers "would rather put up with the occasional supply shortage than put up with any change in their hand-made bourbon."

The strong response from customers revealed the brand's marketing effectiveness: people had reacted as if Maker's Mark were their own private whiskey company, forgetting that no such personal relationship actually exists and that the company is part of a cutthroat industry designed to make money. Maker's Mark had broken the spell of its own mythology by undermining the sense of intimacy it had so carefully crafted. When Jack Daniel's—much less of a connoisseur's quaff than Maker's—made a similar decision to drop proof a few years earlier, there wasn't a peep from customers.

Bill's mood noticeably changes when I mention Suntory, the Japanese whiskey company that bid to buy Beam Inc., the parent company of Maker's Mark, for $16 billion in early 2014 (a week before our afternoon together). The announcement sparked a flood of xenophobic outrage in the United States as people interpreted the move as a loss of treasured American icons to a foreign power. Most didn't realize that by this point in history, half of the eight big companies that control nearly every drop of American whiskey are owned by corporations

---

* Since Maker's Mark rotates its barrels during aging, a laborious measure not adopted by most companies, its whiskey ages a little differently than most brands, thus the absence of an age statement.

headquartered overseas. It's the reality of the world economy, and many U.S.-based liquor companies likewise own many foreign brands (for instance, Beam-owned Courvoisier cognac, a treasured French icon that features a lock of Napoleon's hair in its visitor center). But regardless of who owns what, the 1964 resolution mandates that bourbon can only be made in America, keeping domestic jobs secure. This point was lost on many, and Bill called the outcry from angry Americans a bunch of "bullshit."

Japan has a deep and abiding love for whiskey.* The nation first started building its own whiskey industry after World War I, modeled after the scotch world. The drink wasn't popular at first, but was reinvented after World War II as the glamorous drink of the occupiers. Slowly, the industry matured and today Japanese spirits are coveted by whiskey geeks the world over. In many cases, the companies that make them carry reputations for focusing on the product more than on marketing. "It's reverential. They geek out on it," Bill said. "When you go to their distilleries, it's like going to church." In contrast, he said the American approach was focused more on "instant gratification." Under Suntory's ownership, Maker's Mark would no longer be publicly traded, meaning shareholders' short-term views of profitability and their obsession over quarterly returns would be less likely to undermine what is a long-term business. "Goddamn, I wish we had had them twenty-five years ago," Bill said about Suntory, welcoming the change and acknowledging the kind of pressures inevitably faced by companies that have given up some of their independence under corporate buyouts. Fortunately for Maker's, Japanese spirits companies have an excellent track record. For example, under Kirin's ownership, Four Roses has regained the reputation it lost under Seagram's control; products made by France's Louis Royer Cognac have improved under Suntory's influence; and likewise, Suntory's ownership of scotch legend Morrison Bowmore has generally been good for the company. These are all strong

---

* Even by 2014, with overall whiskey sales up in the United States, Four Roses, Wild Turkey, and Buffalo Trace continued to make super-premium bourbons exclusively for the Japanese market, unavailable to Americans stateside.

indicators that Suntory might actually respect the product integrity of Maker's Mark bourbon more than a publicly traded U.S. company that feels greater pressure to reap short-term profits.

But even though the Japanese whiskey companies excel at making good products, Bill Jr. thought they were weak on marketing. "They are *totally* ineffective at making those products into international brands," he said. As far as Japanese whiskey brands in the United States were concerned, "*nobody* knows about them," Bill said with a shrug. "They could benefit from having some of this ruthless U.S. marketing competency laid against their wonderful products."

In this way, two empires become one.

. . .

With bourbon's revival Maker's Mark has become a celebrity alongside a few other star brands. As the excitement reached a fever pitch in the century's first decade, a few of those celebrities turned into divas. None is more famed than Pappy Van Winkle, which is sold in fifteen, twenty, and twenty-three-year-old expressions. After the brand was created in the early 1990s, it often went ignored, but eventually became so famous it was given its own clothing line and appearances on popular TV shows. The brand's popularity has even spurred a black market, where empty bottles sold online can be filled with far less expensive bourbons that taste surprisingly similar (like some of the W.L. Weller brands) and resold for three or four digits. In 2013, a dramatic heist of Pappy cases at Buffalo Trace, where it is made, sparked national headlines.

Bill Samuels Jr. grew up around Pappy Van Winkle but rolls his eyes at the craze surrounding the brand that is named after the man. "I've never tasted a twenty-year-old whiskey I could drink, because it's just all wood, it's all tannins. But you get your mind adjusted—'I paid all this money, I gotta like it,'" he said. The comment illustrates two oft-forgotten truths of bourbon: that much of the connoisseurship is all in our heads, and that some of the most celebrated brands, despite the buzz surrounding them, aren't necessarily worth the effort.

Bill's attitude is echoed among various other members of the bourbon cognoscenti, who have long considered the popularity behind many of these "oak bomb" bourbons more a product of hype than of craft. Behind closed doors, master distillers often describe bourbons in the range of twenty years old as having a taste similar to "sucking on a pencil," an expression that many of them are fond of using. They quickly point out that bourbons that old are often coveted simply for their relative rarity. The Pappy line manages to avoid this pitfall—it is clearly aged in very mild parts of the warehouse—but nonetheless falls far short of the hype surrounding it. Scores of other brands, most of them easier to find and far less expensive, match or surpass the Pappy labels. Nevertheless, the reality of Pappy is beside the point—what is far more interesting than its flavor is how it arrived at its lofty perch and helped create a new dimension of bourbon marketing.

Julian Van Winkle III created the brand named after his grandfather in the early 1990s. At the time, Americans had little interest in old bourbon and he was easily able to procure leftover glut stocks from the Stitzel-Weller and Old Boone distilleries, both of which were now shuttered. By the early 2000s the old stocks Van Winkle was sourcing from were running low and the brand was preserved when Buffalo Trace agreed to make a very similar version of it under contract. Bottles originally cost in the range of fifty to seventy dollars, which was the high end of what anybody would really pay for a bourbon. For that reason, bottles of Pappy usually lingered on liquor store shelves collecting dust.

Then, around 2007, Pappy blew up after receiving several relatively high ratings from liquor marketing services such as the Beverage Testing Institute. By 2011 it had become the "ultimate cult brand," according to *Fortune* magazine. When the magazine asked Julian Van Winkle III to explain how he had created it, he replied that it was built through a "strategy of scarcity." Each year, roughly seven thousand cases were released, just enough to get it nationwide attention with a few bottles in most of the country's higher-end liquor stores. It had presence, but not so much as to undermine its own sense of exclusivity. This careful positioning, combined with a catchy name and the flashy age statements, put Pappy into the marketing sweet spot bound to attract the celebrity chefs, food writers, and other various apparatchiks of the foodie-industrial complex who are responsible for converting their fetishes into national obsessions. After that, Pappy passed into the vocabulary of people who might not know a single other bourbon brand but at least knew that one and wanted to try it.

Everything had come together perfectly. Bottles of Pappy became nearly unobtainable—finding one required hard-earned connections at the liquor store and a pile of cash. During the times of year when Pappy was released, those lucky enough to get a bottle lit up social media to proudly boast of their prize. Pappy became a quintessential bauble of bourgeois bling, akin to what Porsches were to New York stockbrokers in the 1980s and rare tulip bulbs to Dutch merchants in the 1600s. Everybody knew Pappy's price, but few knew its value, save for Julian Van Winkle III. Thanks to the three-tier system, he watched much of the money people were paying for his brand go to middlemen merchants. When the *Wall Street Journal* asked him about the astronomical prices people were paying, he just replied, "If they're dumb enough to pay that much, that's their prerogative."*

The Pappy phenomenon helped create a new kind of top-shelf bourbon. Up until that point, the whiskey industry had divided brands into three categories: premium, high-end premium, and super premium, distinctions based entirely around price and branding rather than production methods. Between 2000 and 2013, sales of the first two categories, which include classic old brands such as Wild Turkey, Old Forester, Maker's Mark, and Four Roses, only increased by about 17 percent as a group, whereas sales of super-premium brands—anything priced above about fifty dollars—increased by almost 90 percent, according to DISCUS data. People wanted brands they perceived as exclusive, as the Pappy craze indicated, and the market responded predictably: new brands increasingly priced themselves for the higher shelves, even if they didn't always deserve to be there.

The trend was quickly noticed. In a 2013 interview, one market analyst told *Whisky Advocate* that top-end whiskies were increasingly

---

* Because of the three-tier system, high prices for certain brands are often set by retailers rather than producers.

marketed to people who were simply rich, rather than true connoisseurs. As a result, the quality of the highest-price offerings had slid as a group because their new customer base was less likely to realize when the product didn't live up to the price tag. Many of these high-priced whiskies were still excellent, but there was indeed a notable uptick in the number of lukewarm reviews they received in knowledgeable ratings publications.

As always, marketing filled the gaps between what people thought they were getting and what they were actually getting. In the 1950s, the *New York Times* had pointed out the tactic of upmarketing whiskey through fancier glass bottling in an article headlined "Can't Improve Whiskey, So Distillers Turn to Its Container." A half century later, the tactics became more sophisticated. In 2013, Michter's created a new category of whiskey, one it called "ultra-premium," when it released its Celebration Sour Mash brand. It was $4,000 per bottle, the highest retail price in history for an American whiskey. The price was arbitrary, but by setting it so high Michter's was able to grab media attention that doubled as free advertising from the kind of magazines—*Robb Report*, *Elite Traveller*, and so on—found littered about airport business-class lounges. By offering Celebration Sour Mash as a "limited edition" release, Michter's also employed a marketing tactic bourbon drinkers were finding more common since the 1990s, one that created urgency by suggesting scarcity, pushing customers to buy a bottle before the apparently "limited" supply ran out.

Was Celebration Sour Mash worth it? That was hard to tell. The brand was sourced, and when connoisseurs asked for specifics—the who, what, when, where, why, and how of what was actually inside the bottle—Michter's skirted the issue by citing "confidentiality agreements," a common industry response that, while legally binding, also allows companies to hide a bourbon's provenance and details (preventing customers from finding the identical spirit offered for a lower price under a different label). Hidden in the roar of press about the world's most expensive bourbon were the faint voices of savvy whiskey bloggers and other industry watchers. They quickly pointed out the shrewd marketing mechanics behind Celebration Sour Mash and gave the brand nicknames like "Billionaires' Bourbon" and "Fool's Gold."

Of course, marketing to people with money to burn is nothing new. Companies had offered "exclusive" brands even when bourbon was a staunchly blue-collar drink and the industry was cratering in the 1960s and '70s. But even so, those predecessors—such as Stitzel-Weller's Very Old Fitzgerald and a line extension called Very Very Old Fitzgerald—rarely cost more than two or three times the average. Even Maker's Mark, which famously advertised, "It tastes expensive . . . and is," was only a few dollars pricier than its downmarket competition.

The astronomical prices behind brands like Pappy and Michter's Celebration Sour Mash are partly driven by increased demand, but they are also a result of "irrational exuberance," the term that former Federal Reserve chairman Alan Greenspan used to describe how overvalued markets led to the dot-com bubble of the 1990s and the world financial meltdown of 2008. Longtime whiskey drinkers regularly complain that the Pappyification of bourbon is causing a pricing and buying arms race leading to market bubbles.

The whiskey market always has and always will undergo ups and downs. Brokers in the nineteenth century created volatile boom-and-bust cycles when they traded whiskey as a commodity. The bullish whiskey market of the early twenty-first century is merely a reflection of its own era, as consumers attempt to capitalize on bourbon's resurgent popularity by trading bottles at events like the Universal Whisky Experience in Las Vegas. After reading about new "exclusive" or other hard-to-find releases on the Internet, collectors buy and stockpile bottles with the hope of flipping them after they increase in value.* These vast collections of whiskey stockpiled in closets and basements have

---

*Whiskey companies sometimes exacerbate these impulsive cycles by speaking broadly of "whiskey shortages." These announcements often come during the times of year when whiskey sales are traditionally low (such as summer), and can help boost sales by generating urgency. What tends to go unexplained is that the "shortages" are usually very temporary, for brands that are on allocation (meaning that individual distribution networks are allocated a specific amount of a certain brand for a set time period). But even though a certain brand might be unavailable for this temporary period, there will still be plenty of other labels to choose from, easing the worries of drinkers concerned about a potential drought.

been nicknamed "bourbon bunkers." Here bottles sit in sad loneliness, waiting for somebody to drink them instead of checking their prices against auction indexes. The death of one renowned collector in 2013 created shock waves among whiskey hoarders when people realized that the departed hadn't been able to take his collection of more than a thousand bottles with him into the afterlife. Collectors swarmed the auction at which his wife decided to dump them, ensuring that the bottles would remain unopened and unenjoyed. *Whisky Advocate* called the emerging scene a "paradigm shift" for whiskey. Other die-hard whiskey fans worried that bourbon was becoming a snob's drink.

Either way, the phenomenon offered a new chapter in bourbon's story, and perhaps a glimpse into a corner of its future. Bourbon will forever prove the old maxim that it's life simple pleasures that matter most, but the smoke and mirrors of creative marketing and misinformed hype sometimes upends that truth. Whenever that's the case, it's worth remembering that the Bourbon dynasty of France, the ultimate source of the spirit's name, was toppled after it became an inbred and calcified aristocracy that lost touch with its people. We'll know we've reached a similar point when we hear the cry, "Let them drink Pappy!"

But enough melodrama. When I first mentioned Pappy to Bill Samuels Jr. during our afternoon together, he rolled his eyes at a drink he described as doing strange things to people's minds. But he also had another point he wanted to make about the brand: "Even though [Pappy's handlers] don't make whiskey, and all those details that are supposed to matter, people are buying it, and they're happy," he said. Then he smiled and put a finer point on what his business is about: "Anything that aggrandizes what Kentucky has a monopoly on, is a good thing."

· CHAPTER SEVENTEEN ·

ANOTHER SECOND ACT

America is experiencing a second Whiskey Rebellion. This century, the number of craft distilleries in the United States has mushroomed from just a handful in 2000 to almost six hundred by 2015, aided by the loosening of state and local laws that had previously restricted small-scale distilling. The phenomenon carries the distinct feel of the "locavore" movement that has already revolutionized beer and wine culture.

The rise of craft movements in the United States, food or otherwise, often seem like a response to the sense that Hamilton's vision is outweighing Jefferson's. The relative strengths and weaknesses of each side rely on one another for equilibrium, yet it seems like the nation's destiny is pooling into the hands of just a few corporations and banks. Ever fewer Americans are truly their own bosses. Scott Harris, who runs Catoctin Creek Distillery in Purcellville, Virginia, alongside his wife, Becky, summed up the attitude of many upstart distilleries when he told me why he got into distilling: he said he wanted to build something of his own, and that to do it he had gladly ditched the beige cubicles of a government contractor job where he had been making "ungodly sums of money."

Food has become one of the ways we have chosen to battle the creeping trend of consolidation and homogenization. Historically, food has usually been a chore. Over the course of the twentieth century, America minimized the nuisance by churning out increasingly processed foods to save time: TV dinners, powdered breakfast shakes, precut vegetables resembling something off an assembly line. But looking back on the numbing effects of what these changes in our eating habits represent, many Americans have decided to change course. They have decided to make food a pleasure again, a therapeutic release that can be used to escape the stresses of modern life and reconnect with friends and family. The very names of the Slow Food and locavore movements declare a crusade to slow things down and move them closer to home. The do-it-yourself aesthetic of these campaigns suggests they intend to shift things back to individuals and restore proper balance to life. The boom in new distilleries is a part of this, a way to take back control, achieve independence, and satisfy a desire to tinker.

The few large companies that dominate America's whiskey scene make good products, but two centuries of consolidation have made their handful of winning formulas narrow examples of whiskey styles that used to be more diverse. What was once a sprawling road trip down America's highways and byways—and through the occasional grimy alley—became a short jaunt through a couple of counties in Kentucky before hopping over the border into Tennessee.

America's new distillers promise to reintroduce variety. Corsair Distillery in Nashville is at the forefront of America's "alt-whiskey" movement, meaning whiskies made with unconventional ingredients (buckwheat, quinoa, all-wheat mashes) and aging techniques. Corsair's Triple Smoke label uses barley malted in three different ways (with smoke from cherrywood, peat, and beechwood) and it's a distinctly American take on smoky scotch styles of whiskey. The Citra Double IPA uses hops in the distillation process and has a long, constantly evolving finish—it's the whiskey version of Willy Wonka's Everlasting Gobstopper. Another style that Corsair calls "Grainiac" uses nine different grains, including spelt. As of 2015, new distilleries in the United States still only produced less than 5 percent of American spirits— compared to the eight companies controlling the other 95 percent—but the exciting nature of their endeavors would give them press coverage far out of proportion to their actual output. Established distilleries like Buffalo Trace and Jim Beam quickly noticed, and both would start experimenting more—Jim Beam in 2014 announced plans to release spirits made from triticale (a rye/wheat hybrid), brown rice, and rolled oats.

Of course, vanguard new whiskey styles such as those made by Corsair aren't as new as they first seem. Their roots reach back to the experimentation exhibited in distilling manuals from the late eighteenth and early nineteenth centuries, when Americans gladly fermented whatever ingredients lay at hand and threw them into a still to see how they turned out. Corsair doesn't make a bourbon for wide release—established distilleries already do this style well. Instead, the distillery focuses on making something different, a strategy that's probably its best chance at success. David Pickerell, the former master distiller at Maker's Mark who would go on to consult for many new upstart distilleries, calls Corsair's strategy the "spaghetti-on-the-wall approach," meaning, "Just throw a bunch of ideas on the wall and see what sticks."

Nor is this strategy all that new—it is in fact how bourbon got its start. As the distiller Harrison Hall pointed out in 1811, coastal Americans were initially skeptical of the West's corn-based whiskey. Many Europeans before that called corn a grain "fit only for beasts." But all were eventually convinced, and bourbon would become the undisputed king of American whiskey. Pickerell's "spaghetti-on-the-wall" comment also hints at another reality of wildly experimental entrepreneurial startups: there is a lot of failure. Despite Corsair's successes, the taste of its Quinoa Whiskey conjures up a sense of wet dust, and its Wry Moon label is equally unpleasant. Nevertheless, the sheer audacity of the distillery's ambition and its guts to try these new things is still thrilling—the efforts are always interesting, if not always worth revisiting.

Regardless of the occasional missteps, many of America's new distilleries have already mastered gin, rum, and other spirits that require little or no aging. But there is one success that has largely eluded them: bourbon. Making exceptional bourbon requires the better part of a decade, which is an eternity for a craft distiller on a shoestring budget.

With other spirits or beer, craft producers can make hundreds of batches, working out any kinks, in the time that it takes to make one batch of bourbon or any of the more traditional styles of whiskey.

Unfortunately, avoiding the time crunch tempts many new distillers to rely on questionable methods that threaten to undermine their "craft" status as quality producers and jeopardize their potential to truly improve American whiskey. The most obvious of these is the common and long-standing practice of simply relabeling whiskey from a bigger supplier and marking up the price. This is acceptable as long as companies are open about it, but many try to disguise this fact. Whiskey geeks, channeling the spirits of consumer protection heroes like E. H. Taylor Jr. and Harvey Wiley, have attempted to step in and help overburdened federal regulators keep up with violations that have slipped through the cracks. In 2014, at the TTB's request, a group of whiskey enthusiasts on one social media site even supplied to the government a list of almost thirty violations of CFR Section 5.36(d), requiring that brands note distillation location on the label. Some of the infractions seemed like the honest mistakes of new companies learning the ropes of a heavily bureaucratized industry, while others appeared suspiciously like deliberate attempts to convey misleading impressions.

The other way to avoid the time crunch is by making what could be described as "insta-whiskey." Some upstart distilleries claim that the use of smaller barrels, wood chips, ultrasound machines, or pressure cookers age their whiskies in months rather than years. These methods have limited potential, but their use is problematic in an industry that so heavily emphasizes tradition and high standards. Because the craft distilling movement can sometimes resemble the heady days of the early dot-com boom, drinkers who balk at the use of controversial aging shortcuts are sometimes accused of resisting progress, of failing to see the future. But perhaps we should look to the past for a glimpse at the future, and remember that companies that have already made claims about quick-aging—such as Publicker in the 1930s—never had very good reputations and ultimately went out of business. Experimentation and innovation are always laudable, but cheap shortcuts masquerading as such things are still just cheap shortcuts.

In 2009, a man named Tom Lix created a brand called Cleveland Whiskey. He claimed he had made, in just six months, a whiskey that tasted as if it were aged ten years. The basics of his process were simple. He purchased new whiskey from outside suppliers, then dumped the spirits into stainless steel tanks along with barrels chopped into small pieces. The whiskey was pressure-cooked into the wood chunks like a sponge. Soak, squeeze, repeat. Co-opting the language of Silicon Valley, he called his process a "disruptive technology" and promoted the brand with T-shirts that read, "Screw Tradition."

Normally, six-month old whiskey is pale, but Cleveland Whiskey is black as coffee. The nose is sweet but with a kind of chemical aroma— almost like a garbage bag full of sugar that has melted in a microwave— and is plagued by the worst qualities of both extremely young and extremely old whiskey: hot grain notes alongside the kind of eye-wateringly bitter tannins you might get from boiling a tea bag for hours. Lix sometimes urges drinkers to compare his whiskey with Knob Creek, a brand that is far less expensive but aged for close to an actual decade, rather than six months in a pressure cooker.

According to Lix, sales of his whiskey are good in Cleveland. This is no doubt due to the loyalty of a local community wanting to support one of its own, per the rules of a locavore movement that instinctively roots for the hometown team even if it's not a champion. However, when people outside of Cleveland first start trying the whiskey, the reaction is less polite. In reviews, drinkers treat Lix as brutally as he himself treats the dismembered barrels dumped into his whiskey. Chuck Cowdery, a longtime contributor to *Whisky Advocate* and *Whisky Magazine,* wrote on his blog—where such writers' insights are usually more colorful than they are in the magazines—that Lix's "Frankensteinian" process was a "strangler-of-babies-in-their-cradles." Cowdery then harangued against national media outlets NPR and *Forbes,* which had covered Lix's company under the approved narrative that it was a courageous smallholder shaking up an old-fashioned industry through innovation. "Nobody tells the emperor he's buck naked," Cowdery complained. That was the real story.

Cowdery's comment about Lix's whiskey and media coverage of it underscored another trait of America's emerging whiskey renaissance: most are hesitant to disparage underdogs they naturally want to support, even if the whiskey is subpar. The backlash against Cleveland Whiskey also made another message clear: neither producers nor consumers are done a favor when a whiskey's obvious flaws are overlooked in favor of an inspiring backstory. Craft whiskey won't rise to its true potential unless drinkers stay focused on, and truly honest about, the liquid in the glass and nothing else.

Of course, Cleveland Whiskey is an extreme example. A more common aging shortcut is the use of small barrels, a method that's problematic but has shown potential when used in moderation. By increasing the amount of surface area coming into contact with the whiskey, the use of ten- or fifteen-gallon barrels has given insta-whiskies the same dark color and much of the sweetness as whiskey aged for years in conventional barrels. However, small barrels often fail to temper the coarse, moonshiney qualities of young whiskey. They tend to simply cover up undesirable qualities, rather than transform them the way that large barrels do. Though a small-barrel-aged whiskey might have gained sweet notes of vanilla from a quick blast of wood extraction, it often carries a nose reminiscent of cut plywood or the smell one might associate with the inside of a Home Depot outlet, a sure sign that little esterification has occurred. Sometimes this youth can have a pleasing vitality—similar to the freshness of a Beaujolais or other kind of wine meant to be enjoyed young—but the lack of other parts of the maturation process often undermine the kind of complexity that keeps the whiskey interesting until you reach the bottom of the glass.

Even so, some new distilleries claim that small-barrel aging allows them to cultivate flavors they are specifically seeking. It's a reminder that taste is subjective, as well as that whiskey distillers, dating back to the days of nineteenth-century drummers, always promote and rationalize whatever it is they're selling. But with that said, Catoctin Creek makes a pleasing rye that is aged in thirty-five-gallon barrels, only slightly smaller than the fifty-three-gallon standard. Even at a young age—less than two years—the whiskey's grain notes balance nicely with the wood. Balcones, a small Texas distillery, has produced some intriguing young whiskies aged with both small and large barrels (meaning that the whiskey is transferred at some point, which helps limit some of the properties that typically plague small-barrel aging).

Nevertheless, most insta-whiskies are expensive, made by small companies with relatively high overhead and low economies of scale. Their price tags threaten to prevent them from ever becoming more than one-time novelty purchases for drinkers caught in craft whiskey's early glow. When the whiskey market is good, everything flies off the shelves, but when it inevitably dips, as it has always done, other business fundamentals will matter. Because of this, many new distilleries quietly admit that they plan on eventually upgrading to traditional barrels. Small barrels only allow them to save money by getting whiskey out the door faster, not because they are cheaper. (Surprisingly, there isn't much of a price difference between small and large barrels. Also, because small barrels use more wood relative to liquid, they are arguably worse for the environment.) Not only do large barrels provide more complexity—if one can afford the time—they provide economies of scale that help distilleries lower costs as they grow. And if there is one eternal truth of the whiskey industry, it is that cost always matters.

But regardless of whether or not unconventional aging techniques create good whiskey, there is no doubt they create valuable hype. When Tuthilltown Spirits in Gardiner, New York, opened in 2006, thumping bass music made the distillery resemble a dance rave. Visitors learned that the music gently helped vibrate whiskey into the wood of the small barrels the distillery uses. The approach was gimmicky but nonetheless grabbed the attention of reporters in nearby New York City, who helped turn Tuthilltown's line of Hudson whiskies into an early darling of the craft whiskey movement. The only thing missing from the stories about the distillery—which followed the predictable format of championing a couple of likable entrepreneurs—was a critical and honest evaluation of the rather mediocre whiskey that struggled to justify its astronomical price.

Tuthilltown blew up with the speed of a Silicon Valley start-up, aided in large part because it could reap valuable "local" cred within New York City, one of the world's biggest whiskey markets. In 2010, just four years after the distillery started, Tuthilltown sold its Hudson line of whiskies to William Grant & Sons, a 140-year-old Scottish company (under a temporary contract). Of course, the whiskey inside the bottle might have been beside the point. In 2014, a Nielsen rating survey revealed that Gen Xers and Millennials—important demographics—ranked "local" and "authentic" higher as qualities they valued in liquor than did baby boomers, who held the quaint notion that "taste" was most important.

American whiskey's renewed popularity is forcing the industry to define what, exactly, is "authentic": Kentucky's big distilleries peg it to their state's long history of distilling, while new craft outfits claim their entrepreneurial spirit and smallholder individualism best embody American business ideals. But both positions also contain inconsistences. The big companies in Kentucky bear zero resemblance to the industry's mythic beginnings; for new craft producers, their lack of capital and experience threatens their progress. Herein lies a paradox: Success for many smallholders will entail a compromise. Take Tuthilltown; its success arguably wasn't built with exceptional whiskey, but by cultivating the aura of smallholder independence that modern foodies crave. Then it partnered with a large corporation overseas.

Under the temporary buyout, however, the distillery still maintains control of production. Here is an oft-overlooked opportunity distillers can seize to flip the traditional thinking about buyouts. When Hiram Walker bought Maker's, the brand was at its peak, on guard against its standards diminishing. The Hudson line, however, could benefit from Grant's expertise and experience. If Tuthilltown leverages the larger company's resources to better its whiskey and lower its price, it puts a silver lining around Bill Samuels's comment that "they're all being built to sell out."*

---

*Indeed, Tuthilltown's whiskey has improved since the buyout. By 2015, it was also using more large barrels, a positive and telling omen.

The intense but sometimes undeserved buzz created by some new distilleries worries other small producers. In March 2014, the American Craft Distillers Association held its first convention, and many attendees fretted that overrated outfits—those that had mastered the art of marketing whiskey rather than making it—would cause fatigue among consumers. Despite a surging growth rate that had prompted many first-wave craft distilleries to expand, the mood at the convention was surprisingly somber, according to Wayne Curtis, who covered it for the *Atlantic*. "Some expressed anxiety, sotto voce, that many of the new spirits being released aren't yet ready for prime time: the liquor is too rough-edged or funky, pitiably less valuable than its $40-a-bottle price tag promises," he wrote. "Given the current fad for local, 'authentic' products, selling a consumer that first bottle isn't too hard . . . but if the quality doesn't measure up to the price, it's not hard to imagine a nation of home bars each containing a single, largely untouched bottle of disappointing 'craft spirit.'"

This in mind, the most promising new American distilleries are often the most obscure. They don't usually have the buzzy closeness to media centers like New York, and spend their time perfecting their products before talking about them, a plan that's admittedly problematic in a world where marketing matters. Their strategies follow that of New Columbia Distillers in Washington, D.C., which decided to forgo marketing an insta-whiskey and instead started socking away standard-size barrels of rye whiskey the company decided it wouldn't sell for at least six years. In the meantime, New Columbia survives by making a very good gin called Green Hat, which uses botanicals like cardamom instead of the traditional juniper, and doesn't need to be aged. The Great Lakes states and the Pacific Northwest—craft brewing strongholds—also have many new distilleries that have shown great promise but get very little buzz. Westland Distillery in Seattle creates single-malt whiskies, which, due to the delicate nature of that grain, peak with relatively little time in new wood and are rich and complex (they use standard barrels and cask at a low proof, a welcome return of an old method). The company caters to connoisseurs, eagerly providing geeky details about fermentation times and exactly how their barrels are toasted and charred. It's this kind of new distillery—devoted to process, willing to divulge geeky details, and focused on the long term—that will bring America's whiskey renaissance to its full potential in the next decade or two.

Relatively obscure distilleries like New Columbia and Westland are the kind that most excited Bill Samuels Jr., the de facto patron saint of the craft movement, when I asked him his opinion of whiskey's changing landscape. Bill receives calls almost every day from new distillers seeking his guidance. "I can tell within four or five minutes which ones are interested in the product, and which ones are interested in piggybacking on the trend, sell it off for five or six million dollars. There's a *lot* of that," he said. "The nose-holding part of our industry is coming from all of these start-ups which are more interested in a gimmicky approach," he added. Maker's Mark created its own success with a few tweaks on tradition—wheat instead of rye, rotating its barrels in the rackhouse—but Bill's comments warn against mistaking true innovation for the mere appearance of innovation with questionable shortcuts or crass slogans like Cleveland Whiskey's "Screw Tradition."

In any case, the first wave of this century's new American whiskey companies are coming of age in a radically different business environment than the one navigated by Maker's Mark just three decades earlier. Today's upstart companies operate in a world where the concept of time has become compressed—instantly, new businesses can find themselves multibillion-dollar entities existing only in a nebulous digital realm, whereas their predecessors were built of bricks and steel and took decades to grow. Distilleries like Tuthilltown match the trend perfectly—it was able to sell out to William Grant & Sons in roughly the same amount of time it took Maker's Mark to make its first batch of whiskey. But even though everything moves faster now, the standards for truly superlative bourbon don't budge. Bourbon became great by having the self-discipline to *delay* gratification, by sitting aboard boats on the Mississippi River waiting for the water level to change so it could meander down to New Orleans. This is one of the reasons we've returned to drinking it today—because it's an antidote to modern chaos, and refuses to be rushed.

· CHAPTER EIGHTEEN ·

THE STORY

When Vietnamese people open a bottle of liquor or soda, they expect to hear a popping sound—like a muted version of a champagne bottle opening. The noise tells them that the liquid is good, and listening for it is part of Vietnamese drinking culture. "The 'pop' is important," a scientist in a white lab coat explains to me while holding a can of Jim Beam Cola, a product that the bourbon maker has developed for Asian markets.

I'm standing in what's called the "Liquid Arts Studio," the room where Jim Beam evaluates new products. It's housed within Beam's Global Innovation Center and sits on the campus of the main Jim Beam Distillery in Clermont, Kentucky, but is off-limits to most visitors. The fifty-seven-thousand-square-foot complex was built in 2012 for $30 million. Sleek and modern, it was designed by the same firm that has built similar research facilities for companies like Adidas, Office Depot, White Castle, and J.P. Morgan. Natural light streams through giant windows that frame the rural Kentucky landscape where, a couple of centuries earlier, thousands of farmer-distillers, sans white lab coats, plied their craft.

Two guides give me a tour, and they are joined along the way by various other scientists. MaryKay Bolles is Beam's vice president of global research and development. Over the decades she has amassed a wealth of knowledge about how to navigate major brands through a global marketplace. For a previous employer, she once worked on a campaign to develop a "taco-flavored" sports drink for Latin American markets.

My other guide is Adam Graber, Beam's global innovation director. Adam is politely soft-spoken, in his early forties, and has a background keenly appropriate for managing the stable of scientists, psychologists, and other researchers responsible for charting bourbon's path through the future. After drifting in and out of a few uncompleted PhD programs in fields such as South Asian languages, cultural anthropology, and soil science, he got an MBA and landed in the marketing world. At Beam, Adam tells me, his job is to "combine science plus consumer needs and trends to create the product story."

Few people associate the stories of liquor brands, especially bourbon, with scientists in white lab coats. Pappy Van Winkle famously hung a sign over the door at the Stitzel-Weller distillery reading "No Chemists Allowed." Here at Beam's Global Innovation Center, however, multiple floors are crammed with equipment such as texture analyzers, spectrophotometers, nanophotometers, and ultrasound equipment. It begs the question: how does a cobalt-60 irradiator help create a product story?

Much of the equipment actually helps *protect* the product story, as Adam and MaryKay demonstrate. One lab contains counterfeit bottles of Jim Beam products that were seized in China. The liquor inside one bottle is dark as squid ink, another is full of what looks like tobacco juice. China today is a bit like America during the Gilded Age: the world's factory, following its own set of rules. The technicians are testing the counterfeit liquid for the same kind of poisons America added to whiskey during its own Gilded Age, in case they need to alert foreign public health officials. As America today toils away in its role as global policeman, Beam has become the world's bouncer.

Other parts of brand protection simply involve keeping costs down. Technicians study bottle structures and packaging materials designed to minimize breakage. A "pallet transport simulator" helps the company determine how much rough handling can be endured during international voyages. A cork extractor evaluates how much pressure it requires to pull a cork, a task that's harder in warmer temperatures. Like James Crow learned 150-odd years before and a few counties over, God is in the details, as are additional profits.

As for actual product development, that happens in a series of other rooms. In one I'm given a sample of Jacob's Ghost, a white whiskey Beam offers to capitalize on the faux-moonshine fad (the irony of a scientist serving moonshine in the middle of a multimillion-dollar laboratory is lost on nobody in the room). Admittedly, a lot of new product development at Beam isn't focused specifically on bourbon as much as it is on creating products that capitalize on the bourbon maker's powerful brand name. Like Jim Beam Cola, many new products are tailored specifically for markets other than the United States. Heather Daines, a food scientist, walks me through a collection of sample cups full of base spirits and paper test strips containing aromas of lemongrass and lime—someday it might all become some sort of bourbony mojito concoction.

Along the walls are bottles of other flavored drinks such as Red Stag, a bourbon base mixed with cherry flavor that takes its cue from the flavored vodka market. It has become a big seller in the United States, although predictably not to whiskey geeks, who view such things as a kind of sacrilege. A member of the extended Beam family once told me that other family members also sniff at flavored whiskies ("sticky cup" bourbons, he called them, referring to whiskies mixed with syrups carrying the flavors of honey, cinnamon, cherry, and so on). They think it cheapens the name of a family known for straight bourbon, but their argument has been drowned out by the lucrative profits these products generate.*

The lineup of different products reflects Beam's growth from a midsize bourbon maker in the 1950s into a large company with a vast portfolio. By 2014, Beam Global had acquired many onetime competitors:

---

*Flavored whiskies also offer liquor companies an excellent way to dispose of whiskey that didn't age well (the opposite of honey barrels), masking it with sugary sweeteners.

Canadian Club, Laphroaig scotch, Courvoisier, Old Overholt, Old Grand-Dad, and Maker's Mark. Outside of whiskey, it owns a stable of other brands, including tequilas, rums, vodkas, and even the line of Skinnygirl wines that was started by a reality TV star. When the Global Innovation Center opened, Beam CEO Matt Shattock announced that 25 percent of the company's annual sales growth would come from new products.

But regardless of Beam's other brands, bourbon is still at the core of the company's mystique. Ninety-five percent of the world's bourbon is made in Kentucky, and Beam alone is responsible for 50 percent of it. At the center of it all is the flagship Jim Beam Kentucky Straight Bourbon Whiskey, easily recognized by its signature white label.* This is the brand that was developed in the 1930s and carried the company through its twentieth-century rise—it's the one that was popular on military bases during the Cold War, positioning itself as a taste of home for soldiers and a symbol of America for foreigners. As with any icon with such primacy—and perhaps in conjunction with the United States' own parallel international ascent—this famous brand is both loved and hated.

Jim Beam has become an icon by mastering the sort of nonfussy tone that's the holy grail of mass marketing. It's a relatively modern creation, but draws from the wellspring of frontier iconography that strikes just the right notes of rugged individualism, self-sufficiency, and practicality that people admire. This marketing triumph has turned it into the sort of affordable, mid-tier workhorse that's beloved at tailgate parties and backyard barbecues. It's not the best bourbon out there, but it's far from being the worst.

Beam's ubiquity also draws a predictable amount of snobby criticism, although most serious professional whiskey writers recognize its charms, even though few can remember the last time they bought a bottle of it for their home bar. It uses a wild yeast strain that gives it a foxy, spicy quality, and it's smoother than most other four-year-old

---

*Technically, Jack Daniel's is a bigger brand, but due to regional pride (recall chapter 6) it pointedly considers itself "Tennessee Whiskey" rather than bourbon. It is also an iconic brand, but a bit of an anomaly in the whiskey world due to its use of the Lincoln County Process and the way it has positioned itself.

bourbons that cost far more. It's a little thin at only 80 proof, and its youth shows through with a few too many grain notes and not quite enough wood. Yes, you can do better, but you don't always need to. Prestige aside, it's the world's best-selling bourbon brand, and has made Beam a juggernaut success.

The public face of Beam is Fred Noe, the great-grandson of James "Jim" Beam. He is in charge of more than a dozen whiskies that the company makes, including all the Jim Beam labels, Knob Creek, Baker's, Booker's, Basil Hayden's, Old Crow, and Old Grand-Dad, among others. Admittedly, the recipes and production for these brands is well established, and Fred's role as a master distiller is defined less by sweating over a mash tub than it is by serving as a brand spokesperson (master distiller positions at the biggest companies require comfort with posing for publicity photos: nose buried in a snifter of bourbon, eyes closed, an expression of serenity across the face). On the strictly business side of things, there's a fair argument that the most influential person in the Beam empire is its biggest shareholder—a billionaire hedge fund manager named Bill Ackman resided in the wings when the company was bought by Suntory—but Fred is the public face who helps provide a sense of history and heritage for customers.

Beams are to bourbon what the Kennedys are to politics—they are *everywhere,* and even like to call themselves the "first family of bourbon," not that the word bourbon needs any more dynastic connotations than it already has. Many Beams have even landed outside the confines of the company bearing their name, working for competitors. Charles Beam was a master distiller for Seagram in Baltimore, and Everett Beam made bourbon for a distillery in Pennsylvania after World War II. Go back far enough, and you'll find Beam blood in competing brands such as Pappy Van Winkle, Four Roses, Elijah Craig, and Evan Williams. During Prohibition, Guy Beam ran a distillery in Canada, while Joseph and Harry Beam made liquor in Juárez, Mexico. Joseph was the one who helped found the Heaven Hill distillery, and two Beams, Parker and Craig, remain master distillers at the competing company today. Fred Noe's son, Freddie Noe IV, currently works for

Beam, and appears set to assume his father's position when he's ready to retire, maintaining the company's valuable connection to its legacy name.

The Beam dynasty's patriarch—the man at the top of the family tree—is Johannes Jacob Boehm. Jacob was a German Mennonite farmer who was part of that early wave of settlers to Kentucky in the last part of the eighteenth century. Very little is known about him, and the company explains that he got his start selling a brand called "Old Jake Beam Sour Mash." No such thing ever actually existed—the term "sour mash" wasn't widely used and brand names weren't common until decades after Jacob's death. Nonetheless, the invention of the brand and the Americanization of the name are helpful ways for the company to place Jacob in a context that modern consumers can easily understand. Whatever kind of whiskey Jacob made was vastly different from the bourbon we know today.

James Beauregard Beam, born in 1864, was Jacob's great-grandson. During his career, Jim was a respected part of that small group of distillers who earned an adequate living by making quality whiskey during the era when the wider industry was highly corrupt and unaccountable. The names within this coterie paled in comparison to big-wheel distillers like Joseph Greenhut, but after Progressive Era legislation like the 1906 Pure Food and Drug Act, the path was cleared for distillers like Beam and the other well-known names of today to build their reputations. Then, after Prohibition, when Congress rebuilt the shattered whiskey industry in a way that favored larger producers, Beam reentered the industry by pairing with that trio of Chicago financiers who knew nothing about making whiskey but understood that the heritage and knowledge of old names was an important asset. That's when the James B. Beam Distilling Company, in the form we recognize it today, was born.

More than any of the ancients filling the Beam family tree, it is twentieth-century Beams like Booker Noe, Fred's father, who are arguably the real reason why the Beam legacy today is so strong. The company's highest-end bourbon is named after Booker, and it is bottled at cask strength straight from the barrel, meaning no water is added to lower a

high-octane kick that runs between 120 and 130 proof and will knock
the wind out of you if drunk straight. The bourbon is brisk and complex,
loaded on the front end with spices and leather that eventually give way
to a dry lingering finish reminiscent of sweet tea.

Booker was stern but caring, and Fred's voice cracks a little when he
talks about his dad. As a youth, Fred was a hellraiser and a late bloomer
who had failed out of numerous colleges, as he explains to me one eve-
ning over dinner. Booker finally convinced Fred to join the family business so he could begin the Sisyphean task of breaking in his wayward
son. Fred is self-deprecating and acknowledges the role luck played in
his incredible fortune, straying from the bootstrapping narrative commonly heard about most bourbon legends. He instead tells the story of
a prodigal son given a second chance. Bourbon is Fred's life now, and
he is in a way a living embodiment of the industry.

But even though the sentiments that Fred expressed during that
dinner were honest and real, that doesn't mean they weren't also part of
the brand's salesmanship. On the way back to my hotel after dinner, I
passed through the Beam gift shop and picked up a copy of *Beam,
Straight Up*, an autobiography that Fred wrote with the assistance of
one of the company's public relations representatives. Almost verbatim,
for all the world to see, the book contained the same heartfelt details
about Fred's upbringing as I had learned them during our dinner. Here
was a reminder that success in the whiskey industry is the prize for
whoever most convincingly creates a mythology and sense of intimacy
around ideas of heritage and authenticity. And in the bourbon business,
victory goes to whoever tells the story best.

· · ·

Angus MacDonald is a man who once distilled a wedding cake. He
mashed it up, fermented it, ran the gloopy mess through a still, and
bottled what was essentially cake moonshine to serve at a friend's wedding. On another occasion, he distilled a pile of Cap'n Crunch cereal.
The verdicts on each spirit? For the wedding cake: "Acceptable," Angus
tells me in a tone suggesting that the wedding guests might not have

taken a charitable view of the effort. The Cap'n Crunch: "Unreal," he whispers in a hushed manner suggesting that distilled junk food cereals could overtake the whiskey market if people would just give them a chance. "It's all basically refined corn products anyway," he explains.

Angus is a jovial man in his fifties with a gravelly voice and a graying beard. He wears overalls and work boots while standing in the middle of an old warehouse in West Park, New York, tucked into the Hudson Valley's Ulster County, the name a reminder of America's most storied early distillers. The warehouse was a printing shop for the Holy Cross Monastery across the street years before Angus and his partners started Coppersea Distilling there in 2012. Before then, the warehouse stood abandoned. When Coppersea moved in, Angus and his tiny cohort swept out the cobwebs and set up their distilling equipment. The space is pretty rough. The bathroom is a toilet poking out of the concrete floor with a washbasin rigged up next to it. Plywood boards serve as makeshift walls. There's no mirror in the bathroom, but Angus has helpfully solved this problem by posting a sign over the basin that reads, "You Look Great Today."

Appearances aside, Coppersea is another kind of "liquid arts studio," albeit very different from the one at the Beam Global Innovation Center. Whereas Beam's facility presents a very modern vision of the future, Coppersea's idea of the future is inspired by the past. It uses "heritage distilling" techniques—a term they coined for their unique process of resurrecting long-forgotten methods—to make whiskey. This includes processes such as green malting, a method mostly used about two hundred years ago. By not drying malted grains before they are ground up, you can introduce clean fruit notes to the drink. At Coppersea, pot stills are used and spirits are often barreled at around 100 proof, which is far lower than most producers barrel at today, but helps preserve the flavor of the ingredients. Coppersea grows their own grain nearby and their stills are direct-fired, a method akin to using a blazing-hot masonry oven to cook bread. Direct firing a still is rare today because it is fickle and can scorch the ingredients (think of the dark crust on a loaf of bread baked in a masonry oven). It requires close supervision and careful timing, but can bring additional nuance and complexity to spirits. Coppersea's approach is "incredibly primitive," Angus explains.

But Coppersea isn't just simply reintroducing old methods in an effort to mimeograph the whiskey of yesteryear. Its nod to the past is accompanied by the revelation that American history is really just a series of new beginnings. Coppersea's resurrection of old methods is done with a distinct spirit of innovation. The distillery utilizes modern technology when it makes sense and can still achieve the end result of an old method. Angus shows me a 1921 Hobart food chopper and a 1936 A&P coffee grinder that are sturdy as battleships, built with the chunky permanence of an era that had a less disposable view of such equipment. These tools grind the malt more consistently than other pieces of equipment—antique or modern—that Angus and the distillery manager, Christopher Williams, have encountered thus far, which gives Coppersea more control over the fermentation process. Sitting nearby is an electrified chiller that the men built themselves, which also gives them precise control over production. This mishmash of methods from different eras proves that the distillery isn't limited by a sense of historical purism that could limit the quality of the final product.

This hybrid mind-set is important. Christopher isn't duped by sentimental nostalgia, and recognizes that much of history's whiskey was probably unpleasant, but not necessarily because the methods used to make it didn't work. In the era before brand names existed, when whiskey was mainly sold as a bulk commodity, distillers had little incentive to swing for the fences. Some of the old methods, however, held the ability to produce a superb product, but just weren't economically feasible on the large scale the whiskey industry would grow to achieve. Coppersea's goal is to graft a modern culinary mind-set to old methods that truly have something unique to offer.

Angus and Christopher use the term "folk" instead of "craft" to describe their approach to whiskey, wary of the way the latter expression is often appropriated within the food world. Christopher elaborates by drawing a comparison to the folk musician John Fahey, who had training in classical music theory, but spent his career prowling rural

America to learn unconventional but brilliant playing methods devised by self-taught musicians. Decades ago, Angus spent time with a fading subculture of rural American distillers—those whose legacy was most rooted in the era before the Civil War's whiskey tax—who made their own liquor as a matter of self-sufficiency. They took pride in their craftsmanship, oftentimes devising creative but contrarian distilling methods akin to the unique musical methodology of folk musicians.

Some of the folk distilling methods Angus learned worked wonders, while others were "extremely questionable," he explains. For instance, some distillers would implement a sweet mash only under moonlight, letting wild yeast spores at night infiltrate the mash tub (it's an alternative definition for the term "moonshine"). There's also a scientific logic behind it that researchers would later discover: ultraviolet rays from the sun can apparently alter wild yeast. Sweet mashes like this occasionally did strange and wonderful things to the whiskey, but the wildly fickle and unpredictable nature of the process ultimately renders it unpractical for commercial distillers.

"We are to whiskey what, say, alt-country bands like Wilco or the Old 97's or the Jayhawks are to American country music," Christopher explains. "Those guys aren't trying to sound like Hank Williams or Roy Acuff, but what they do is the natural extension of that aesthetic: small, twangy, perplexing, weird." Nirvana was another comparison: "People don't think about how steeped Cobain was in old-time American music like Leadbelly and Dock Boggs, as well as the deep-catalog punk and garage bands of his own youth," Christopher says. These two musical comparisons paint a hybrid picture of what Coppersea is attempting to accomplish. The reference to Roy Acuff is a nod to the distillery's attempt to revive the lost world that cultural critic Greil Marcus once called "the old, weird America." Nirvana, on the other hand, highlights an antiestablishment vibe apparent in many of America's craft food endeavors, albeit one that, like the band, can be a huge commercial success if packaged appropriately. Christopher is a fan of many big whiskey brands, particularly Four Roses, but he can't help contrasting his whiskey to some of the industry's more ubiquitous crowd pleasers: "Jim Beam, Jack Daniel's, etcetera. Those guys are like Brooks & Dunn or Taylor Swift: huge, bland, obvious, familiar."

Whereas most distilleries understandably let you taste only at the end of your visit, giving them the time to tell you stories and set the mood, Coppersea let me sample its whiskey first thing. This way, the rest of my visit would help inform what I already knew about the product. This wasn't a calculated move. The distillery is tiny, isolated, and visited by appointment only—shortly after I arrived, it became clear that Angus was struggling a little to determine how a tour guide is supposed to behave. Instead, he acted more like a host, and the first thing a good host does is offer his guest a drink.

We started with Coppersea's "Raw Rye," an unaged whiskey made with rye the distillery grows down the street. We taste through distillate made from grains harvested during different seasons. As starch and sugar levels evolve over the course of months, the whiskey transforms accordingly. The tight, green notes of the spring distillate were followed by summer, which carried strong honey notes. The spirits made in autumn had a nose that was floral and delicate, melting into a palate of ripe cantaloupe. Unaged whiskey is admittedly a hard sell. The harsh vegetative notes spur most knowledgeable drinkers to ask of the whiskey's "potential," and the gimmicky way it's usually marketed is an immediate turnoff. But drinkable unaged whiskies do exist, and are best acknowledged as a kind of fleeting miracle, akin to spotting a rare species on the verge of extinction—finding one is like a birdwatcher scouring the forests for a decade in order to catch a quick glimpse of a scarlet tanager. Coppersea's autumn expression of its Raw Rye is one of the rarities. It can fairly be called "exquisite," harboring layered complexities missing from many superlative aged whiskies.

Notes of fresh, ripe fruit are rare in white dogs, but Coppersea's bourbon distillate (made with 53 percent corn) is also full of them. Angus then hands me a sample of whiskey that had been aging in the barrels. It had already achieved a rich complexity even though it was young. The finish was eternal, constantly morphing the way light does during a sunset. In many ways, Coppersea's whiskies were the equivalent of funky cheeses—unexpected and complex, but always managing to achieve their own kind of harmony. None of the unique flavors was a mere novelty—lesser distillers will sometimes try to spin obvious flaws as being the same kind of weird nuance that Coppersea very deliberately cultivates.

There are no gimmicks at Coppersea. The distillery's labels are simple: there is no fabricated backstory and the space on the label is instead filled with the kind of information that whiskey geeks covet but that some brands hide: mash bills, ingredients, methods used, age statements. A few small barrels lie around for the purpose of experimentation, but much of the whiskey they plan on selling is aged in large barrels. "We're not bullish on small barrels. There's a difference between flavoring and maturing whiskey," Angus explains, immediately distancing Coppersea from a method used by many small distillers that has left many critics skeptical. No corners are cut. To borrow the words of Bill Samuels Jr., Angus and Christopher are "product guys."*

· · ·

So what else has been erased from American whiskey as the industry has consolidated? Compared to the past, many of today's most famous brands are the same in name only. They all used to be made by different distilleries that all did things a little differently: ground the grains to different levels of coarseness, used a wider array of yeast strains, malted differently, seasoned barrel wood in different fashions or had barrels customized. As brands got bought out, flocks of labels increasingly migrated to a fewer number of larger distilleries. Processes were streamlined and standardized approaches were implemented: yeast strains and recipes shared, cooking processes batched. Other parts of the industry, such as the cooperages that make the barrels, also consolidated, meaning even more of the little variations among brands would inevitably be lost. Much as different parts of America have lost their distinct dialects, America's regional whiskey

---

* In 2014, Coppersea partnered with a local cooper to begin production of barrels specifically for the distillery, giving its whiskies additional *terroir*. A sample of Coppersea's malted rye that had been aged in the small barrels was also quite pleasing, reminding those who are skeptical of that method—including myself—that there are always exceptions to the rule.

styles—whiskey *terroir*, if you will—faded. Bourbon edged out rye to become the nation's norm, and then Kentucky edged out other states to largely define that style. The product was still good, although it admittedly began to fall within an increasingly narrow range.

The eight companies making the vast majority of America's whiskey do a great job—their relatively few individual expressions all represent winning formulas—but it's hard not to sense that some good things have been lost. America's economic history has always been a struggle to balance different systems, like those reflected in the policies of Thomas Jefferson and Alexander Hamilton. Each offers its own unique benefits, but also its own disadvantages. In 1952, John Steinbeck addressed this balancing act when he wrote, "A group can build automobiles quicker and better than one man, and bread from a huge factory is cheaper and more uniform." But Steinbeck also acknowledged a flip side to such advantages: "When our food and clothing and housing all are born in the complication of mass production, mass method is bound to get into our thinking and to eliminate all other thinking." Coppersea is a part of new distilling trends that promise to restore balance. "At this point in American culture, the pendulum has swung so far in one direction," Christopher explains. "We're pushing back."

The Coppersea Distillery is almost entirely bereft of marketing. In an age of gratuitous self-promotion, its rough edges carry a welcome vitality. But as refreshing as Coppersea's apparent disdain for crass commerciality might be, it's admittedly problematic when you're running a commercial endeavor. Angus winces when I ask him how business has been in the two years since Coppersea opened in 2012. Despite the distillery's closeness to the New York City food media stronghold, coverage had been scant. There's an almost cosmic injustice to this—Coppersea's whiskey is far more interesting and nuanced than most other spirits made in the state. As some of Coppersea's more successful neighbors prove, marketing matters, even if it doesn't result in the best whiskey.

Angus simply shrugs at the notion that success should be measured by whether or not you can create an empire, which is the model that many of America's whiskey producers, big and small alike, seem determined to follow. This well-blazed path echoes Bill Samuels's comment that "they're all being built to sell out," suggesting that there's only one true model for an American business to pursue.

But Christopher disagrees. "There's an element that's decidedly un-American in the way we're doing this," he acknowledges. His goal is to keep his scale at a manageable level that might not make him fantastically wealthy, but will allow him to do well enough, taking care of his needs, paying for his kids to go to college, and living a comfortable life. It will never grow to a size where he loses complete control. He can take absolute pride in his product and never have to apologize for what it became after a franchise took it over and the accountants began poking their heads through the doorway every quarter.

Coppersea carries many contradictions: it rejects tradition and embraces it at the same time, breaking some rules while strictly following others. The story of bourbon has been told a lot of different ways, a curious pastiche of charming truths and strange little lies. In the end, it might not matter which are which because the myth has already been created, and that tells the ultimate truth. But then again, why not rewrite the rules and rethink things, because really, who made up the rules and the stories in the first place?

Before I departed Coppersea for the day, Angus reflected on the history of American whiskey, how that story has been told by the industry that dominates it, and how it's always open to change. His comment spoke not just to bourbon, but to the nation that invented the spirit: "If you can come up with a plausible lie, with a set of logical reasons why that would be the truth, you might actually be right. And who's to say whether or not the last person to tell the 'real truth' about how it really was before somebody forgot didn't do the same thing?"

ACKNOWLEDGMENTS

In order to write a book like this—a blend of commentary and history—one must have a lot of conversations. Mike Veach of Louisville's Filson Historical Society was always gracious with his time. Chuck Cowdery, as the dean of American whiskey writers, was also an invaluable source of insight, be it through his blog (www.chuckcowdery.blogspot.com), books, industry newsletter, or occasional e-mail in response to a question. My afternoon spent with Dixie Hibbs, the former mayor of Bardstown and the author of a book on Nelson County distilleries, was one of my favorite memories about this project.

There were many helpful people within the whiskey industry, but here are some of the standouts: Greg Davis, Matt Hofmann, Freddie Johnson, Angus MacDonald, Chris Morris, Amir Peay, David Pickerell, Paul Pogue, Bill Samuels, Jr., Amy Preske, John Uselton, and Christopher Williams. At the Distilled Spirits Council of the United States, Frank Coleman, Lisa Hawkins, and Alexandra Sklansky were always helpful and informative.

Finally, there is a small group of whiskey bloggers whose work I love. Many were gracious enough to share research and leads with me; others I've never spoken with, and that's my fault. In any case, they helped clear the fog of click bait that dominates spirits coverage in today's media. Josh Feldman at www.cooperedtot.com is a joy to read and somebody who truly "gets" whiskey; Jack Sullivan at www.pre-prowhiskeymen.blogspot.com writes wonderful histories of pre-Prohibition era distillers and was a great help; Steve Ury at Sku's Recent Eats, www.recenteats.blogspot.com, is tireless, thorough, and thoughtful; Brian Haara at www.sippncorn.blogspot.com is a lawyer dominating the niche of people who write about the whiskey industry of the late 1800s from the perspective of lawsuits; www.thebourbontruth.tumblr.com shall remain anonymous, as he likes it; the *Whisky Advocate* blog, www.whiskyadvocate.com/blog, is always informative; David Driscoll at California wine retailer K&L Merchants writes one of the most thoughtful and smart blogs in the business at www.spiritsjournal.klwines.com; Fred Minnick, author of *Whiskey Women* and regular contributor to *Whisky Advocate* and *Whisky Magazine,* also provides gems of whiskey knowledge at www.fredminnick.com. Other good blogs include: www.ellenjaye.com; www.inwithbacchus.com; www.whiskyfun.com; www.bourbonguy.com; www.whiskycast.com; www.alcademics.com; www.themashnotes.com; www.matthew-rowley.blogspot.com (now defunct, but the old posts are great); www.sourmashmanifesto.com; www.bourbonr.com; and the discussion forums found at www.straightbourbon.com and www.bourbonenthusiast.com.

Thanks to Michelle Brower at Folio Literary Management for finding this project the best home possible. At Viking, Liz Van Hoose got everything aimed in the right direction. Melanie Tortoroli helped me land it without crashing.

A few writers, often unbeknownst to them, served as valuable guides: William Hogeland, Henry Crowgey, Marni Davis, Wayne Curtis, William Grimes, W. J. Rorabaugh, Thomas Slaughter, and Richard Taylor.

Here are other people I owe a drink for at some point having a conversation that provided some gem of insight, or many such gems: Derek Brown, Lew Bryson, Doug Campau, Sierra Clark, Mickey Meece, Maureen Petrosky, Lawrence Powell, Clay Risen, Adam Rogers, Allan Roth, Jay Somerset, Brian Spatola, Lauren Viera, and Amy Zavatto. Other friends who read early drafts or gave needed advice: Eric Broxmeyer, Austin Considine, Matt Ryan, Ryan Stahl, Ryan Stayton, Alison Thomas, and Todd Zwillich.

And of course I owe my parents far more than a brief mention in an acknowledgments section, as well as my siblings, Sara and Pete. I'm also lucky to have great in-laws, Dave and Pat, whose handiwork produced my wife, Lauren, who gets the most credit of all.

SELECTED BIBLIOGRAPHY

BOOKS AND ARTICLES

Adams, George Worthington. *Doctors in Blue: The Medical History of the Union Army in the Civil War.* New York: Henry Schuman, 1952.

Ade, George. *The Old-Time Saloon: Not Wet—Not Dry, Just History.* New York: Ray Long & Richard R. Smith, Inc., 1931.

Anderson, Oscar. *The Health of a Nation: Harvey W. Wiley and the Fight for Pure Food.* Chicago: University of Chicago Press, 1958.

Bailyn, Bernard. *The Peopling of British North America: An Introduction.* New York: Vintage, 1988.

———. *The Barbarous Years: The Peopling of British North America; The Conflict of Civilizations, 1600–1675.* New York: Knopf, 2012.

Bakeless, John. *Daniel Boone: Master of the Wilderness.* New York: William Morrow, 1939.

Barr, Andrew. *Drink: A Social History of America.* New York: Carroll & Graf, 1999.

Belasco, Warren. *Appetite for Change: How the Counterculture Took on the Food Industry, 1966–1988.* New York: Pantheon, 1989.

Bernheim, Isaac Wolfe. *The Story of the Bernheim Family.* Louisville, KY: John P. Morton & Co., 1910.

Bolton, Charles Knowles. *The Private Soldier Under Washington.* New York: Charles Scribner's Sons, 1902.

Brinton, John H. *Personal Memoirs of John H. Brinton.* New York: Neale Publishing Co., 1914.

Brookhiser, Richard. *Alexander Hamilton, American.* New York: Free Press, 1999.

Brown, George Garvin. *The Holy Bible Repudiates "Prohibition": Compilation of All Verses Containing the Words "Wine" or "Strong Drink," Proving that the*

Scriptures Commend and Command the Temperate Use of Alcoholic Beverages. Louisville, KY: self-published by George Garvin Brown, 1910.

Bryce, J. H., and G. G. Stewart, eds. *Distilled Spirits: Tradition and Innovation.* Nottingham: Nottingham University Press, 2004.

Bunting, Chris. "Japanese Whisky." In *Whiskey and Philosophy: A Small Batch of Spirited Ideas,* edited by Fritz Allhoff and Marcus Adams. Hoboken, NJ: John Wiley & Sons, 2010.

Burns, Eric. *The Spirits of America: A Social History of Alcohol.* Philadelphia: Temple University Press, 2004.

Carr, Jess. *The Second Oldest Profession: An Informal History of Moonshining in America.* Englewood Cliffs, NJ: Prentice-Hall, 1972.

Carson, Gerald. *The Social History of Bourbon.* New York: Dodd, Mead, 1963.

Cashman, Sean Dennis. *America in the Gilded Age.* New York: New York University Press, 1993.

Cecil, Sam. *Bourbon: The Evolution of Kentucky Whiskey.* New York: Turner Publishing Company, 2010.

Chernow, Ron. *Alexander Hamilton.* New York: Penguin Press, 2004.

Clark, Norman. *Deliver Us from Evil: An Interpretation of American Prohibition.* New York: Norton, 1976.

Clay, Karen, and Werner Troesken. "Strategic Behavior in Whiskey Distilling, 1887–1895." *Journal of Economic History* 62, no. 4 (December 2002).

Coffey, Thomas. *The Long Thirst: Prohibition in America, 1920–1933.* New York: Norton, 1975.

Collins, Lewis. *Historical Sketches of Kentucky.* Cincinnati: Collins & James, 1847.

Cook, William A. *King of the Bootleggers: A Biography of George Remus.* Jefferson, NC: McFarland, 2008.

Coulter, Ellis Merton. *The Confederate States of America, 1861–1865.* Baton Rouge: Louisiana State University Press, 1950.

Cowdery, Charles K. *Bourbon, Straight.* Chicago: Made and Bottled in Kentucky, 2004.

———. *The Best Bourbon You'll Never Taste.* Chicago: Made and Bottled in Kentucky, 2012.

———. *Small Barrels Produce Lousy Whiskey.* Chicago: Made and Bottled in Kentucky, 2012.

Crèvecoeur, J. Hector St. John de. *Letters from an American Farmer.* New York: Dutton, 1957. Originally published 1782.

Crowgey, Henry. *Kentucky Bourbon: The Early Years of Whiskey Making.* Lexington: University Press of Kentucky, 1971.

Curtis, Wayne. *And a Bottle of Rum: A History of the New World in Ten Cocktails.* New York: Three Rivers Press, 2007.

Dabney, Joseph Earl. *Mountain Spirits.* Asheville, NC: Bright Mountain Books, 1974.

David, Elizabeth. *Harvest of the Cold Months: The Social History of Ice and Ices.* New York: Viking, 1995.

Davis, Marni. *Jews and Booze: Becoming American in the Age of Prohibition.* New York: New York University Press, 2012.

Davis, Marni. "Despised Merchandise: American Jewish Liquor Entrepreneurs and Their Critics." In *Chosen Capital: The Jewish Encounter with American Capitalism,* edited by Rebecca Kobrin. New Brunswick, NJ: Rutgers University Press, 2012.

Davis, William C. *The Pirates Laffite: The Treacherous World of the Corsairs of the Gulf.* New York: Harcourt, 2005.

Dickens, Charles. *Martin Chuzzlewit.* New York: University Society, 1908.

Dowd, William, ed. *Barrels and Drams: The History of Whisk(e)y in Jiggers and Shots.* New York: Sterling Epicure, 2010.

Edmunds, Lowell. *Martini, Straight Up: The Classic American Cocktail.* Baltimore: Johns Hopkins University Press, 1998.

Embury, David. *The Fine Art of Mixing Drinks.* New York: Mud Puddle Books, 2008. Originally published 1948 by Doubleday.

Faith, Nicholas. *The Bronfmans: The Rise and Fall of the House of Seagram.* New York: Thomas Dunne, 2006.

Felten, Eric. *How's Your Drink?: Cocktails, Culture, and the Art of Drinking Well.* Evanston, IL: Surrey Books, 2007.

Fishlow, Albert. "Antebellum Interregional Trade Reconsidered." *American Economic Review* 54, no. 3, Papers and Proceedings of the Seventy-sixth Annual Meeting of the American Economic Association (May 1964).

Foner, Eric. *The Story of American Freedom.* New York: Norton, 1999.

Gethyn-Jones, Eric. *George Thorpe and the Berkeley Company.* Stroud, UK: Sutton Publishing, 1981.

Getz, Oscar. *Whiskey: An American Pictorial History.* New York: David McKay Company, 1978.

Gjelten, Tom. *Bacardi and the Long Fight for Cuba: Biography of a Cause.* New York: Penguin, 2008.

Greene, Graham. *Our Man in Havana.* New York: Viking, 1958.

Grimes, William. *Straight Up or On the Rocks: A Cultural History of American Drink.* New York: Simon & Schuster, 1987.

Hall, Harrison. *The Distiller.* Philadelphia, 1811.

Hamilton, Alexander. "Report on the Difficulties in the Execution of the Act Laying Duties on Distilled Spirits." In *The Papers of Alexander Hamilton,* edited by Harold C. Syrett. New York: Columbia University Press, 1962.

Handlin, Oscar, ed. *This Was America: As Recorded by European Travelers in the Eighteenth, Nineteenth, and Twentieth Centuries.* New York: Harper & Row, 1949.

Hanes, Merv, MD. "The Search for the Old Forrester." http://innominatesociety .com/Articles/The%20Search%20for%20the%20Old%20Forrester.htm.

Harwell, Richard Barksdale. *The Mint Julep.* Charlottesville: University Press of Virginia, 1975.

Herman, Arthur. *How the Scots Invented the World.* New York: Three Rivers Press, 2001.

Hibbs, Dixie. *Before Prohibition: Distilleries in Nelson County Kentucky, 1880–1920.* New Hope, KY: St. Martin de Porres Print Shop, 2012.

Hofstadter, Richard. *The Age of Reform.* New York: Vintage, 1960.

———. *The American Political Tradition and the Men Who Made It.* New York: Vintage, 1989.

Hogeland, William. *The Whiskey Rebellion: George Washington, Alexander Hamilton, and the Frontier Rebels Who Challenged America's Newfound Sovereignty.* New York: Scribner, 2006.

Hopkins, Kate. *99 Drams of Whiskey: The Accidental Hedonist's Quest for the Perfect Shot and the History of the Drink.* New York: St. Martin's Press, 2009.

Horne, Gerald. *Class Struggle in Hollywood, 1930–1950: Moguls, Mobsters, Stars, Reds, and Trade Unionists.* Austin: University of Texas Press, 2001.

Horwitz, Tony. *Confederates in the Attic: Dispatches from the Unfinished Civil War.* New York: Vintage Departures, 1998.

Hudson, Karen. "Millville and the Old Taylor Distillery: Industry and Community." In *Kentucky's Bluegrass Region: Tours for the 11th Annual Meeting of the Vernacular Architecture Forum, May 10 & 11, 1990,* edited by Julie Riesenweber and Karen Hudson. Frankfort: Kentucky Heritage Council, 1990.

Jefford, Andrew. "Scotch Whisky: From Origins to Conglomerates." In *Whiskey and Philosophy,* edited by Fritz Allhoff and Marcus P. Adams. Hoboken, NJ: John Wiley & Sons, 2010.

Keneally, Thomas. *American Scoundrel: The Life of the Notorious Civil War General Dan Sickles.* New York: Anchor, 2003.

Kosar, Kevin. *Whiskey: A Global History.* London: Reaktion, 2010.

Krafft, Michael. *American Distiller: Or, the Theory and Practice of Distilling, According to the Latest Discoveries and Improvements, Including the Most Improved Methods of Constructing Stills, and of Rectification.* Philadelphia: Thomas Dobson, 1804.

Krass, Peter. *Blood and Whiskey: The Life and Times of Jack Daniel.* Hoboken, NJ: John Wiley & Sons, 2004.

Labunski, Richard. *James Madison and the Struggle for the Bill of Rights.* New York: Oxford University Press, 2006.

Lacour, Pierre. *The Manufacture of Liquors, Wines, and Cordials Without the Aid of Distillation.* New York: Dick and Fitzgerald, 1863.

Lender, Mark Edward, and James Kirby Martin. *Drinking in America: A History.* New York: Free Press, 1982.

Lukacs, Paul. *Inventing Wine*. New York: Norton, 2012.

McCary, Ben C. *Indians in Seventeenth-Century Virginia*. Charlottesville: University of Virginia Press, 1980.

McCusker, John J. *Rum and the American Revolution: The Rum Trade and the Balance of Payments of the Thirteen Continental Colonies*. New York: Garland, 1989.

Mancall, Peter. *Deadly Medicine: Indians and Alcohol in Early America*. Ithaca, NY: Cornell University Press, 1995.

Maurer, David. *Kentucky Moonshine*. Lexington: University Press of Kentucky, 2003.

Meier, Kenneth J. *The Politics of Sin: Drugs, Alcohol, and Public Policy*. Armonk, NY: M.E. Sharpe, 1994.

M'Harry, Samuel. *The Practical Distiller*. Harrisburg, PA: John Wyeth, 1809.

Mill, John Stuart. *Auguste Comte and Positivism*. London, 1865.

Minnick, Fred. *Whiskey Women: The Untold Story of How Women Saved Bourbon, Scotch, and Irish Whiskey*. Lincoln: University of Nebraska Press/Potomac Books, 2013.

Mintz, Sidney. *Tasting Food, Tasting Freedom: Excursions in Eating, Culture, and the Past*. Boston: Beacon, 1996.

Morgan, Robert. *Boone: A Biography*. Chapel Hill, NC: Algonquin Books, 2007.

Murdock, Catherine Gilbert. *Domesticating Drink: Women, Men, and Alcohol in America, 1870–1940*. Baltimore: Johns Hopkins University Press, 1998.

Newman, Peter C. *The King of the Castle: The Making of a Dynasty; Seagram's and the Bronfman Empire*. New York: Atheneum, 1979.

Nickell, Joe. *The Kentucky Mint Julep*. Lexington: University Press of Kentucky, 2003.

Noe, Fred. *Beam, Straight Up*. Hoboken, NJ: John Wiley & Sons, 2012.

Ogle, Maureen. *Ambitious Brew: The Story of American Beer*. New York: Harcourt, 2006.

Okrent, Daniel. *Last Call: The Rise and Fall of Prohibition*. New York: Scribner, 2010.

Pacult, F. Paul. *American Still Life: The Jim Beam Story and the Making of the World's #1 Bourbon*. Hoboken, NJ: John Wiley & Sons, 2003.

Park, Peter. "The Supply Side of Drinking: Alcohol Production and Consumption in the United States Before Prohibition." *Contemporary Drug Problems* 12 (Winter 1985).

Perkins, Edwin. *The Economy of Colonial America*. New York: Columbia University Press, 1980.

Pierce, Daniel S. *Real NASCAR: White Lightning, Red Clay, and Big Bill France*. Chapel Hill: University of North Carolina Press, 2010.

Powell, Lawrence. *The Accidental City: Improvising New Orleans.* Cambridge, MA: Harvard University Press, 2013.

Regan, Gary, and Mardee Haidin. *The Book of Bourbon and Other Fine American Whiskies.* Shelburne, VT: Chapters, 1995.

———. *The Bourbon Companion.* Philadelphia: Running Press, 1998.

Risen, Clay. *American Whiskey, Bourbon, and Rye: A Guide to the Nation's Favorite Spirit.* New York: Sterling Epicure, 2013.

Rogers, Adam. *Proof: The Science of Booze.* New York: Houghton Mifflin Harcourt, 2014.

Root, Waverley. *Eating in America: A History.* New York: Morrow, 1976.

Rorabaugh, W. J. *The Alcoholic Republic: An American Tradition.* Oxford: Oxford University Press, 1979.

Rothbaum, Noah. *The Business of Spirits: How Savvy Marketers, Innovative Distillers, and Entrepreneurs Changed How We Drink.* New York: Kaplan, 2012.

Rowley, Matthew B. *Moonshine!* New York: Lark, 2007.

Rutkow, Eric. *American Canopy: Trees, Forests, and the Making of a Nation.* New York: Scribner, 2012.

Samuels, Bill Jr. *Maker's Mark—My Autobiography.* Louisville, KY: Saber, 2000.

Schlesinger, Arthur M. "A Dietary Interpretation of American History." *Proceedings of the Massachusetts Historical Society,* 3rd series, vol. 68 (October 1944–May 1947).

Simmons, James C. *Star-Spangled Eden: 19th Century America Through the Eyes of Dickens, Wilde, Frances Trollope, Frank Harris, and Other British Travelers.* New York: Carroll & Graf, 2000.

Sismondo, Christine. *America Walks into a Bar: A Spirited History of Taverns and Saloons, Speakeasies and Grog Shops.* Oxford: Oxford University Press, 2011.

Slaughter, Thomas. *The Whiskey Rebellion: Frontier Epilogue to the American Revolution.* Oxford: Oxford University Press, 1998.

Smith, Daniel Blake. "This Idea in Heaven." In *The Buzzel About Kentuck,* edited by Craig Thompson Friend. Lexington: University Press of Kentucky, 1999.

Smith, George. *A Compleat Body of Distilling.* London: Henry Lintot, 1731.

———. *The Nature of Fermentation Explained.* London: n.p., 1729.

Steinbeck, John. *East of Eden.* New York: Penguin, 1952.

Sullivan, John Jeremiah. *Blood Horses: Notes of a Sportswriter's Son.* New York: Farrar, Straus & Giroux, 2004.

Taylor, Richard. *The Great Crossing: A Historic Journey to Buffalo Trace Distillery.* Frankfort, KY: Buffalo Trace Distillery, 2002.

Thompson, Neal. *Driving with the Devil.* New York: Three Rivers Press, 2006.

Timberlake, James H. *Prohibition and the Progressive Movement, 1900–1920.* Cambridge, MA: Harvard University Press, 1963.

Tocqueville, Alexis de. *Democracy in America.* 2 vols. New York: Vintage, 1959. Originally published 1835–40.

Trachtenberg, Alan. *The Incorporation of America: Culture and Society in the Gilded Age.* New York: Hill & Wang, 1982.

Trollope, Frances. *Domestic Manners of the Americans.* Mineola, NY: Dover Publications, 2003. Originally published 1832.

Van Winkle Campbell, Sally. *But Always Fine Bourbon: Pappy Van Winkle and the Story of Old Fitzgerald.* Frankfort, KY: Old Rip Van Winkle Distillery, 2004.

Veach, Michael. *Kentucky Bourbon Whiskey: An American Heritage.* Lexington: University Press of Kentucky, 2013.

Wallace, Benjamin. *The Billionaire's Vinegar.* New York: Crown, 2008.

Watman, Max. *Chasing the White Dog: An Amateur Outlaw's Adventures in Moonshine.* New York: Simon & Schuster, 2010.

Weightman, Gavin. *The Frozen Water Trade.* New York: Hyperion, 2003.

Wiley, Bell I. *The Life of Johnny Reb: The Common Soldier of the Confederacy.* Indianapolis: Bobbs-Merrill, 1943.

Young, Al. *Four Roses: Return of a Whiskey Legend.* Louisville, KY: Butler Books, 2010.

Zoeller, Chester. *Bourbon in Kentucky: A History of Distilleries in Kentucky.* Louisville, KY: Butler Books, 2010.

PERIODICALS AND NEWSPAPERS

American Economic Review
Atlantic Monthly
Baltimore Sun
Barron's National Business and Financial Weekly
Bonfort's Wine and Spirit Circular
Boston Daily Globe
Boston Globe
Bourbon County Reader
Chicago Tribune
Collier's Weekly
Contemporary Drug Problems
Drinks Business
Economist
Esquire
Fortune
Japan Times

Lexington (KY) *Leader*
Louisville Courier-Journal
McClure's Magazine
National Tribune (Washington, D.C.)
The New Georgia Encyclopedia
New Republic
New York Times
New Yorker
Proceedings of the Massachusetts Historical Society
Prologue
Punch
Salon
Seagram Spotlight (company newsletter)
Shanken News Daily
Slate
Smithsonian
Spirits Business
Spirits Magazine
Sports Illustrated
Tasting Panel
Time
Wall Street Journal
Washington Post
Whisky Magazine
Whisky Advocate
Wine and Liquor Journal

ARCHIVES

Brown University: Alcoholism and Addictions Collection.
Filson Historical Society: Atherton Family Papers; Taylor-Hay Family Papers; Weller Family Papers.
University of Kentucky: Louie B. Nunn Center for Oral History, Bourbon in Kentucky Oral History Collection.
Smyth of Nibley Papers (1673–74) at the New York Public Library (copy courtesy of Berkeley Plantation staff).

INDEX